Networking Made Easy

Networking From Beginners to Advanced

By

Chris Marshal

This document is intended to provide correct and detailed information on the topic and problem. The publication is marketed with the understanding that the publisher does not make any accounts, officially approved services or otherwise suitable services. If legal or medical advice is required, an adult working in the field should be requested.

From a Theory Statement approved and ratified similarly by the American Bar Association Committee and the Publishers 'and Affiliates' Committee;

It is in no way permissible for any of this text to be copied, duplicated or distributed in any electronic or written media.

Recording of this publication is strictly forbidden, and the preservation of this text is not allowed until the publisher gives written permission.

The rights are all reserved.

The material presented herein is accurate and clear because the recipient's reader is alone and entirely

CONTENTS

Introduction

What is Networking?

Networking Glossary

Here are a few terms in networking Connection: In networking, connection refers to bits of related information that are transmitted over a network. It generally implies that the connection is established before the transfer of data (by following the procedures laid down in the protocol) and then deconstructed at the end of the data transfer.

Packet: Generally speaking, a packet is the simplest unit to be transmitted over a network. While communicating over the network, packets are envelopes that carry data (in parts) from one endpoint to the other. Packets have a header segment that contains information about the packet, including source and destination, network hops, timestamps, etc. The key component of a packet contains the data being transmitted. Sometimes it's called the body or the payload.

Network Interface: The network interface may refer to any kind of networking hardware-software interface. For instance, if there are two network cards in your device, you can control and configure each network interface connected with them individually.

A network interface may be connected to a physical device or may be a representation of a virtual interface. An example of this is the "loopback" device, which is a virtual interface to a local machine.

LAN: LAN means local area network. It refers to a network or part of a network that is not accessible publicly to the wider internet. An example of a LAN is a home or office network.

WAN: WAN means "wide area network." This means a network that is much wider than a LAN.

Although WAN is the relevant term to be used to describe large, distributed networks in general, it is generally meant to mean the Internet as a whole. If the device is said to be connected to the WAN, it is generally believed that it can be accessed through the internet.

Protocol: Protocol is a set of regulations and standards that basically describe the language that devices can use to communicate with each other. A large number of protocols are commonly used in networking and are mostly implemented in various layers.

Several low-level protocols are UDP, TCP, IP, and ICMP. Some common examples of application layer protocols based on these lower protocols are HTTP, SSH, TLS / SSL, and FTP.

Port: Port is an address on a single machine which can be connected to a particular piece of software. It's not a physical interface or location, but it allows servers to connect with more than one application.

Firewall: Firewall is a program that determines whether the traffic to or from a server should be allowed. Firewalls usually work by creating rules for which type of traffic is permissible on which ports. Normally, firewalls block ports that are not used by a particular application on a server.

NAT: NAT means network address translation. It's a way to translate incoming requests into a routing server to the relevant servers or devices it knows about on the LAN. This is usually done in physical LANs as a way to route requests to the appropriate backend servers through one IP address.

VPN: VPN means virtual private network. It is a way of linking separate LANs via the internet while preserving privacy. It is used as a means of connecting remote systems, like they were on a local network, mostly for security reasons.

Network Layers: Although networking is often addressed horizontally between hosts in terms of topology, its implementation is layered vertically throughout a network or computer. This means that there are several technologies and protocols that are built on top of each other to make communication easier. Every successive, higher layer summarises raw data a little more, making it easier to use for applications and users. It also enables people to exploit lower layers in new ways without having to invest time and energy to develop protocols and applications that handle such types of traffic.

The terminology we use to speak about each of the layering schemes vary considerably depending on what kind of model you use. The path of the data is the same irrespective of the model used to analyze the layers.

As data is sent out from one computer, it starts at the top of the stack and filters down. Actual transmission to another system takes place at the lowest level. At this stage, the data will travel back through the layers of the other device.

Each layer has the ability to include its own "wrap" around the data it receives from the adjacent layer, which helps the layers that come after in determining what to do with the data when it is passed off.

OSI Model:

Traditionally, the OSI model is one way to talk about different layers of network communication. OSI means Open System Interconnect. This model describes seven different layers. The layers in this model are

Application:

Application layer is the layer most commonly interacted with by users and user applications. Network communication is discussed on the basis of availability of resources, communication partners, and data synchronization.

Presentation:

Presentation layer is responsible for the mapping of resources and the creation of context. It is used to translate lower-level networking data into data that the applications hope to see.

Session: Session layer is a connection handler. It creates, maintains, and breaks connections between nodes in a persistent manner.

Transport: transport layer is responsible for handling the layers above it with a dependable connection. In this sense, dependable refers to the ability to confirm that a piece of data has been received intact at the other end of the connection.

This layer is capable of resending information that has been lost or corrupted and can acknowledge receipt of data to remote computers.

Network:

Network layer is used to route data between various nodes on the network. It uses addresses to know which computer to send the information. This layer can also break up larger messages into smaller pieces to be reassembled at the other end.

Data Link:

The data link layer is implemented as a means of establishing and maintaining dependable links between different nodes or computers on a network using established physical connections.

Physical:

The physical layer is responsible for managing the actual physical devices used to make connections. This layer includes the software that handles physical connections and the hardware itself (such as Ethernet).

There are a lot of different layers that can be discussed depending on their closeness to bare hardware and the functionality they offer.

Tcp / Ip Model

The TCP / IP model, commonly known as the Internet Protocol suite, is a simpler and more widely adopted layering model. It defines four different layers, some of which intersect with the OSI model:

Application: In the application model, the application layer is responsible for creating and sharing user data between applications. Applications may be on remote systems and should tend to function as if they were local to the end-user.

The communication is said to have taken place between peers.

Transport: The transport layer is in charge of communication between the processes. This level of networking uses ports to access different services. Depending on the type of protocol used, it can create reliable or unreliable connections.

Internet: Internet layer is used to transfer data from node to node on a network. This layer is informed of the endpoints of the connections, but it does not worry about the actual connection required to get from one place to another. In this layer, IP addresses are defined as a way to access remote systems in an addressable manner.

Link: The link layer implements the actual local network topology that allows the Internet layer to display an addressable interface. It establishes connections between neighboring nodes for the transmission of data.

The TCP / IP model is a little more abstract and fluid. This made it much easier to implement and made it the dominant way for networking layers to be categorized.

Interfaces: Interfaces are communication networking points of the network for your computer. Each interface is connected to a virtual or physical networking device.

Normally, your server should have one configurable network interface for every Ethernet or wireless internet card you have.

In addition, a virtual network interface called the "loopback" or localhost interface will be defined. It is used as an interface to connect processes and applications to other processes and applications on a single computer. You will see this referred to as the "lo" interface in a number of tools.

Several times, administrators configure one interface to service traffic to the internet and another LAN or private network interface.

Protocols networking operates by piggybacking several different protocols on top of each other. By this, one piece of data can be transmitted using several protocols encapsulated within each other.

We'll talk about some of the common protocols that you might find and try to explain the difference, as well as the context of what part of the process they're concerned with.

We will start with protocols implemented on lower layers of networking and work our way to higher abstraction protocols.

Media Access Control

Media Access Control is a communication protocol used to distinguish different devices. During the manufacturing process, each device must have a unique MAC address that distinguishes it from any other computer on the internet.

Addressing hardware by MAC address enables you to refer to a device by a unique value even when the software above may modify the name of the device during operation.

One of the only link layer protocols that you are likely to deal with regularly is the media access control.

IP

IP protocol is one of the essential protocols that allow the internet to run. IP addresses are unique for each network and allow machines to address each other across the network. It is implemented in the IP / TCP model on the Internet layer.

Networks may be linked together, but traffic must be diverted when the boundaries of the network are crossed. This protocol assumes an unstable network and multiple routes to the same destination that can be dynamically modified.

There are a variety of different protocol implementations. The most common implementation presently is IPv4, although IPv6 is gaining popularity as an alternative due to the scarcity of usable IPv4 addresses and improved protocol capabilities.

ICMP

ICMP means Internet Control Message Protocol. This is used to send messages between devices to show the conditions of availability or error. These packets are used in a wide range of network diagnostic tools, such as ping and trace route.

ICMP packets are usually transmitted when a packet of another kind encounters some kind of problem. They are essentially used as a feedback mechanism for network communications.

TCP

TCP means transmission control protocol. TCP is implemented in the transport layer of the IP / TCP model and used to create stable connections.

TCP is one of the protocols that embodies data in packets. They are then moved to the remote end of the connection using available methods on the lower layers. On the other end, it can search for errors, request resending of certain pieces, and reassemble the information into one logical piece to be sent to the application layer.

The protocol establishes a connection before data is transmitted using a method called a three-way handshake. It is a method for the two ends of the communication to recognize the request and to agree on a method of ensuring data reliability.

After the data is sent, the connection is broken using a similar four-way handshake.

TCP is the main protocol for several of the most common uses on the Internet, including WWW,

SSH, FTP, and email. It's fair to say that the internet wouldn't be here without TCP.

UDP

UDP means user datagram protocol. It is a common TCP companion protocol and is also implemented in the transport layer.

The main difference between UDP and TCP is that UDP offers insecure data transfer. It does not check that the data was received at the other end of the connection. It could seem like a negative thing, and it is for a lot of purposes. However, it is also highly important for other functions.

Because there is no need to await confirmation that the data was received and forced to resend the data, UDP is much faster than TCP. It does not create a connection to a remote host, it simply sends data to that host, and it does not bother whether it is accepted or not.

Due to the fact that it is a simple transaction, it is effective for basic communication, such as a query for network resources. It also does not maintain a state that makes it great to transmit data from one machine to several real-time clients. This makes it suitable for games, VOIP, and other applications that can not tolerate delays.

HTTP

HTTP means hypertext transfer protocol. It is a protocol specified in the application layer that forms the basis for web communication. HTTP describes a variety of functions that tell the remote system what you are asking for. For example, POST, GET, and DELETE all communicate in a different way with the requested data.

FTP

FTP means file transfer protocol. This is also in the application layer and offers a way to transfer full files from one host to another.

It is inherently unsafe, so it is not recommended for any external network unless it is introduced as a public download-only resource.

DNS

DNS means domain name system. This is an application layer protocol used to provide a human-friendly naming system for Internet resources. DNS connects a domain name to an IP address and enables you to access sites by name in your browser.

SSH

SSH means secure shell. It is an encrypted protocol incorporated in the application layer which can be used to communicate with a remote server in a secure manner. Thanks to its end-to-end encryption and ubiquity, several additional technologies are developed around this protocol.

Computer Network

Computer network is a digital telecommunications network for the sharing of information between nodes, which are computing devices that use standard telecommunications technology. Data transmission between nodes is facilitated over data links consisting of physical cable media, such as twisted pairs or fibre optic cables, or through wireless methods such as Wi-Fi, free-space optical communication, or microwave transmission.

The computer network is a link between two or more computers for the purpose of electronic communication of data. Apart from physically connecting computers and communication devices, a network infrastructure plays a significant role in establishing a cohesive architecture that enables a variety of equipment types to transmit information in a nearly seamless manner. Two common architectures are IBM Systems Network Architecture (SNA) and ISO Open Systems Interconnection (OSI).

Network nodes are network computing devices that initiate, route, and terminate data communications. They are generally known by network addresses, which can include hosts such as phones, personal computers, servers, and networking hardware such as switches and routers. Two of such devices can be considered to be networked when one device is capable of exchanging information with the other device, whether or not they have a direct link to each other. In most cases, application-specific communication protocols are layered over other more general communication protocols.

Computer networks provide support for a wide variety of applications and services, including access to the World Wide Web, digital audio, digital video, mutual use of data and storage servers, fax machines and printers, and use of email and instant messaging applications.

Computer networks can be classified according to a number of criteria, such as transmission medium used to carry signals, bandwidth, communication protocols for managing network traffic, network size, topology, traffic control system, and organizational purpose. The Internet is the most well-known computer network.

Types Of Network

1. Personal Area Network (PAN)

The smallest and most common form of network, the PAN, consists of a wireless router, a computer or two, printers, phones, tablets, etc., and centres on one person in a single building. This type of network is usually located in small offices or homes and are operated by one individual or company from a single device.

2. Local Area Network (LAN)

LANs are the most widely discussed networks, one of the most original, one of the most common, and one of the simplest types of networks. LANs link groups of computers and low-voltage devices over short distances (within the building or between two or three buildings in proximity to each other) to share resources and information. Enterprises usually operate and manage LANs.

Using routers, LANs can connect to wide area networks (WANs) in order to transfer data quickly and securely.

3. Wireless Local Area Network (WLAN)

Running as a LAN, WLANs use wireless network technologies such as Wi-Fi. Usually found in the same types of applications as LANs, these types of networks do not need devices to rely on physical cables to connect to the network.

4. Campus Area Network (CAN)

They are larger than LANs but smaller than Metropolitan Area Networks (MANs), these types of networks are usually located in colleges or small businesses. These can be distributed around a variety of buildings that are relatively close to each other so that users can share resources.

5. Metropolitan Area Network (MAN)

They are larger than LANs but smaller than WANs – and combine elements of both types of networks. MANs cover an entire geographical area (usually towns or cities, and sometimes a campus). Ownership and management are handled either by a single individual or company.

6. Wide Area Network (WAN)

It is a little more complex than a LAN. WAN connects computers over longer distances. This enables computers and low-voltage devices to be remotely connected to each other over a large network, even though they are miles apart.

The Internet is the simplest example of WAN connecting all computers around the world. Due to the wide scope of the WAN, it is usually managed and operated by various administrators or the public.

7. Storage-Area Network (SAN)

SAN is a dedicated high-speed network that links shared storage pools to multiple servers. This type of network does not rely on LAN or WAN. Instead, they transfer storage resources away from the network and position them in their own high-performance network. SANs can be used in the same way as a drive connected to a server. Storage Area Network Types include Virtual, Converged, and Unified SANs.

8. System-Area Network (also recognized as SAN)

This is a fairly local network designed to provide high-speed connectivity in storage area networks (also called "SANs"), server-to-server applications (cluster environments), and processor-to-processor applications. The computers connected to the SAN work as a single system at high speeds.

9. Passive Optical Local Area Network (POLAN)

POLAN technology as an alternative to conventional switch-based Ethernet LANs, can be incorporated into standardized cabling to address concerns about adopting traditional Ethernet protocols and network applications such as PoE (Power over Ethernet). A point-to-multipoint LAN architecture, POLAN uses optical splitters to split the optical signal from one strand of single-mode optical fibre into different signals to support users and devices.

10. Enterprise Private Network (EPN)

This type of network is developed and operated by companies who want to securely connect their different locations to share computer resources.

11. Virtual Private Network (VPN)

By expanding a private network over the Internet, a VPN allows users to send and also receive data as if their computers were connected to a private network – even though they are not. Users can access a private network remotely through a virtual point-to-point connection.

LANs link computers and peripheral devices in a limited physical environment, such as a business office, laboratory, or college campus, by means of connections (wires, Ethernet cables, fibre optics, Wi-Fi) that transmit data quickly. A typical LAN comprises of two or more personal computers, printers, and high-capacity disk storage devices called file servers that allow each computer on the network to access a common collection of files. LAN operating system software, interpret input and instructs networked machines, and allows users to communicate with each other; share printers and storage devices; and simultaneously access centrally located processors, data, or programs (instruction sets). LAN users are also able to access other LANs or WANs. LANs with similar architectures are connected by "bridges," which act as transfer points. LANs with different architectures are connected by "gateways" that convert data as it moves between systems.

WANs link computers and smaller networks to larger networks across wider geographic regions, including different continents. They can connect computers via cables, optical fibres or satellites, but their users typically access the networks through a modem (a system that enables computers to communicate over telephone lines). The largest WAN is the Internet, a series of networks and gateways connecting billions of computer users across every continent.

LOCAL AREA NETWORKS (LAN)

Local Area Networks (LANs) link computers inside a building or a small group of buildings. A LAN can be configured as

1) a bus, a major channel to which nodes or secondary channels are linked in a branching structure,

2) a ring in which each computer is linked to two neighbouring computers to create a closed circuit, or
3) a star in which each computer is connected directly to a central computer and only indirectly to each other. Each of these has advantages, although the configuration of the bus has become the most common.

Even if just two computers are connected, they must obey the rules or protocols to communicate with each other. For example, one may signal "ready to send" and hold on for the other to signal "ready to receive." When several computers share one network, the protocol may include "talk only when it's your turn" or "don't talk while someone else is talking." Protocols must also be configured to manage network errors.

The most popular LAN architecture since the mid-1970s is the bus-connected Ethernet, originally developed at Xerox PARC. Each computer or other device on the Ethernet has a unique 48-bit address. Any device that wants to transmit listens for a carrier signal, which shows that a transmission is ongoing. If it does not detect any, it will start transmitting the address of the receiver at the beginning of its transmission. Every system on that particular network receives each message but ignores those that are not addressed to it. While the system is transmitting, it also listens, and if it discovers a simultaneous transmission, it pauses, waits for a random time, and retries. The random time delay before retry reduces the likelihood that they will collide again. This is known as carrier sense multiple access with collision detection (CSMA / CD) control. It works very well when the network is moderately heavily loaded, and then degrades with more frequent collisions.

The very first Ethernet had a capacity of about two megabits per second, and now 10-and 100-megabit-per-second Ethernet is popular, with gigabit-per-second Ethernet also in use. Ethernet transceivers (transmitter-receivers) for PCs are low-cost and easy to install.

A new standard for wireless Ethernet, known as Wi-Fi, has become popular for small office and home networks. Using frequencies ranging from 2.4 to 5 gigahertz (GHz), these networks are able transfer data at a rate of up to 600 megabits per second. In early 2002, another Ethernet-like standard was released, called HomePlug. The first version was able to transmit data at about eight megabits per second through the existing electrical power infrastructure of a building. A later version could reach speeds of 1 gigabit per second.

Applications Of Lan

One computer in a network can be allocated as a server that allows all other computers to be managed.

The LAN allows the software to be stored on the server and to be used by all users of the network.

It lets you connect all the workstations in a building to enable them communicate with each other locally without the need for internet access.

Helps to share resources such as printers and scanners • Software developers can also use the LAN network to share development/testing tools within the office or within the factory with the aid of a networking device client-server model.

Advantages Of Lan

Computer resources such as hard disks, DVD-ROMs, and printers can share local area networks that dramatically reduce the cost of hardware purchases.

The same software can be used over the network instead of buying the licensed software for each device on the network.

The data of all network users can be stored on a single hard disk of the server computer.

Data and messages can be easily transferred over networked computers.

It will become easier to manage data at just one location, making data more secure.

The Local Area Network provides the facility to share a common Internet connection for all LAN users.

Lan Disadvantages

The LAN admin can inspect the personal data files of any LAN user so that they do not provide good privacy.

The LAN network lets you save costs due to shared computing resources. Nevertheless, the initial cost of building Local Area Networks is very high.

Unauthorized users can access sensitive company data in the event that the LAN admin is unable to protect a centralized data repository.

Local Area Network requires constant LAN management because there are issues related to device configuration and hardware malfunction

Wide Area Networks (Wan)

Wide Area Networks (WAN) around cities, countries, and the globe, usually use telephone lines and satellite connections. The Internet connects many WAN networks; as its name implies, it's a network of networks. Its popularity originated from early support from the U.S. Department of Defense, which created its precursor, ARPANET, to enable researchers interact easily and share computer resources. Its popularity is also attributed to its versatile communication technique. The advent of the Internet in the 1990s as not only a networking medium but also one of the key focal points of computer use may be the most important developments in computing in the last few decades.

Applications Of Wan

The head of the corporate office department needs to share some of the data with his regional office colleagues, and then they can share the data by saving it to a centralized node.

Military operations require a highly secure communication network. WAN is used for these operations.

Train reservations and airlines use WAN networks.

Dean and university lecturers can easily share data or resources with each other as they share a common network.

WAN enables workstations to be linked locally, which helps each node to communicate with each other without needing any internet connection.

Resources such as printers, scanners, hard disk, and fax machines make it possible for all nodes to be shared publicly.

Advantages Of Wan

WAN enables coverage of a larger geographical area, making it easy for business offices located at longer distances to communicate.

Includes devices such as cell phones, laptops, tablets, computers, game consoles, etc.

WLAN connections operate with radio transmitters and receivers built into client devices.

Share software and resources by connecting to different workstations.

Exchange information/files across a wider region.

Disadvantages Of Wan

The initial set-up cost of the WAN network is high

It is difficult to manage the WAN network because you need trained technicians and network administrators.

More time is required to address problems due to the presence of various wired and wireless technologies.

The WAN network has lower security compared to other types of networks.

MAIN DIFFERENCES BETWEEN LAN and WAN

LAN has a higher data transfer rate, while WAN has lower data transfer rate.

LAN is a computer network that extends over a specific geographical region, such as the home, workplace, or group of buildings, while WAN is a computer network that covers a wider area.

The LAN speed is high, while the WAN speed is slower than the LAN speed.

LAN has more fault tolerance, but WAN gives less fault tolerance.

On the other hand, LAN design and maintenance is simple, WAN design and maintenance is difficult.

Network Topologies

Topology Types

There are five types of topology in a computer network:

1. Mesh Topology
2. Star Topology
3. Bus Topology
4. Ring Topology
5. Hybrid Topology

Mesh Topology

In a mesh topology, each device is linked to every other device on the network via a dedicated point-to-point connection. When we say dedicated, this means that the connection only carries Data for the two connected devices. Let's assume we have n devices in the network; then, each device must be linked to (n-1) network devices. The number of links in the n device mesh topology will be n(n-1)/2.

Advantages of mesh topology

1. No data traffic problems, as there is a dedicated link between two devices, which means that the link is only available for these two devices.
2. Mesh topology is durable and reliable as the failure of one link does not impact other connections and communication between other devices on the network.
3. Mesh topology is safe because there is a point-to-point connection, so unauthorized access is not possible.
4. It's very easy to detect faults.

Disadvantages of Mesh Topology

1. The amount of wires needed for each device to be linked is exhausting.
2. Since each device needs to be connected to other devices, the number of I / O ports needed must be large.

3. Scalability problems as a system can not be connected to a large number of devices with a point-to-point link.

Star Topology

In star topology, every device on the network is linked to a central system called a hub. Unlike Mesh Topology, Star Topology does not allow direct communication between devices; a system would have to communicate via a hub. When one computer wishes to transfer data to another computer, it must first transfer the data to the hub and then transmit the data to the specified device.

Advantages Of The Star Topology

1. Less costly, as each system requires only one I / O port and requires to be linked to a single link hub.
2. It's easier to run

3. Less number of cables needed since each system only needs to be connected to the core.
4. Robust, so if one connection fails, the other link will work just fine.
5. It's easy to detect faults since the connection can be easily identified.

Disadvantages to Star Topology

1. When the hub goes down, everything goes down as well, none of the systems can operate without the hub.
2. Hub needs more money and frequent maintenance since it is the fundamental feature of star topology.

Bus Topology

There is the main cable in the bus topology, and all devices are connected to this main cable via drop lines. There's a system called a tap that links the drop line to the main cable. Since all data is transmitted over the main cable, there is a limitation on the drop lines and the distance the main cable can have.

Bus topology advantages

1. Easy to install, each cable must be linked to the backbone cable.
2. Fewer cables needed than Mesh and Star Topology Bus topology

Disadvantages

1. It's difficult to detect faults.
2. Not scalable, because there is a limit on how many nodes you can connect to the backbone cable.

Ring Topology

In a ring topology, each device is connected to the two devices on either side of it. There are two dedicated point-to-point connections between the devices on either side of the device. This structure forms a ring, so it is known as a ring topology. If the system wishes to transmit data to another system, then it sends data in one direction, each device in the ring topology has a repeater, if the received Data is intended for another device, then the repeater forwards that Data before the intended device receives it.

Advantages of Ring Topology

1. It's easy to install.
2. Managing is simpler because adding or removing a system from the topology requires changing only two links.

Disadvantages of Ring Topology

1. The entire network will fail when there is a link failure, as the signal does not move forward due to failure.
2. Data traffic problems, as all data circulates in a ring.

Hybrid Topology

A hybrid topology is a fusion of two or more topologies known as hybrid topology. For example, a combination of mesh and star topology is referred to as a hybrid topology.

Benefits of Hybrid Topology

1. We can choose a topology based on the requirement, For instance, if scalability is our concern, we can use star topology instead of bus technology.
2. It is Scalable because we can further link other computer networks to existing networks with different topologies.

Disadvantages of Hybrid Topology

1. It is difficult to detect faults.
2. It is difficult to install.
3. Design is complex, so maintenance is high and therefore, costly.

Peer To Peer Network

Unlike the Client-Server, the Peer-to-Peer model does not differentiate between the client and the server; rather, each node may be either a client or a server depending on whether the node requests or provides services. Every node is considered to be a peer.

In order to become part of peer-to-peer, the node must first join the network. After joining, services must begin to be provided to and must be requested from other nodes in the peer-to-peer network. There are two ways to determine which node offers which services; these are as follows: when a node joins the peer-to-peer system, it must register the services it will provide in a centralized search database on the network. If a node desires a particular service, it will contact centralized search services to see which node can provide the services requested. The rest part of the communication is handled by the desired node, and the node providing the service.

A node seeking a specific service must broadcast a request for services to all other nodes in the peer-to-peer network. The node providing the requested service responds to the node making the request.

The benefit of the Peer-to-Peer network over the client-server is that the server is not filtered because the services are delivered by a variety of nodes distributed in a peer-to-peer environment.

Advantages from Peer to Peer Network

1. Failure of one computer does not interrupt the whole system.

A peer-to-peer network does not rely on a centralized system to transfer information. This means that each terminal functions independently of each other. When one of the computers goes down for whatever reason, there will be no damage to the rest of the network. The only negative outcome that would arise in this case would be a loss of access to files on the terminal experiencing problems.

2. You can eliminate the cost of having and managing a server.

A Peer to Peer network does not need a server since individual terminals function as an information repository. Registered users may use their assigned or personal devices to access any computer connected in this way. This benefit greatly reduces operating costs for large organizations as each workstation interacts automatically with each other on the assigned network.

This benefit also means that staff will become more efficient as file access is immediate rather than requiring a transfer from station to station.

3. Peer to peer networks does not need a network operating system.

A peer-to-peer network does not require the proper functioning of a network operating system. This advantage is also a result of this setup's independent structure. Every computer acts as its own "server" in a way that stores Data for individual users while providing access to local files – often under different profiles. You can then link each system to the Internet or to cloud-based services as required to manage the network. Without the need for an operating system, users can be more efficient, and businesses can reduce technology and staffing costs without adversely affecting their workers.

4. This system does not require the use of advanced knowledge.

Peer to Peer networks are much simpler to set up and operate than client-server networks. This method does not require specialized expertise during the start-up process. As long as the user knows how to connect the terminal to those in close proximity to the station, peer-to-peer functionality is instantly attainable.

Also, when computers move through copper wire connections in a hardwired office, most systems use a plug-and-play method that allows almost everyone to create the connectivity needed for continuous productivity.

5. It eliminates the need for technical workers to be available.

Peer to peer networks does not need the same number of specialized workers as other links as everything happens at the user terminal. Each individual is able to set their own permissions as to which files they want to share with the rest of the network. While this means that it is theoretically possible to set up an independent system that has nothing to share, the arrangement eliminates the need for network technicians and system administrators to be available for support desk services and ongoing maintenance.

When a user understands how to build file permissions on a peer-to-peer network, that individual is ready to be productive.

6. You can start file retrieval process at any time.

Ever tried downloading a large file only to disrupt your Internet connection in the middle of the process? When you use a peer-to-peer network protocol, this problem goes away. If there is a stoppage for any reason, such as a sudden shutdown of your terminal, there is no need to start the download process from the start. When you can get your computer back online or connected to the rest of the network, you can proceed with the retrieval process.

7. You can find an entire library of files online.

You can easily find and download files online from peer to peer network, particularly if you prefer torrent files. Many online outlets and directories provide large libraries with high-quality material that you can access at any time. While it is up to you to decide the legality of every file or folder you download to your device, this information sharing method makes it easy to collaborate on projects or to get feedback on creative work.

8. Your internet speed may not have an effect on the loading time of your files.

Based on the number of terminals that serve as seeds for peer-to-peer networks, the speed of your Internet connection does not have an effect on the efficiency of your download. Even when users have poor connections, some torrent files can be downloaded very quickly compared to the conventional way. This benefit is possible because of the sharing structure in this way. You're getting tiny bits of information from hundreds or thousands of machines instead of just one storage location.

Disadvantages of Peer to Peer Network

1. Files or resources are not centrally coordinated on a peer to peer network.

A peer to peer network stores files or resources on individual computers instead of using a centrally structured shared space. This means that it could be difficult for some people to find specific files when the PC owner doesn't seem to have a logical file system. You must search each database manually to decide which files you need to download to your device. If you don't have a dependable Internet connection to support these efforts, you may find yourself wasting a lot of time.

2. The risk of introduction of viruses increases with peer-to-peer networks.

Once a peer-to-peer network is used, it is the duty of each individual user to avoid the introduction of viruses, malware, and other issues into the system. One individual making a mistake will adversely affect the effectiveness of the entire team indefinitely.

Even though the entire network runs antivirus software and works with a firewall, there is no guarantee that an individual user can prevent any problems they experience online.

3. Peer to Peer networks usually have very little security.

Most peer-to-peer networks have very little security to secure information stored on individual terminals or devices. If the IT department grants permissions to a particular device, anyone with access to it will share that level of access. Most users don't even need to sign in to their workstations because of the systems employed. This means the front door is the first line of protection for homeowners or companies using P2P networks. If a workstation requires a password, it is useful to have one set up to secure files and resources.

4. There is no way to remotely back up files or directories.

The only way you can back up files using peer-to-peer networks is to store them on separate computers. This means that you will have separate duplicate files that each user can adjust independently of each other. The lack of a centralized system causes problems with coordination due to this drawback, as the information is mainly terminal-based without a server. If something tempers with a workstation and files are lost, there's no way to recover from it unless the backup drive is part of the terminal.

5. Peer to Peer networks suffer performance issues.

When users operate in a peer-to-peer network, each terminal has the ability to access any other computer that is connected to it. This implies that any device could be accessed by every other user on the system at any time. Direct connections result in slower performance, even if the terminal user is not trying to access any other information than what is stored locally.

This drawback is the primary reason why most peer-to-peer connections require only two computers. As the number of terminals continues to increase, performance problems are almost always at higher risk of occurring.

6. The structure can allow remote access to some terminals.

As with most network systems, peer-to-peer networks can experience the disadvantage of having unsecured or unsigned codes on a particular terminal. If this circumstance has occurred, it can allow anyone to remotely access files on a connected device without permission. This means that it is often possible to compromise the entire system when this incident happens.

Because each device is operated on its own, there is no way to tell the difference between authorized and unauthorized use of this framework.

7. You may need to use a particular interface to read the file.

If you use torrent downloads as a means of accessing files, you typically need a special software program or platform to make the file accessible. Specific codex specifications may be required to read the information. Even if you have all the elements in place to access the data, a large network has a higher chance of file corruption because various components of the seeding process operate on a number of different systems.

Since larger systems do not give many options or knowledge about where your data originates, peer-to-peer networks force users to depend on a trust-based system.

8. Peer to peer networks does not have a way to access files before downloading.

This drawback does not extend to a network that allows individual terminals to remotely access files from approved systems. It applies to all other systems because there is no way to check the details you want to access before the file appears on your computer. Most systems will give you an opportunity to see what the file contains as a sample, but it will not allow you to access the quality of the data.

The only way for users to prevent problems with this issue is to conduct a quality check through online reviews from others or to request files from sources that you personally trust.

9. You can exchange personal information through peer-to-peer network activities.

The peer-to-peer protocol would automatically reveal your IP address to the people participating in your swarm. If you are concerned about guarding your privacy when uploading files, the only way you can do this is to use a virtual private network. A VPN helps you to funnel your traffic via various online servers in different countries so that your home address can be hidden. Even your ISP is not permitted to break through this tunnel.

If you want to start using a VPN, you'll want to make sure that the service provider has a good reputation for preventing leaks.

10. Some peer-to-peer protocols require you to upload and download at thesame time.

When you make use of the BitTorrent protocol to manage peer-to-peer networking solutions, you upload and download files simultaneously. This behaviour can have a huge effect on the speed of your Internet connection in adverse ways. Basic tasks can not be carried out during the download process due to this drawback, including the inability to access a specific web page.

Some networks allow this traffic to be somewhat isolated, but they will still impact users who multitask projects as part of their work duties. If you access files at home, it won't take a lot of time to overcome a standard DSL link.

Client Server Network

Description Of Client-Server

The Client-Server network model, is commonly used as a network architecture. The server is a strong device that stores data or information in it. On the other hand, the client is a device that allows users to access data on the remote server.

The system administrator manages the server's data. Client devices and servers are connected to the network. It enables clients to access data even though the client computer and server are far apart.

In the Client-Server model, the client process on the client device sends the request to the server on the server device. When the server receives a request from the client, it checks for the requested data and sends it back with the reply.

As all services are provided by a centralized server, there could be a risk that the server may become bottlenecked, slowing down the performance of the system.

Purpose Of Client Server Network

We are in an age in which information technology plays a key role in business applications, which is perceived to be an environment in which a company would invest significantly in order to expand the opportunities available to compete in the global market. A dynamic global economy would cause obsolescence and obscurity for those who are unwilling or unable to compete, which means that it is important for companies to retain their market position by re-engineering the existing organizational structures and business practices to achieve their business objectives. In short, with the shift in technological dimensions, there is a profound need to develop. Organizations would also be subject to a system to collect and process their corporate data in order to make business operations more effective in order to succeed or thrive on the global market. The client/server model provides a functional viewpoint of distributed business processing where the server manages and processes all client requests. This can also be seen as a groundbreaking achievement for the data processing industry. "Client/server networking is the most effective method for empowering workers with authority and responsibility. Workstation power, workgroup dominance, protection of existing investments, remote network management, and market-driven business are the forces that generate the need for client/server computing. Client/server computing is moving a long way in the computer industry, leaving no field or corner untouched. Hybrid skills are often required for the development of client/server applications, such as database design, transaction processing, communication skills, graphical user interface design, and development, etc. Advanced applications require the knowledge of distributed objects and the infrastructure of components. The most widely known client/server strategy today is the PC LAN implementation designed for group/batch group/batch use. This has effectively set a standard for many modern distributed businesses as it removes host-centric computing.

Characteristics of the Client-Server Network

- Client and server machines, require a variety of hardware and software resources.
- Clients and server machines can belong to different vendors.
- Horizontal scalability (an increase of client machines) and vertical scalability (migration to a more efficient server or multi-server solution) The client or server application interacts directly with the

transport layer protocol to communicate and send or receive information.

- The transport protocol instead uses lower-layer protocols to send or receive individual messages. Thus, a device requires a full collection of protocols to operate either a client or a server.
- A single server-class computer may provide multiple services at the same time; a separate server program is required for each service.

Three-Tier Client Server Network

The conventional client/server network consists of two levels, the level of the client and the level of the server. Another typical design of the client/server system uses three layers:

- A client that communicates with the user
- An application server that holds the business logic of the application
- A resource manager that stores the data

Advantages of the Client-Server Network

Companies also pursue ways to retain functionality and competitive efficiency in order to preserve their market place with the aid of the technologists. Deployment of client-server computing in an enterprise would effectively increase its efficiency through the use of cost-effective user interface, enhanced data storage, robust networking, and efficient application services.

Improved data sharing: data stored by normal business processes and manipulated on a server is accessible to approved users (clients) through authorized access.

Services integration: every client has the ability to access corporate information through a desktop interface, removing the need to log in to a terminal mode or processor.

Shared Resources Between Different Platforms: Application used for the client-server model is developed regardless of the hardware platform or technological background of the software (operating system software) that provides an open computing environment, enables users to obtain services from clients and servers (database, application and communication services).

Easy Maintenance: Client-server architecture is a distributed model reflecting shared roles between independent computers incorporated across the network. It is also easy to replace, upgrade, patch and transfer a server while the client remains intact. This unconscious change is called Encapsulation.

Security: Servers have stronger control access and resources to ensure that only approved clients are able to access or modify data and that server updates are efficiently administered.

Disadvantages of Client-Server Network

Overloaded Servers: If there are multiple simultaneous client requests, the system becomes seriously overloaded, resulting in network congestion.

Effect of Centralized Architecture: Because it is centralized when a vital server fails, client requests are not completed. Therefore, client-server lacks the stability of a strong network.

Key Differences Between Client-Server and Peer-to-Peer Network

1. The main difference between Client-Server and Peer-to-Peer network is that there are dedicated servers and specific clients in the Client-Server network model, while peer-to-peer nodes will act as both server and clients.

2. The server offers services to the client in the client-server model. However, in peer-to-peer cases, each peer may provide services and may also request services.

3. Information exchange is more important in the client-server model, whereas peer-

to-peer system connectivity is more important.

4. In the client-server model, data is stored on a centralized server, while in peer-to-peer, every peer has its own data.
5. In a peer-to-peer model, servers are spread around the network, so there is less risk of a server getting bottlenecked, but in a client-server model, there is a single server serving customers, and there is more risk of a server getting bottlenecked.
6. The client-server model is more complex to implement than the peer-to-peer model.
7. The client-server model is more efficient and stable than the peer-to-peer model.

Network Infrastructure

Network infrastructure is the hardware and software resources of the entire network that allow network connectivity, communication, operation and management of the enterprise network. It offers communication paths and resources between users, applications, software, utilities and external networks/internet.

Network connectivity is usually part of the IT connectivity that is used in most business IT environments. The whole network infrastructure is interconnected and can be used for internal communication, external communication or both. Networking Hardware: Routers Switches LAN Wireless Routers Cables Networking Software: Network Operations and Management Operating Systems Firewall Network Protection Applications Network Services: T-1 Line DSL Satellite Wireless Protocols IP Addressing NETWORK SPEEDS What is Network Speed?

In certain situations, a network interruption will only last a few milliseconds and have a marginal effect on what you're doing. In other situations, network delays can cause severe slowdowns. Typical scenarios that are particularly sensitive to network speed issues include time to set a new connection, time to download an app, an operating system patch, time to load a web page, or other file ability to stream video content for long periods of time without glitches.

The Role of Bandwidth in Network Performance

Bandwidth is a vital factor in determining the speed of a computer network. Providers use the bandwidth ratings of their internet service in product ads prominently, and you already know how much you have and what your network router can handle.

Computer networking bandwidth refers to the data rate provided by a network connection or interface. It reflects the total capacity of the connection. The greater the capacity, the more likely it will be to produce better results.

Bandwidth applies to both theoretical ratings and actual performance, and it is important to differentiate between the two. For example, a typical 802.11g Wi-Fi link offers 54 Mbps of authorized bandwidth, but in reality, only 50 percent or less of that number is achieved.

Traditional Ethernet networks potentially allow a maximum bandwidth of 100 Mbps or 1000 Mbps, but can not really reach this limit. Cellular (mobile) networks usually do not claim any particular bandwidth classification, but the same concept applies. Communications overheads in computer hardware, network protocols, and operating systems allow a difference between potential bandwidth and actual performance.

Measuring Network Bandwidth

Bandwidth is the amount of data that travels through a network link over time as calculated by bits per second (bps). There are various methods for administrators to calculate the bandwidth of network connections. On LANs (local area networks), such applications include Netperf and Test TCP. There are several bandwidth and speed test services on the internet, and most of them are free for you to use.

Even with these tools at your fingertips, bandwidth usage is difficult to quantify precisely because it varies over time depending on the configuration of the hardware plus the characteristics of the software applications, including how they are used.

Broadband Speeds

The word "high bandwidth" typically distinguishes faster broadband Internet connections from conventional dial-up or cellular network rates. Definitions of "high" and "low" bandwidth differ and have evolved over the years as network infrastructure improved.

Bandwidth is not the only factor related to the perceived speed of the network. A less well-known aspect of network performance-latency-also plays an important role.

Latency in Broadband Speeds

Latency, which can appear as "ping" in some speed tests, is the time required for data to be transmitted from your computer to the server and back. It is measured in milliseconds. A good ping is less than 10 ms. One more than 100 ms can cause issues, however, particularly when you're watching a movie or playing an online game. High latency can cause buffering, stuttering, and delay (or "lag") that can affect output.

NETWORK HARDWARE

Network hardware, also known as network equipment or computer networking devices, is an electronic device that is necessary for communication and interaction between devices on a computer network. Specifically, they mediate data transmission on a computer network. Units which are the last receiver or which generate data are called hosts, end systems or data terminal devices.

Network hardware may include gateways, switches, network bridges, modems, wireless access points, network cables, line drivers, routers, hubs, and repeaters; and may also include hybrid network devices such as bridge routers, multilayer switches, protocol converters, proxy servers, network address translators, firewalls, network interface controllers, multiplexers, wireless network interface controllers, ISDN terminal adapters and other hardware.

The most popular form of networking hardware today is a copper-based Ethernet adapter that is standard on most modern computer systems. Wireless networking has become increasingly common, particularly for mobile and handheld devices.

Computer networking hardware includes data centre facilities (such as database servers, file servers, and storage areas), network services (such as DHCP, DNS, e-mail, etc.) as well as content delivery devices.

More generally, mobile phones and devices associated with the internet of things can also be called networking hardware. As technology progresses and IP-based networks are incorporated into building infrastructure and household services, network hardware may become an uncertain concept due to the increasingly growing number of network-capable endpoints.

Network hardware can be categorized by its network location and function.

1. Network Core

Network components that interconnect other network components.

- Gateway: an interface that offers network compatibility by translating transmission speeds, protocols, codes or security measures.

- Router: a networking system that transmits data packets across computer networks. Routers perform "traffic control" roles on the internet. A data packet is usually routed from one router to another via the networks that make up the internetwork until it arrives at its destination node. It Runs on the OSI layer 3.
- Switch: a device that links devices to a computer network using packet switching to receive, process and forward data to a destination device. Unlike less complex network hubs, a network switch only transfers data to one or more machines that need to access it, rather than forwarding the same data from each of its ports. It Runs on the OSI layer 2.

- Bridge: is a device that links multiple segments of the network. It Runs on OSI layers 1 and 2.
- Repeater: is an electronic device that receives and transmits a signal at a higher level of power or on the other side of a barrier so that the signal can travel longer distances.
- Repeater hub: It connects multiple Ethernet devices together and make them function as a single network node. It has several input/output (I / O) ports in which the signal entered at the input of any port shows at the output of each port except the original incoming one. The hub operates on the physical layer (layer 1) of the OSI model. Repeater hubs also engage in collision detection, transmitting a jam signal to all ports when a collision is detected. Hubs are now essentially redundant, having been replaced by

network switches except for very old systems or specialized applications.

2. Hybrid: Hybrid components may be found in the core or border of the network.

- Multilayer switch: it's a switch that, in addition to switching to OSI layer 2, offers higher protocol layer functionality.
- Protocol converter: it's a hardware device that converts between two different types of transmission to be interoperable.
- Bridge Router: It is also known as a brouter. It's a device that works as a bridge and a router. The brouter routes packets to known protocols and simply forward all other packets as a bridge would.

3. Border Hardware or software components that are usually located at the point of connection of various networks (for instance, between an internal network and an external network) include

- Proxy Server: a computer network service that enables clients to make indirect network connections to other network services.
- Firewall: a piece of hardware or software mounted on the network to prevent certain communications prohibited by the network policy. A firewall usually creates a barrier between a trusted, protected internal network and another external network, such as the internet, that is believed not to be secure or trusted.
- Network Address Translator (NAT): It's a network service (provided as hardware or software) that translates internal to external network addresses and vice versa.

4. End stations Other hardware devices used for networking or dial-up connections include:

- Network Interface Controller (NIC): It's a device that links a computer to a wire-based computer network.
- Wireless network interface controller: It's a device that links a computer to a radio computer network.
- Modem: a device that modulates the analog "carrier" signal (like sound) to encode digital information, and also demodulates the carrier signal to decode transmitted information. For example, it is used when a computer interacts over a telephone network with another computer.
- ISDN terminal adapter (TA): An ISDN specialized gateway.
- Line driver: a system designed to increase the transmission distance by amplifying

the signal; it is used only in base-band networks.

Network Interface Card (Nic)

A network interface card (NIC) is a hardware component without which a computer can not be connected to a network. It's a circuit board installed in a computer and provides a dedicated network connection to the computer. It is often referred to as a network interface controller, a network adapter or a LAN adapter.

Purpose of NIC

- NIC enables both wireless and wired communication.
- NIC facilitates communication between computers connected through the local area network (LAN) as well as large-scale network communication through the Internet Protocol (IP).
- NIC is a physical layer and a data link layer tool, i.e. it provides the hardware circuitry

required so that physical layer processes and some data link layer processes can operate on it.

NIC Card Types

NIC Cards are of two types — Internal Network Card and External Network Card In Internal Network Cards, the motherboard has a network card slot where it can be inserted. Network cables are needed to provide network access. There are two types of internal network cards. The first type makes use of Peripheral Component Interconnect (PCI) connections, while the second type uses Industry Standard Architecture (ISA).

External Network Cards

External NICs are used in desktops and laptops that do not have an internal NIC. There are two types of external network cards which are: wireless and USB-based. The wireless network card must be inserted into the motherboard, and no network cable is needed to be connected to the network. They are useful when travelling or accessing a wireless signal.

Workstations

A Workstation (WS) is a computer dedicated to a user or group of users involved in business or professional activities. It requires one or more high-resolution displays and a faster processor than a personal computer (PC). Workstations also have a higher multitasking capability due to additional random access memory (RAM), drive and drive capacity. Workstations can also have higher-speed graphics adapters and also more connected peripherals.

The term workstation also refers to a local area network (LAN) PC or mainframe terminal. These workstations can share network resources with one or more large client and network servers.

Workstations are typically designed with an optimized layout for complex data manipulation and visualization. Some examples are image rendering and editing, computer-aided design (CAD), animation and mathematical plot. Workstations were the first industry segment to build customer communication tools and innovative accessories and upgrades. These include 3D mice, multiple displays and high-performance data storage devices.

However, the mainstream PCs embraced work station features that led to the downturn in the work station market segment. In fact, the cost difference decreased between lower-end workstations and higher-end PCs. Low-end workstations adopted Intel Pentium 4 or AMD Athlon 64 CPUs, while high-end PCs adopted powerful processors such as Intel Xeon, IBM Power, AMD Opteron or Sun UltraSPARC-a powerhouse for computer-processing. These latter machines are also known as workstation-class PCs and include features such as Error-correcting code (ECC) memory support Extra memory sockets for registered modules Multiple processor sockets for more powerful CPUs

Multiple displays Reliable operating systems with advanced features High-performance graphics cards.

Sun Microsystems currently produces the only workstations that use x86-64 microprocessors and Windows, Solaris 10, Mac OS X, and Linux-distributed operating systems.

Network Administrator

The network administrator is the person appointed in an organization whose role includes the maintenance of computer infrastructures with a focus on networking. Responsibility can vary between organizations, but on-site servers, software-network interactions as well as network integrity/resilience are major areas of focus.

The Role Of The Network Administrator

The role of a network administrator can vary considerably depending on the size, location and socio-economic factors of the organization.

Several organizations focus on a user-to-technical support ratio, while others adopt several other approaches.

Generally, in terms of reactive circumstances (i.e., sudden service failures or service improvements), the IT Support Incidents are generated via the Issue Tracking system. Issues typically work their way through the Help Desk and flow to the appropriate technology field for resolution. In a network related issue, the issue will be addressed to the network administrator. If the network administrator is unable to fix the problem, a ticket will be scaled to a higher level network engineer to restore the service or to a more suitable expertise group.

Network managers are also engaged in proactive work. This type of work also include:

- monitoring of the network.
- Check the network for weakness.
- Keep an eye out for the updates you need.

- Installation and execution of security programs.
- In certain instances, e-mail and Internet filters.
- Evaluation of implementing network.

Network administrators are responsible for ensuring that computer hardware and network infrastructure connected to the data network of the organization are managed effectively. For smaller organizations, they are usually involved in the acquisition of new hardware, roll-out of new software, maintaining disk images for new computer installations, ensuring that licenses are paid for and up to date for software that requires it, maintaining standards for server installations and applications, poor data management practices, monitoring network performance, and checking for security breaches A common problem for a small-medium business (SMB) network administrator is the amount of bandwidth needed to run my business? Usually, within a larger organization, these responsibilities are divided into multiple tasks or functions across various departments and are not carried out by a single individual. Some of these functions are performed by system administrators in other organizations.

As with other technical roles, a network administrator position require a wide range of technical skills and the ability to quickly learn the intricacies of modern networking and server software packages. For smaller organizations, the higher role of network engineer is often linked to the responsibility of the network administrator. It is very popular for smaller organizations to outsource this role.

Collision Domain

A collision domain is a network segment connected by a common medium or via a repeater where simultaneous data transmissions collide with each other. The collision domain applies in particular to wireless networks, but also to early versions of the Ethernet. A network collision happens when more than one device tries to send a packet to the network segment at the same time. Individuals in a collision domain may be involved in collisions with each other. Devices outside the collision domain lack any internal collisions.

Just one computer in the collision domain can transmit at any time, and the other devices in the domain can listen to the network and refrain from transmitting while others are still transmitting in order to avoid collisions. Since only one device can be transmitted at a time, total network bandwidth is shared amongst all devices in the collision domain. Collisions also reduce network efficiency in the collision domain, as collisions cause devices to interrupt transmission and transmit again at a later time.

Since data bits are dispersed at a finite speed, they must be simultaneously specified in terms of size of the collision domain and the minimum size of the packet allowed. A smaller packet size or a larger dimension will make it possible for the sender to finish sending the packet without the first bits of the message reaching the most remote node. So, the node could also start sending, without a hint to the transmission already taking place, thereby destroying the first packet. Unless the size of the collision domain enables the initial sender to receive the second transmission attempt – the collision – within the time required to transmit the packet, it would not be able to detect the collision or repeat the transmission – it is called a late collision.

Broadcast Domain

A broadcast domain is a logical part of a computer network in which all nodes can access each other through broadcast at a data link layer. A broadcast domain may be within the same LAN segment or may be connected to other LAN segments.

As far as current popular technologies are concerned, any device connected to the same Ethernet repeater or switch is part of the same broadcast domain. In addition, every device connected to the same set of interconnected switches/repeaters is a member of the same broadcast domain. Routers and other higher-layer devices are the boundaries between broadcast domains.

This is compared to a collision domain, in which all nodes on the same set of interconnected repeaters, are separated by switches and learning bridges. Collision domains are generally smaller than and included in broadcast domains.

While some layer two network devices are capable of separating collision domains, broadcast domains are only separated by layer three network devices, such as routers or layer three switches. Separating VLANs also separates the broadcast domains.

Networking Cables

Networking cables are networking hardware used to link one network device to another network device or to link two or more computers to share printers, scanners, etc. Depending on the physical layer, topology, and size of the network, various types of network cables, such as coaxial cable, optical fibre cable, and twisted pair cables, are used. Devices may be divided by a few meters (e.g. via Ethernet) or by almost limitless distances (e.g. via Internet connections).

There are a variety of systems used for network connections. Patch cables are used in office and wiring closets, for short distances. Electrical connections using a twisted pair or a coaxial cable are used inside a building. Optical fibre cable is used for long distances or applications requiring high bandwidth or electrical insulation. Many installations use organized cabling practices to improve reliability and maintenance. In some home and commercial applications, power lines are used as network cables.

Twisted pair

Twisted pair wiring is a type of wiring in which pairs of wires (a single circuit's forward and return conductors) are twisted together in order to remove electromagnetic interference (EMI) from other wire pairs as well as from external sources. This type of cable is used by both home and corporate Ethernet networks. Twisted pair cabling is used for short patch cables and standardized cabling in the long run.

The primary types of twisted pair cable industry standards are the shielded twisted pair (STP) and the unshielded twisted pair (UTP). Modern Ethernet cables use UTP wiring because of their lower cost, while STP wiring can be used in other forms of networks like Fiber Distributed Data Interface (FDDI).

USB Cables

Most Universal Serial Bus (USB) cables connect computers to a peripheral devices (such as a mouse or keyboard) rather than to another computer. However, special network adapters (also called dongles) link the Ethernet cable to the USB port. USB cables feature twisted pair wiring.

Fibre optics

An optical fibre cable consists of a central glass core surrounded by many layers of protective material. Optical fibre installation is more costly than copper but provides higher bandwidth and span longer distances. There are two primary types of optical fibre cables: shorter-range multi-mode fibre and long-range single-mode fibre.

Coaxial

Coaxial cables form a transmission line and interconnect the electromagnetic wave within the cable between the centre conductor and the shield. The transfer of energy in the line takes place entirely through the dielectric within the cable between the conductors. Coaxial lines are also bent and twisted (subject to limits) without adverse effects and can be attached to conductive supports without causing unnecessary currents.

Early Ethernet, 10BASE5 and 10BASE2, utilized baseband signalling over coaxial cables. In the 20th century, L-carrier system used long-distance coaxial cables.

Coaxial cables are typically used for television and other broadband signals. Although most home coaxial cables have been designed for the transmission of TV signals, new technologies (like the ITU-T G.hn standard) open up the possibility of utilizing home coaxial cable for high-speed networking applications (Ethernet over coax).

Patch

A patch cable is an optical or electrical cable that connects one electronic device to another for the creation of a signal routing infrastructure. Devices of various types (e.g. switch connected to a computer, or switch connected to a router) are connected with patch cables. Patch cables are typically made in several different colours so that they can be easily distinguished and most of them are fairly thin, not more than a few meters long. In comparison to on-site wiring, patch cables are more versatile.

Power lines

While AC power wires are not intended for networking applications, power line communication (PLC) often enables such wires to be used to interconnect home computers, peripherals and other networked consumer products. The HomePlug protocol family was an early development of the PLC. In December 2008, ITU-T introduced Recommendation G.hn / G.9960 as the world's first standard for high-speed powerline communications. G.hn also defines communication methods for existing

Category 3 cables used by phones and coaxial cables used by home-based cable television.

Serial and parallel cables Since many PCs lacked Ethernet capabilities in the 1980s and early 1990s, and USB had not yet been developed, serial and parallel interfaces (now useless on modern computers) had often been used for PC-to-PC networking. Null model cables, for instance, connected the serial ports of two PCs and allowed data transmission at a speed range of 0.115 and 0.45 Mbps.

Crossover Cables

One example of a crossover cable type is the null modem cables. A crossover cable links two network devices of the same kind, such as two PCs or two network switches. The use of Ethernet crossover cables was popular on older home networks years ago when two PCs were connected directly together.

Externally, Ethernet crossover cables tend to be similar to ordinary cables (sometimes referred to as straight-through cables), the only noticeable distinction is the pattern of colour-coded wires found on the cable end connector. For this purpose, manufacturers usually added special identifying marks to their crossover cables. Nowadays, however, most home networks use routers that have built-in crossover capabilities, removing the need for such special cables.

Wireless Networking

A wireless network, simply put, is a computer network that utilizes wireless connections between network nodes.

Wireless networking is a system by which households, telecommunication networks and business installations bypass expensive processes of cable integration into a building or as a connection between various locations of an equipment. Admin telecommunications networks are typically established and operated by means of radio communication. This implementation is carried out at the physical layer of the OSI model network structure. Examples of wireless networks include cellular networks, wireless sensor networks, wireless local area networks (WLANs), satellite communication networks and terrestrial microwave networks.

History Of Wireless Networks

Wireless networks The first modern wireless network was established under the ALOHAnet brand at the University of Hawaii in 1969, and in June 1971, it became operational.

The first commercial wireless network was a WaveLAN products family developed by NCR in 1986.

In 1973, Ethernet 802.3 was developed In 1991 2G mobile phone network was developed In June 1997, 802.11 'WiFi' protocol was first released In 1999, 803.11 VoIP integration was introduced Underlying technology Developments in MOSFET (MOS transistor) wireless technology facilitated the development of digital wireless networks. , The widespread adoption of RF CMOS (radio frequency CMOS), MOSFET and LDMOS (lateral diffuse MOS) devices contributed to the introduction and growth of digital wireless networks in the 1990s, with further developments in MOSFET technology contributing to an increase in bandwidth in the 2000s. Most of the fundamental elements of wireless networks are developed from MOSFETs, including mobile transceivers, routers, base station modules, telecommunication circuits, RF circuits, and radio transceivers, in networks such as 2G, 3G, and 4G.

Wireless links

Terrestrial microwave – Terrestrial microwave communication make use of Earth-based transmitters and receivers that resemble satellite dishes. Terrestrial microwaves are in a low gigahertz range, which restricts all communications to the line of sight. Relay stations are roughly 48 km (30 mi) apart.

Communications satellites – Satellites communicate through microwave radio waves that are not deflected by Earth's atmosphere. The satellites are located in space, typically in a geosynchronous orbit 35,400 km (22,000 mi) above the equator. Such Earth-orbiting networks are capable of receiving and transmitting voice, data and TV signals.

Cellular and PCS systems use a range of radio communications technologies. The systems divide the region into different geographic areas. Each area has a radio relay antenna system or low-power transmitter to relay calls from one area to the next.

Radio and Spread spectrum technologies – Local wireless networks use high-frequency radio technology close to modern cellular and low-frequency radio technology. Wireless LANs use spread spectrum technology to allow communication between multiple devices in a limited region.

Free-space optical communication makes use of visible or invisible light for communication purposes. For most situations, line-of-sight propagation is used, which restricts the physical location of communication devices.

Types Of Wireless Networks

Wireless PAN

Wireless Personal Area Networks (WPANs) link devices within a fairly limited region, which is usually within the reach of a person. For example, Bluetooth radio and invisible infrared light provide a WPAN for connecting a headset to a laptop. ZigBee also supports WPAN applications. WiFi PANs are becoming common as equipment designers start incorporating WiFi into a range of consumer electronic devices.

Wireless LAN

A wireless local area network (WLAN) connects two or more devices over a short range using a wireless communication system, typically providing an Internet access connection. The use of spread-spectrum or OFDM technology that allows users to move around within a local coverage area and remain connected to the network.

Products that use IEEE 802.11 WLAN standards are known as WiFi. Fixed wireless technology offers point-to-point communications between computers or networks at two distant places, typically utilizing dedicated microwave or modulated laser light beams along a line of sight paths. It is mostly used in cities to link networks in two or more buildings without a wired connection being built. Often devices such as a router or mobile smartphones connect to WiFi through hotSpot.

Ad-hoc wireless network

An ad-hoc wireless network, also known as a wireless mesh network or a mobile ad-hoc network (MANET), is a wireless network composed of radio nodes arranged in a mesh topology. Every node sends messages on behalf of the other nodes, and each node performs routing. Ad hoc networks "self-heal" by automatically re-routing round a node that has lost power. Various network layer protocols are needed to implement ad hoc mobile networks, such as distance sequenced vector routing, ad hoc on-demand distance vector routing, Associativity-based routing, and dynamic source routing.

Wireless MAN

Wireless Metropolitan Area Networks are a form of wireless network that links multiple wireless LANs.

WiMAX

WiMAX means Worldwide Interoperability for Microwave Access. WiMAX refers to the interoperable implementation of the IEEE 802.16 family of wireless network standards approved by the WiMAX Board. (Similarly, WiFi refers to interoperable IEEE 802.11 Wireless LAN specifications certified by the WiFi Alliance.) WiMAX Forum certification enables retailers to market fixed or mobile devices as WiMAX accredited, providing a degree of interoperability with other authorized products as long as they match the same profile.

The original IEEE 802.16 standard (now known as "Fixed WiMAX") was released in 2001. WiMAX has adapted some of its WiBro technology, a service promoted in Korea.

Mobile WiMAX (which was originally based on 802.16e-2005) is a revision that has been adopted in several countries and is the foundation for future revisions, such as 802.16m-2011.

WiMAX can be used for a variety of applications, including wireless networks, cellular backhauls, hotspots, etc. It is similar to long-range WiFi, but it can be used at a much greater distance.

Uses of WiMAX

It has a scalable physical layer architecture that enables data rates to be easily scaled with the available channel bandwidth, and WiMAX range makes it ideal for the following potential applications: delivering portable mobile broadband connectivity across towns and countries via different devices.

Provide a wireless option to cable and digital subscriber line (DSL) for "last mile" access to broadband.

Data provision, telecommunications (VoIP) and IPTV services (triple play).

Provides Internet access as part of a business continuity strategy.

Intelligent grids and metering.

Access To The Internet

WiMAX provides home or mobile Internet connectivity across cities and countries. In certain cases, this has led to rivalry in markets that usually only had access to them through an existing incumbent DSL (or similar) operator.

In addition, despite the comparatively low costs associated with the implementation of WiMAX networks (compared to 3G, xDSL, HSDPA, FTTx or HFC), it is now commercially feasible to provide last-mile broadband Internet connectivity in remote areas.

Advantages of WiMAX

1.WiMAX is very common because of its low cost and versatile nature. It can be built faster than other internet technology as it can use shorter towers and fewer wiring to accommodate even non-line-of-sight coverage across an entire city or country.

1. WiMAX isn't only for fixed connections, like at home. You may also connect to the WiMAX service for mobile devices, as USB dongles, laptops and phones also have built-in technology.
2. In addition to internet access, WiMAX provides voice and video transmission features and telephone access. Since WiMax transmitters can cover a distance

of several miles with data rates of about 30-40 megabits per second (1 Gbps for a fixed station), it is easy to see its advantages, particularly in areas where wired internet is difficult or too expensive to implement.

3. WiMAX supports various models of networking usage as a way of transmitting data through the Internet Service Provider Network — commonly referred to as backhaul A type of fixed wireless broadband Internet access, replacing satellite internet service A type of mobile internet access which competes directly with LTE technology Internet connectivity for users in remote areas where the wiring will be too expensive.

Disadvantages of WiMAX

Because WiMAX is wireless in nature, the further away from the source the client gets, the slower their connection becomes. This means that while a user can pull down 30 Mbps at a single spot, travelling away from the cell site will reduce the speed to 1 Mbps or close to nothing.

Similar to multiple devices pulling away at a bandwidth when linked to a single router, multiple users in one WiMAX radio sector decreases efficiency for others.

WiFi is far more common than WiMAX, and more devices have built-in WiFi capabilities than WiMAX. However, most WiMAX implementations possess hardware that allows an entire household to use the WiFi service, for example, just as a wireless router provides the Internet for a variety of devices.

WiFi

WiFi is a group of wireless networking technologies that is based on the IEEE 802.11 series of standards that are widely used for local computer networking and Internet access. WiFi is a trademark of the non-profit WiFi Alliance, which limits the use of the name WiFi Certified to devices that have successfully completed interoperability certification testing. As of 2010, the WiFi Alliance consisted of over 375 companies from around the world. As of 2009, WiFi integrated circuit chips shipped approximately 580 million units annually.

WiFi uses various parts of the IEEE 802 protocol family and is intended to communicate seamlessly with its wired Ethernet sibling. Compatible devices can be connected to each other through wireless access points as well as to wired devices and the Internet. The various versions of WiFi are defined by specific IEEE 802.11 protocol standards, with different network technologies defining frequency bands, maximum ranges and speeds that can be achieved. WiFi uses 2.4 gigahertz (120 mm) UHF and 5 gigahertz (60 mm) SHF ISM radio bands most commonly; these bands are subdivided into several channels. Channels can be exchanged between networks, but only one transmitter can broadcast locally on a channel at any time.

WiFi wavebands have fairly high absorption and are ideally suited for line-of-sight application. Many common obstacles, such as walls, pillars, home appliances, etc., can significantly reduce the range, but this also helps to minimize interference between different networks in crowded environments. The access point (or hotspot) typically has a range of around 20 meters (66 feet) indoors, while some modern access points have a range of up to 150 meters (490 feet) outdoors. Area covered by the hotspot can be as small as a single room with walls that obstruct radio waves, or as wide as several square kilometers using a number of overlapping roaming access points permitted between them. The speed and spectral quality of WiFi have increased over time. As of 2019, some models of WiFi operating on appropriate hardware will achieve speeds of more than 1 Gbit / s (gigabit per second) at close range.

WiFi is actually more vulnerable to attack than wired networks, as anyone within the range of a wireless network interface controller can attempt entry. Typically, a user requires a network name (SSID) and a password to connect to a WiFi network. The password is used to encrypt WiFi packets to block intruders. WiFi Protected Access (WPA) is designed to secure information passing through WiFi networks and provides versions for personal and business networks. Developing the security features of WPA required better protections and new security practices.

Uses Of Wifi

Internet

WiFi technology can be used to provide local network and internet connectivity to devices within the WiFi range of one or more routers connected to the internet. The area covered by one or more interconnected access points (hotspots) may extend from an area as small as a few nearby rooms to as many square kilometres as possible. Coverage in the wider region can involve a group of access points with overlapping coverage.

WiFi is accessible in private residences, businesses and public spaces. WiFi hotspots can be set up either free of charge or commercially, often using a captive website for connectivity purposes. Organizations, fans, authorities and companies, such as airports, hotels and restaurants, also provide free or paid-to-use hotspots to draw tourists and offer business support services in selected areas.

Routers also have a digital subscriber line modem or cable modem, and a WiFi connection point is often set up in homes and other buildings to provide access to the internet and networking for the system.

A cellular Internet radio modem and a WiFi access point may also be included in battery-powered routers. When connected to a cellular data carrier, it allows local WiFi stations to access the Internet through 2 G, 3 G or 4 G networks using a tethering technique. Many smartphones have built-in capabilities of this type, including those based on Android, iOS (iPhone), BlackBerry, Windows Phone, and Symbian, but carriers often disable the functionality, or charge a separate fee to allow it, particularly for customers with unlimited data plans. "Internet packs" often have stand-alone facilities of this kind, without the use of a smartphone; examples include MiFi devices. Some laptops with a cellular modem card can also serve as mobile Internet WiFi connection points.

Geolocation

WiFi positioning systems use WiFi hotspot positions to determine the location of the device.

WiMAX vs WiFi

The main difference between Wimax technology and WiFi technology is cost, speed, distance, and so on. WiMAX coverage is approximately 30 miles, and WiFi coverage is quite limited to a small area.

Wimax network is just like an ISP without any cable as Wimax signal gets internet access to your home or business, while WiFi is used within your local area network (LAN) to access the internet.

The Wimax architecture is designed to make Metropolitan Area Networking (MAN) possible. WiMAX base station is capable of providing connectivity to business and hundreds of homes, while WiFi only offers local area networking (LAN) services.

The Wimax and WiFi network deployments are the same as ISP will have access to their T3 network. The line of sight antennas used to link the tower to Wimax technology. The tower shared the non-line of sight to the MAN.

The Wimax Line of Sight Antennas operates at a frequency of 60 MHz while the non-lined tower operates on a range much like the WiFi.

The Wimax base or tower station would beam a signal to the WiMAX receiver. Similarly, the WiFi access point transmit signal to the receiving device.

The Wimax network offering QoS (Quality of Service) also allows a large number of people access to the tower at the same time. The built-in algorithm will automatically move the user to another tower or Wimax station cell. Unlike WiFi users, they have to fight to remain linked with a defined access point.

The most important issue between Wimax and WiFi discrepancy is pricing as Wimax is a high-cost network, whereas WiFi is a low-cost network, and most people use WiFi due to lower prices and avoid Wimax due to costly installations.

WiMax won't place WiFi out of reach at home as WiFi is much stronger in terms of pace and technology. With the passage of time, technological development introduces a new version in 802.11. Wimax provides high speed, but if a client resides away from the tower or base station speed may be decreased.

Wimax provide high-speed internet as a broadband link that transmits data, voice and video at a very high speed. Although WiFi provides a short range of data transfer. WiFi can only be linked in designated areas so that only file sharing is possible.

Wimax long-distance design in a licensed spectrum or an unlicensed spectrum. Wimax enables point to point or point to multi-point connection. Various WiMAX standards such as 802.16e, 802.16b for fixed location mobile connection. Thus WiFi offers quality services to a fixed Ethernet where packets have priority over their tags. WiFi hotspots are generally hauled back over ADSL in small companies, cafes, etc., and connectivity is typically very difficult. The upload speed of WiFi relative to Wimax is also very poor between the internet and the router.

Wireless WAN

Wireless Wide Area Networks (WAN) are wireless networks that usually span vast areas, such as between neighbouring cities and towns, or between cities and suburbs. These networks may be used to connect business branch offices or as a public Internet access system. Wireless connections between access points are typically point-to-point microwave links using parabolic dishes on the 2.4GHz and 5.8Ghz bands, rather than omnidirectional antennas used on smaller networks. A Typical system comprises base station gateways, access points and wireless bridge relays. Certain setups are mesh systems where each connection point also serves as a relay. When paired with renewable energy systems such as photovoltaic solar panels or wind turbines, they may be stand-alone turbines.

Cellular network A cellular network (also known as mobile network) is a wireless network spread over land areas called cells, each of which is served by at least one fixed-location transceiver, known as a cell site or base station. Within a cellular network, each cell usually uses a separate set of radio frequencies from all its immediate neighbouring cells to prevent interference.

When these cells are joined together, they provide radio coverage over a large geographic region. This allows a large number of portable transceivers (e.g. mobile phones, etc.) to communicate with each other and with fixed transceivers and phones anywhere on the network, through base stations, even though some transceivers pass via more than one cell during transmission.

Although originally intended for mobile phones, with development of smartphones, cellular telephone networks regularly carry data in addition to telephone conversations: the Global System for Mobile Communications (GSM): the GSM network is divided into three main systems: the switching system, the base station system, and the operation and support system. The cell phone connects to the base station system, which then connects to the operation and support station, and then connects to the switching station where the call is conveyed to where it needs to go. GSM is the most common standard used for most cell phones.

Personal Communications Service (PCS): A PCS is a radio band that can be found on mobile phones in North America and South Asia.

D-AMPS: Digital Advanced Mobile phone Service, is an upgraded version of AMPS, which is being phased out due to technological advancements. Newer GSM networks are replacing the older GSM infrastructure.

Global Area Network

The Global Area Network (GAN) is a network used to support mobile networks across a random number of wireless LANs, satellite coverage areas, etc. The primary challenge in mobile communications is to handle user communications from one local coverage area to another. This includes the succession of terrestrial wireless LANs in IEEE Project 802.

Space Network Space Networks are networks used to communicate between spacecraft, mostly in the vicinity of Earth. The NASA Space Network is an example of this.

Uses

Many examples of use involve mobile phones that are part of everyday wireless networks, allowing simple personal contact. Another example, Intercontinental Network Systems, uses radio satellites to communicate around the world. Emergency services, such as the military, often use wireless networks to effectively communicate. Individuals and companies use wireless networks to send and exchange data easily, whether in a small office building or around the world.

General Properties

In a general context, wireless networks provide a wide range of applications for both business and home users.

The industry is now embracing a range of different wireless technologies. Each wireless technology is described by a standard that defines the specific features of both the data and physical link layers of the OSI model. These standards differ, among other things, in their specified signalling methods, geographic ranges and frequency usages. Such differences make certain technologies better suited to home networks and others better suited to networking with larger organizations.

Performance Each standard varies in geographical range, making one standard more suitable than the next depending on what you want to achieve with a wireless network. Wireless network performance supports a number of applications, such as voice and video. The use of this technology also provides room for extensions, such as 2 G to 3 G and 4 G and 5 G systems, which represent the fourth and fifth generation of mobile phone networking standards. Since wireless networking has become a standard, complexity increases with the modification of network hardware and software, and wider capacity to transmit and receive larger volumes of data is accomplished more quickly. The wireless network is now based on LTE, a 4G mobile networking standard. Consumers of the LTE network have a maximum speed that is 10x higher than the 3 G network.

Space Space is another aspect of wireless networking. Wireless networks offer several advantages when it comes to difficult-to-wire areas when trying to communicate, probably across a river or street , a warehouse on the other side of the premises or buildings that are physically separate but operate as one. Wireless networks allow users to identify a certain space that the network will be able to communicate with other devices via that network.

Space is also generated in homes as a result of the removal of wiring clutters. This technology offers an alternative to the installation of physical network media such as TPs, coaxes or fibre optics, which can also be costly.

Home Wireless technology is an effective option for homeowners compared to Ethernet for sharing printers, scanners and high-speed Internet connections. WLANs help save the cost of installing cable media, saves time of physical installation, and also provide mobility for devices linked to the network. Wireless networks are straightforward and require as few wireless access points as possible that are directly connected to the Internet through a router.

Wireless Network Elements

The physical layer telecommunications network often consists of a variety of interconnected wireline network elements (NEs). Such NEs can be stand-alone systems or goods that are either supplied by a single supplier or assembled by a service provider (user) or a system integrator with parts from a variety of different manufacturers.

Wireless NEs are the products and services used by the wireless carrier to support the backhaul network as well as the mobile switching centre (MSC).

Reliable wireless coverage relies on the physical layer network elements to be secured against all operating environments and applications.

The NEs, which are located on the cell tower to the base station (BS) cabinet, are especially significant. Attachment hardware and antenna positioning and associated closures and cables are needed to have adequate power, robustness, corrosion resistance and resistance to wind, storms, icing and other weather conditions. Requirements for individual parts, such as hardware, wires, connectors and fasteners, shall take into account the structure to which they are attached.

Difficulties

Interference

In contrast to wired systems, wireless networks are also subject to electromagnetic interference. It could be triggered by other networks or other types of equipment that produce radio waves inside or near the radio bands used for communication. Interference can disturb the signal or cause the system to malfunction.

Absorption and reflection

Certain materials cause electromagnetic wave absorption, which prevents electromagnetic waves from reaching the receiver, in certain situations, in particular with metallic or conductive material reflection. It can trigger dead zones where there is no reception. Aluminium foiled thermal insulation in modern homes can potentially reduce indoor mobile signals by 10 dB, often leading to concerns about poor reception of long-distance rural cell signals.

Multipath Fading

In the multipath fading of two or more separate signal paths, due to reflections, the signal can be cancelled at some locations and made stronger at other locations (upfade).

Hidden node problem

The hidden node problem arises in certain types of network when a node is accessible from a wireless access point (AP) but not from other nodes that connect with that AP. This leads to difficulties in the regulation of media access (collisions).

Exposed terminal node issue

The problem with the exposed terminal is that a node on one network is unable to transmit because of co-channel interference from a node on another network.

Shared resource issue

Wireless spectrum is a finite resource shared by all nodes within the range of its transmitters. The allocation of bandwidth is complex with several participating users. Most times, users are not aware that advertised numbers (e.g. for IEEE 802.11 devices) are not their capacity but are shared with all other users and therefore the individual user rate is much lower. For the rising competition, the capacity shortage is increasingly likely to happen. User-in-the-loop (UIL) can be a solution to upgrading to newer over-provisioning technologies.

Network

Total network bandwidth depends on how dispersive the medium is (more dispersive medium usually has stronger total bandwidth as it minimizes interference), how many frequencies are available, how noisy are they, how many aerials are utilized and whether a directional antenna is in use, whether nodes use power control, and so on.

Cellular wireless networks typically have a strong range as a result of their use of directional aerials and their ability to use radio channels again in non-adjacent cells. In addition, very small cells can be produced using low-power transmitters that are used in cities to provide network capacity that scales linearly with population size.

WIRELESS NETWORK HARDWARE

Wireless Network Adapter: Wireless Network Adapters are definitely what you need when you set up a small local area network (LAN). Such adapters carry a radio transmitter and a receiver inside them. When every system on the network has been equipped with a network adapter, they can be made to communicate with each other. Some of the newest laptops have been pre-installed with these wireless network adapters. However, whether you are using a desktop or an old laptop, wireless network cards are still found in the market in two form factors – the PCMCIA form or the USB form factor. Choose the one that suits your machine best, and your LAN is more than ready.

If you want to set up a LAN that can handle more devices, a wireless network adapter is not enough, here's what else you'll need.

Wireless Network Router: a wireless router that works identical to a traditional wired Ethernet. It effectively guides data packets to their respective destinations and also serves as an access point for wireless networks. Guests can connect to your internal wired network and use Internet services using these access points. However, the operation of the guests over the network resources can be fully managed by using firewalls.

But for a wireless router to allow resource sharing between computers, computers must be fitted with a wireless network adapter.

Wireless Access Points: Wireless access point or WAP serves as an interconnector and links wireless clients to Ethernet. The access point will either help you connect to the Ethernet or to another access point. Wireless Access Points are ideally designed for companies with multi-stored offices. This is because using access points will help you build a WLAN (wide local area network) that is larger than the LAN.

However, thousands of these access points can be installed inside the same network, and all computers can access each of them as necessary. Notice also that the access point present in the network may be a device that is in turn connected to the router (or an essential part of the router itself).

Tip: If you already have a network-based wired broadband router in your home, you can expand it to a wireless network using the Wireless Access Points.

Wireless Range Extenders: The function of the Wireless Range Extenders is to expand the degree to which a wireless network is spread. The key role of the wireless network is to improve the efficiency of the overall signal strength by overcoming barriers. These devices are often referred to as signal boosters or range extenders. A wireless range extender links to a router or WiFi access point.

In short, the efficiency of devices on the network in the presence of a wireless range extender is much greater than when they are directly connected to the signal source.

Service Set Identifier (Ssid)

Service Set Identifier (SSID) is a series of characters that uniquely identify a wireless local area network (WLAN). SSID is often referred to as a "Network Name." This unique name allows stations to connect to the same network while several different networks operate within the same geographic area.

A set of wireless devices that communicate directly with each other is called the Basic Service Set (BSS). Several BSSs can be joined together to create a single logical WLAN segment referred to as the Extended Service Set (ESS). The Service Set Identifier (SSID) is simply an alphanumeric 1-32 byte name given to each ESS.

For example, a departmental WLAN (ESS) can consist of several access points (APs) and dozens of stations, all of which use the same SSID. Another organization in the same building can run its own departmental WLAN, consisting of APs and stations using a separate SSID. The goal of SSID is to help stations in Department A locate and connect to APs in Department A while ignoring APs belonging to Department B.

Each AP advertises its presence several times per second by transmitting beacon frames bearing the name of the ESS (SSID). Stations may discover APs by passively listening to beacons, or by sending probe frames to actively search for an AP with the desired SSID. If the station locates a properly named AP, an associated request frame containing the requested SSID can be submitted. The AP responds with an associate response frame, often containing an SSID.

Some frames are allowed to hold a null (zero-length) SSID called a broadcast SSID. For example, a station can send a probe request that carries a broadcast SSID; the AP must return its actual SSID to the probe response. Some APs can be programmed to send a zero-length SSID to beacon frames instead of sending their real SSID. However, it is not possible to keep the SSID value secret because the real SSID (ESS name) is stored in many frames.

Main features of an SSID

One common thing you'll find in an SSID, whether it's the default set by the ISP or router maker, or you've changed it, is that it features up to 32 case-sensitive letters and numbers. Despite the fact that you can use up to 32 characters, there is no lower limit. However, it is advised that you don't make the SSID so short that it creates confusion (for example, "me" or a few digits).

SSIDs are usually issued as part of the setup materials and written on a sticker attached to the outside of the router, which often contains a password. Alongside the SSID and password, there should also be a username and password for the router administrator console, which provides access to network data and configuration options, including the SSID.

How devices utilize SSID to connect to the Internet

When you first set up a connected device, or when you try to connect to a new network, you will be required to configure your connection to the network. Usually, you will be prompted to search for available networks in your region and select the one best suited to your needs, often a home or business WiFi. They will be displayed as either open and free of any instant authentication checks (although they may come later via a browser) or locked, symbolized by a padlock symbol. If you plan to connect to a locked network, you will be asked to enter a password before your device attempts to contact the host.

However, only those that have been configured to publicly view their SSID or personalized name will be included in this list of available networks. You will need to enter their SSID or name manually, along with your password, if necessary, to access any secret networks. To prevent a network from appearing on the list of available connections, you will need to select 'hidden' or 'disable SSID' in the router settings.

When your computer is connected to a network, you can save its information and automatically connect to it any time you allow WiFi.

SSID security While SSID is used by almost every wireless network in the world, it is considered to be a fairly unsafe way to connect to the Internet because even though you have decided to mask your SSID so that it can't be detected by anyone, software and apps have been created to expose any secret networks.

Even if such an app or software is not used by people trying to find secret networks, some data packets drop traces of the SSID they're going through when you send requests. If these are intercepted, hackers can reveal the name of your network if they want to.

Another reason why SSIDs are not very useful is that if many of your neighbours use the same ISP as you, their default SSID will probably be very close to yours, and since very few people change their default network name, it's pretty easy to unintentionally try to link to the wrong one.

So, for example, if one of you doesn't have protection turned on, you can find that smartphones and other devices set up to connect to the strongest network will use the wrong connection by default. If a security-free network does not have broad download limits, it may result in high overage billing or throttled speeds.

Bluetooth

Bluetooth is a wireless technology system used to transmit data between mobile and fixed devices over short distances using short-wave UHF radio waves in scientific, commercial, and medical radio bands, from 2.402 GHz to 2.480 GHz, and to create personal area networks (PANs). It was originally planned as a wireless alternative to RS-232 data cables.

Bluetooth is regulated by the Bluetooth Special Interest Group (SIG), which has more than 35,000 member companies in the telecommunications, computer, networking and consumer electronics industries. IEEE has defined Bluetooth as IEEE 802.15.1, but no longer retains the standard. The Bluetooth SIG controls the creation of the specifications, manages the qualification system and protects the trademarks. The product must comply with the Bluetooth SIG guidelines in order to sell it as a Bluetooth device. The patent network refers to technologies licensed to specific eligible products.

How Bluetooth Functions

Bluetooth sends and receives radio waves in a band of 79 distinct frequencies (channels) of 2.45 GHz, set apart from radio, television and cellphones, and intended for use by scientific, commercial, and medical devices. The short-range Bluetooth transmitters are one of the main plus points. These use virtually no power and, since they do not travel far, are potentially more reliable than wireless networks that run over longer ranges, such as Wi-Fi. (There are some security concerns in practice.) A Bluetooth device automatically detects and connect to another Bluetooth device, and up to eight of them can communicate at any time. They do not disrupt with each other because each pair of devices uses another of the 79 channels available. If two devices decide to communicate, they select a channel randomly and, if this is already achieved, randomly switch to one of the others (a method known as spread-spectrum frequency hopping). To reduce the risks of interference from other electrical devices (and also to improve safety), pairs of devices continuously change the frequency they use — thousands of times in a second.

When a group of Bluetooth devices exchange information together, they form a kind of ad-hoc, mini computer network called a piconet. Other devices can enter or exit an existing piconet at any time. One computer (known as the master) serves as the main controller of the network, while the others (known as slaves) follow its instructions. Two or more independent piconets may also enter and exchange details about what is called a scatternet.

How Bluetooth Is Evolving

Bluetooth has always been very difficult to use: like any wireless technology, it's a battery drainer for mobile devices; you can always move out of range, making contact unreliable or impossible; and even having two Bluetooth devices to connect to each other in the first place isn't always as easy as it should be. The world of mobile devices is shifting as we push towards the so-called Internet of Things (where all sorts of everyday items are net-connected)—and Bluetooth needs to keep evolving to keep up. Recognizing the need to connect a growing number of devices, Bluetooth developers come up with updated versions on a regular basis, faster and more reliable. First, Bluetooth BR / EDR (Basic Rate / Enhanced Data Rate, Technically Bluetooth Version 2.1) offered smoother communication between devices and improved security. Then came Bluetooth Highspeed (Bluetooth Version 3.0), which enabled faster connectivity and lower power consumption. More recently, we've seen Bluetooth Smart or Bluetooth Low Energy (technically known as Bluetooth Version 4.0 +);

as these names indicate, this version is best suited to connect a wider variety of simpler devices, requires much less power, and is far easier to incorporate into mobile (iOS and Android) applications. The new version, Bluetooth 5, provides a further improvement in speed, range and bandwidth.

Wireless Ad-Hoc Network

An ad hoc wireless network (WANET) or a mobile ad hoc network (MANET) is a decentralized wireless network type. It is ad hoc because it doesn't rely on established infrastructure, such as routers in wired networks or access points in regulated (infrastructure) wireless networks. Instead, each node joins in routing by forwarding data to other nodes such that the determination of which nodes forward data is dynamically made on the basis of the network connections and the routing algorithm in use.

Ad-hoc is a mode of communication in the Windows operating system that allows computers to communicate with each other directly without a router. Ad hoc mobile wireless networks are self-configured, distributed networks in which nodes are free to travel.

These wireless networks lack the complexity of infrastructure setup and administration, allowing users to build and connect "on-the-fly" networks – anywhere, at any time.

A true MANET needs, by definition, multicast, not just unicast or broadcast, routing.

Each device in the MANET is free to travel independently in either direction and will, therefore, constantly change its connections to other devices. Each of them must forward traffic unrelated to their own use, and thus be a router. The main challenge in constructing a MANET is to equip each system to keep up to date the information required for proper route traffic. These networks may run on their own or may be linked to the wider Internet. They can contain one or more transceivers between nodes. This results in a highly complex and autonomous topology.

MANETs typically provide a routable networking environment on top of an ad hoc Link Layer network. MANETs consist of a peer-to-peer, self-forming, self-recovering network. MANETs circa 2000–2015 normally communicate at radio frequencies (30 MHz – 5 GHz).

APPLICATIONS Of AD-HOC NETWORK

The decentralized design of ad-hoc wireless networks makes them ideal for a range of applications where central nodes can not be relied on and can increase the scalability of networks compared to wireless networks, while theoretical and practical limitations on the overall capacity of these networks have been found. Minimal setup and fast deployment make ad hoc networks ideal for emergency situations such as natural disasters or military conflicts.

The implementation of dynamic and flexible routing protocols enables the rapid creation of ad hoc networks. Ad-hoc wireless networks can be further categorized by their applications: mobile ad-hoc networks (MANETs) A mobile ad-hoc network (MANET) is a continuously self-configuring, self-organizing, wireless network of mobile devices. It is often referred to as 'on-the-fly' networks or 'spontaneous networks.' Vehicle ad hoc networks (VANETs) VANETs are used for contact between vehicles and roadside equipment. Intelligent ad hoc vehicle networks (InVANETs) are a kind of artificial intelligence that helps vehicles act intelligently during vehicle-to-vehicle collisions and accidents. Vehicles use radio waves to communicate with each other, building immediately on-the-fly communication networks as vehicles drive along the highways.

Smartphone Ad Hoc Networks (SPANs)

SPAN leverages existing hardware (primarily Wi-Fi and Bluetooth) and software (protocols) in commercially accessible smartphones to create peer-to-peer networks without relying on cellular carrier networks, wireless access points or traditional network infrastructure. SPANs differ from traditional hubs and spoke networks, such as Wi-Fi Direct, in that they promote multi-hop relays and there is no concept of group leader so the peers can enter and exit on their own without breaking the network.

iMANETs

Internet-based mobile ad hoc networks (iMANETs) is a type of wireless ad hoc network that promotes internet protocols like TCP / UDP and IP. It makes use of a network-layer routing protocol to connect mobile nodes and set up routes on a distributed and automatic basis.

Wireless mesh networks

The Mesh networks derive their name from the topology of the resulting network. In a fully connected network, each node is attached to any other node, creating a "mesh." Meanwhile, a partial mesh has a topology in which certain nodes are not connected to others, although this concept is seldom used. Ad hoc wireless networks can take the form of mesh networks or other networks. An ad hoc wireless network does not have a fixed topology, and its communication between nodes depends entirely on the behaviour of the devices, their mobility patterns, the distance between them, etc. As a consequence, wireless mesh networks are a particular type of wireless ad hoc networks, with particular emphasis on the resulting network topology. While some wireless mesh networks (especially those within the home) have relatively infrequent mobility and thus infrequent connection breaks, other more mobile mesh networks require regular routing changes to compensate for broken connections. Google Wi-Fi, Google Home, and Google OnHub all support Wi-Fi mesh (i.e. Wi-Fi ad hoc) networking. Apple's

AirPort allows wireless mesh networks to be built at home, links multiple Wi-Fi devices together and provides good wireless coverage and connectivity at home.

Army tactical MANETs

Military or tactical MANETs are utilized by military units for data-rate emphasis, real-time wireless coverage and home connectivity. Ad hoc mobile communications are well adapted to meet this need, in particular its infrastructural design, rapid deployment and service. Military MANETs are utilized by military units with a focus on rapid deployment, infrastructure-less, all-wireless networks (no fixed radio towers), robustness (no connection breaks), stability, range, and instant service. MANETs are used in army "hopping" mines, in platoons where soldiers communicate in foreign lands, giving them dominance in battlefields. Tactical MANETs can be created automatically during the mission, and the network "disappears" when the mission is completed or decommissioned. It is often referred to as a wireless tactical network on-the-fly.

Air Force UAV

Ad-hoc networks Flying ad-hoc networks (FANETs) are comprised of unmanned aerial vehicles, offering high mobility and access to remote areas.

An Unmanned Aerial Vehicle, is an aircraft that has no pilot on board. The UAVs can be remotely controlled (i.e., directed by a pilot at a ground control station) or can operate independently on the basis of pre-programmed flight plans. Civilian UAV uses includes 3D terrain modelling, package delivery (Amazon), etc. UAVs have also been used by the US Air Force for data collection and situation sensing without risking the pilot in an unpleasant foreign environment. With wireless ad hoc network technology embedded in UAVs, multiple UAVs can communicate with each other and function as a team, collaboratively to complete a task and goal. If an attacker damages a UAV, the data can be easily transmitted wirelessly to other nearby UAVs. The ad hoc UAV contact network is also often referred to the Instant Sky UAV network.

Navy ad hoc networks

Navy ships typically use satellite communications and other marine radios to communicate with each other or with ground stations back onshore. However, these communications are limited by delays and insufficient bandwidth. Ad hoc wireless networks allow ship-area networks to be developed while at sea, enabling high-speed wireless communications between ships, improving their sharing of images and multimedia data, and better coordination in battlefield operations.

Wireless sensor networks Sensors are useful instruments that collect information about a given parameter, such as noise, temperature, humidity, pressure, etc. Sensors are increasingly linked via wireless so that sensor data can be collected on a large scale. With a wide sample of sensor data, analytics processing may be used to make some sense of these results. The functionality of wireless sensor networks is based on the concepts behind wireless ad hoc networks, as sensors can now be deployed without any fixed radio towers and can now form on-the-fly networks. Of recent, mobile wireless sensor networks (MWSNs) have also been an area of scientific interest.

Ad hoc home smart lighting

ZigBee is a low-power, ad hoc wireless network that is now making its way into home automation. Its low power consumption, robustness and increased range embedded in mesh networking can provide a variety of advantages for smart lighting in homes and offices. Control includes adjustable lighting, ambient lighting, and ambient or scene. Networks allow a collection or subset of lights to be operated through a smartphone or a computer.

Ad-hoc street light networks

Ad-hoc smart street light networks are starting to grow. The idea is to use wireless control of city street lights to boost energy efficiency as part of a smart city architectural feature. Multiple street lights form an ad hoc wireless network. Up to 500 street lights can be powered by a single gateway device. Using a gateway device, it is possible to switch the individual lights on, off or dim, as well as to find out which individual light is faulty and requires maintenance.

The ad hoc robot network

Robots are mechanical devices that drive automation and perform tasks that would seem difficult for humans. Efforts have been made to organize and monitor a group of robots to perform collective work to complete a task. Centralized control is also based on a "star" strategy, where robots take turns talking to the controller station. However, with ad hoc wireless networks, robots can create an on-the-fly communication network, i.e. robots can now "speak" to each other and cooperate in a distributed way. With a network of robots, robots can interact with each other, exchange local information and agree on how to solve a problem in the most effective and secure manner.

Disaster rescue ad hoc network Public safety is another civilian application of the ad hoc wireless network. In times of disasters (floods, hurricanes, earthquakes, fires, etc.), a fast and instant wireless communication network is required. Particularly in times of earthquakes where radio towers fell or were demolished, ad hoc wireless networks may be established independently. Firemen and emergency personnel may use ad hoc networks to coordinate and emergency the wounded. Commercial radios with this feature are available on the market.

Hospital ad hoc network

Wireless ad hoc networks allow sensors, images, instruments, and other devices to be distributed and interconnected wirelessly for clinical and hospital patient monitoring, for physician and nurse warning notification, and also to make sense of these data quickly at fusion points so that lives can be saved.

Data monitoring and mining

MANETS data management, and mining can be used to enable the processing of data mining sensor for a variety of applications, such as air pollution monitoring and various types of architectures, for such applications. A key feature of these applications is that nearby sensor nodes monitoring and environmental features usually record similar values. This form of data redundancy due to the spatial similarity between sensor observations inspires in-network data aggregation and mining techniques. Through calculating the spatial similarity between data collected by different sensors, a wide range of advanced algorithms can be developed to create more efficient spatial data mining algorithms as well as more reliable routing strategies. Researchers have also developed MANET output models to implement the queueing theory.

Infrastructure Mode

Network mode is an 802.11 networking system in which computers communicate with each other via an Access Point (AP) first. In infrastructure mode, wireless devices may communicate with each other or may communicate with a wired network. If an AP is connected to a wired network and a set of wireless stations, it is known as the Basic Service Set (BSS). An Extended Service Set (ESS) is a collection of two or more BSSs which form a single subnetwork. Most corporate wireless LANs run in infrastructure mode because they need wired LAN access to enable them use services such as file servers or printers.

Infrastructure mode is when a wireless network needs a physical structure to sustain the network. This implies, in fact, that there should be a mechanism for handling the network operations, establishing an infrastructure around which the network retains.

It performs these typical functions:

- Provide connections to other networks
- Forwarding
- Intermediate connections control

In infrastructure-based wireless networks, communication takes place between wireless nodes (i.e. network endpoints such as your device, phone, etc.) and access points (i.e. routers) only.

There might be more than one access point on the same network that manages various wireless nodes.

A common example of a telecommunications network will be mobile phone networks. They need a fixed infrastructure (i.e. network towers) to operate.

When to use an infrastructure network:

1. If you can quickly add more access points to increase the range
2. When you want to set up a more stable network
3. If you need to link to other types of networks (e.g., you can connect to a wired network if needed).

Infrastructure Mode Vs Ad Hoc Mode Network

1. In infrastructure mode, communication occurs only between wireless nodes and access points (AP) but not directly between wireless nodes (s). At the same time, each node interacts directly with other nodes in ad-hoc mode, so no access point control is required.
2. External Communication: In networking, access points function as a link to other wireless / wired networks. Meanwhile, Ad-hoc nodes will interact if they are within the same range.
3. Physical needs: Physical infrastructure in infrastructure mode is required. In the meantime, no physical infrastructure is required in Ad-hoc mode.
4. Complexity: In infrastructure mode, the architecture is simple, because much of

the network functionality is inside AP, and the client is just a simple machine. During ad hoc mode, there is no central control; thus, decentralized MAC protocols such as CSMA / CA need to be used, with all nodes providing the same features. This increases the difficulty and the cost.

5. Infrastructure mode can not be used in critical circumstances such as disaster relief where no infrastructure is left. Ad hoc mode is not always completely connected as two mobile nodes can be temporarily out of control.
6. IEEE 802.11 & HIPERLAN2 implementations are based on network mode. Bluetooth is typically an ad hoc network.
7. Channel Access: Most WLAN-based infrastructure uses TDMA-based protocols. Many Ad-hoc based WLAN uses MAC contention protocols (e.g. CSMA) 8. Topology: Based on topology,

the ability of WLAN networks to provide wired network software and facilities is a major benefit. Ad-hoc WLANs are simpler to set up and do not require any infrastructure.

Communication Protocols

Communication protocols are standard descriptions of the formats and rules of the digital communication. They are needed to exchange messages in or between computer systems and are necessary for telecommunications.

Communication protocols include authentication, error detection and correction, and signalling. They can also define the syntax, semantics, and synchronization of analog and digital communications. Communication protocols are incorporated into hardware and software. There are thousands of communication protocols that are used both in digital and analog communications. Without them, computer networks can not exist.

Communication devices need to agree on certain physical aspects of the data to be transmitted before a successful transmission can take place. The rules that describe transmissions are called protocols.

There are several transmission properties that the protocol can identify. Common ones include transmission speed, packet size, error correction types, handshaking and synchronization techniques, acknowledgement processes, address mapping, flow control, packet sequence controls, routing, address formatting Popular protocols include file transfer protocol (FTP), TCP / IP, post office protocol (POP3), user datagram protocol (UDP), hypertext transfer protocol (HTTP), Simple Mail Transfer Protocol (SMTP), Internet Message Access Protocol (IMAP).

Transmission Control Protocol / Internet Protocol (TCP / IP)

The language used by a device to access the Internet is known as the Transmission Control Protocol / Internet Protocol (TCP / IP). It comprises of a suite of protocols designed to set up a network to provide a host with internet access.

TCP / IP is responsible for complete data connection and for transmitting network end to end by providing additional functions, including addressing, mapping and acknowledgement. TCP / IP comprises four layers, slightly different from the OSI model.

The Technology is so popular that a full name will seldom be used. In other terms, the term itself now widely in use is the acronym.

Almost all computers today makes use of TCP / IP. TCP / IP is a set of protocols named after the two most significant protocols or layers within it – TCP and IP.

As it is with every other form of communication, two things are required: a message to be transmitted and the means to reliably transmit the message. The message part is handled by the TCP layer. The message is split into smaller units called packets. These packets are then transmitted over the network and are received by the corresponding TCP layer in the receiver and reassembled to the original message.

The IP layer is mainly concerned with the transmission part. It is achieved through a specific IP address allocated to each and every active user on the network.

TCP / IP is called a stateless protocol suite because each client connection is formed newly regardless of whether a previous connection has been developed.

File Transfer Protocol (FTP)

File Transfer Protocol (FTP) is a client/server protocol used to transfer data to or share files with a host device. User names and passwords can be authenticated. Anonymous FTP helps users to access files, programs and other data from the Internet without a user ID or password. Websites are often configured to encourage users to use 'anonymous' or 'guest' as a user ID and password e-mail address. Publicly accessible files are often located in a directory called a pub, and can easily be FTPed to a user's device. FTP is also the Internet standard for transferring files from one device to another through TCP or IP networks.

The File Transfer Protocol is also referred to as RFC 959.

The original FTP specification was written by Abhay Bhushan and published as RFC 114 on 16 April 1971. Subsequently, this was replaced by RFC 765 (June 1980). RFC 959 (October 1985) is the latest standard. RFC stands for requests for comments.

The first implementations of the FTP client used the DOS command prompt with standard commands and syntax. Since then, several graphical user interface (GUI) clients have been built within operating systems, making it easier for users to upload and access files.

There are various uses and types of FTP:

1. FTP is a website where users can conveniently upload or download specific files.
2. FTP by mail helps users without access to the Internet to view and copy files using anonymous FTP by sending an e-mail to ftpmail@decwrl.dec.com and typing the word help in the body of the letter.
3. FTP Explorer is a Windows 95 File Manager (Windows 95 Explorer) FTP application.
4. The FTP server is a dedicated computer that provides FTP service. This prompts hackers and includes security hardware or software, such as usernames, passwords and file access control.

5. The FTP client is a computer application that accesses the FTP server. When doing so, users will block incoming FTP connection attempts employing passive mode and search for viruses on all downloaded files.

Hypertext Transfer Protocol (HTTP)

Hypertext Transfer Protocol (HTTP) is a standard protocol used on the Internet to manage data transmission to and from a hosting server while communicating with a web browser.

HTTP is a primary means of communication between web users and servers that manage the websites themselves.

Being a stateless protocol, HTTP does not automatically preserve user settings — so things like cookies are used to help websites and servers "remember" what the user has done.

Application of user-accessible software means that users can opt to erase cookies and other resources and start again as anonymous users, or to save these markers so that they can avoid all the "getting to know" about the hosting server's site again. In several ways, HTTP has been helpful in translating web usage to a fully secure stateful result — but users who erase all cookies and stored data for the first time will be dismayed at how much of their daily web routine is exposed.

Early HTTP The HTTP request and response headers describe the HTTP transaction operating parameters.

Usually, a request structure includes a URL together with a method and identifies the protocol.

Then there are different standard and non-standard request fields, all of which cause different interactions.

An easy way to think about this is that HTTP codes and fields are, again, the way the two transacting parties communicate — the browsers send the request to the server, and the server submits the response, still in HTTP syntax.

Universalizing this in the form of hypertext syntax makes sense and is part of how organizations like the World Wide Web Consortium have approached building the Internet as it is today.

Making HTTP Secure Over time, a protocol known as HTTPS encrypts the contents of HTTP messages with Transport Layer Protection and Safe Dockets Layer or TLS / SSL protocols.

Previously, in many situations, hackers may simply enter and type in additions or changes to the main request in their browser URL bar before the request itself is triggered. This contributed to all kinds of security vulnerabilities where bad players had access to or control of systems.

Since HTTPS encrypts the actual HTTP code, it is successful against this form of operation.

Tracking and Interactivity

As the web becomes more dynamic, HTTP is also changing. The ways in which web users and websites connect have undergone major changes over the last few decades.

For example, the age of Web 2.0 has traditionally been a time when businesses and other websites have become more interactive. More user registration fields and other user activities are usually embedded in web pages, and all of these must be handled with HTTP, or more specifically with HTTPS.

First comes the news of the future web 3.0, which will focus on technologies like JSON to allow more data mapping, more conceptual connection and more client and server interaction automation.

HTTP itself will experience even more future change to accommodate this — but for now, HTTPS remains a key element of Internet security and functionality.

Hypertext Transfer Protocol Secure (HTTPS)

Hypertext Transfer Protocol Secure (HTTPS) is a variation of the Standard Web Transfer Protocol (HTTP) that adds a layer of protection to data in transit via a secure socket layer (SSL) or transport layer security (TLS) protocol connection.

HTTPS allows encrypted communication and secure connections between the remote user and the primary web server.

HTTPS is mainly designed to provide additional protection layer over the unsecured HTTP protocol for confidential data and transactions such as billing information, credit card transactions, user login, etc. HTTPS encrypts every data packet in transition using TLS or SSL encryption technologies to prevent hackers and attackers from stealing data information, even if the connection is breached.

HTTPS is installed and supported by default in most web browsers and automatically opens a secure connection when accessed web servers request a secure connection. HTTPS operates in conjunction with the Certificate Authorities that determine the security certificate of the website accessed.

User Datagram Protocol (UDP)

User Datagram Protocol (UDP) is a part of the Internet Protocol suite utilized by programs running on various computers around the network. It is used to send short messages known as datagrams, but, ultimately, it is an insecure, connectionless protocol. UDP is officially specified in RFC 768 and was developed by David P. Reed.

The User Datagram Protocol is an Open System Interconnection (OSI) transport layer protocol for client-server network applications. UDP uses a basic transmission model but does not use handshaking dialogues for reliability, ordering and data integrity. The protocol assumes that error checks and corrections are not necessary, thereby preventing processing at the level of the network interface.

UDP is commonly used in video conferencing and in real-time computer games. The protocol allows individual packets to be dropped and UDP packets to be obtained in a different order from that in which they were sent, allowing for better efficiency.

UDP network traffic is structured in the form of datagrams consisting of one message unit. The first eight bytes in the datagram contain the header information, while the remaining bytes contain the message data. The UDP datagram header contains four fields of two bytes each:

- Source port number
- Destination port number
- Datagram size
- Checksum

Post Office Protocol (POP)

Post Office Protocol (POP) is a kind of computer networking and Internet standard protocol that collects and retrieves e-mail from a remote mail server for host machine access. It is an application layer protocol in the OSI model that allows end users the ability to accept and receive e-mails.

The Post Office Protocol is the main protocol for e-mail communications. POP operates through a support e-mail software client that incorporates POP to connect to the remote e-mail server and download e-mail messages to the recipient's computer.

POP uses the TCP / IP protocol stack for network connectivity and deals with the Simple Mail Transfer Protocol (SMTP) for end-to-end e-mail communication, where POP extracts messages and SMTP transfers messages to the server.

The Internet Message Access Protocol (IMAP)

Internet Message Access Protocol (IMAP) is a standardized protocol for accessing e-mail from a local client to a remote server. IMAP is an Internet Protocol application layer that uses the underlying transport layer protocols to provide host-to-host communication services for applications. This allows the remote mail server to be used. The well-known IMAP port address is 143.

The IMAP architecture allows users to send and receive e-mails from a remote server without the assistance of a physical computer. This form of e-mail access is perfect for travellers receiving or responding to e-mails from their home desktop or office computer.

This concept is also known as the Interactive Mail Access Protocol, the Interim Mail Access Protocol and the Internet Mail Access Protocol.

IMAP was originally developed by Mark Crispin as a remote mailbox protocol in 1986. This was the case during the famous use of the Post Office Protocol (POP). All IMAP and POP are still supported by most modern e-mail servers and clients. However, IMAP is a remote file server, meanwhile POP stores and forwards. In other terms, with IMAP, all e-mails stay on the server until they are removed by the client. IMAP also allows multiple clients to access and manage the same mailbox.

When an e-mail is requested by the user, it is routed via a central server. It maintains an e-mail file storage document. Some of the advantages of IMAP include the ability to delete messages, check keywords in the content of e-mails, create and manage several mailboxes or folders, and see the headings for quick visual scanning of e-mails.

IMAP is still commonly used, but less relevant now that so many e-mails are sent via web-based interfaces like Gmail, Yahoo mail, Hotmail, etc.

Simple Mail Transfer Protocol (SMTP)

Simple Mail Transfer Protocol is a standard protocol for TCP / IP network e-mail services. SMTP offers the ability to send and receive e-mail messages.

SMTP is an application-layer protocol that enables transmission and distribution of e-mails over the Internet. The Internet Engineering Task Force (IETF) generates and manages the SMTP.

Simple Mail Transfer Protocol is often referred to as RFC 821 and RFC 2821.

SMTP is one of the most common and popular e-mail communication protocols on the Internet and offers intermediary network services between the remote e-mail provider or the organizational e-mail server and the local user who accesses it.

SMTP is typically incorporated into an e-mail system program and consists of four primary components: a local user or a client-end feature known as a mail user agent (MUA) server known as a mail submission agent (MSA) a mail transfer agent (MTA) a mail delivery agent (MDA) SMTP operates by creating a session between the user and the server, while MTA and MDA provide local delivery services and domain searching.

Telnet

Telnet is a series of rules designed to connect one network to another. The connection process here is referred to as remote log in. The device that requests for the connection is the local computer, and the device that acknowledges the connection is the remote computer.

Gopher

Gopher is a set of rules for searching, extracting and viewing documents from isolated sites. Gopher is still operating on the client/server concept.

Some other common protocols serve as co-functioning protocols affiliated with these primary protocols for core functions.

- ARP (Address Resolution Protocol)
- DHCP (Dynamic Host Configuration Protocol)
- IMAP4 (Internet Message Access Protocol)

- SNMP (Simple Network Management Protocol)
- SIP (Session Initiation Protocol)
- RTP (Real-Time Transport Protocol)
- RLP (Resource Location Protocol)
- RAP (Route Access Protocol)
- TFTP (Trivial File Transfer Protocol)
- L2TP (Layer Two Tunneling Protocol)
- PPTP (Point To Point Tunneling Protocol)

Threats to Information Security

In Information Security, there can be like Software attacks, theft of intellectual property, theft of equipment or information, identity theft, sabotage, and information extortion.

A Threat could be anything that can take advantage of a security breach vulnerability and negatively change, delete, damage objects or items of interest.

Software attacks are attacks by malware, Trojan Horses, Worms, etc. Many users think that malware, worms, viruses, bots are all the same thing. But they're not the same; the only link is that they're all malicious software that acts differently.

Malware is derived from two words, malicious and software. So malware essentially means malicious software that can be an invasive program code or something that is designed to perform malicious system operations. Malware can be classified into two categories:

- Infection methods
- Malware Actions malware based on the infection methods are:

Virus – They have the potential to replicate themselves by linking them to the host computer program like songs, images, etc., and then they move all over the Internet. The Creeper virus was first observed on ARPANET. Examples are File Virus, Boot Sector Virus, Macro Virus, Stealth

Virus, etc. Worms – Worms are often self-replicating in nature, but they don't bind to the host computer system. The major difference between worms and viruses is that worms are aware of the network. They will move easily from one computer to another if the network is available and they won't do much damage to the target machine, for example, consuming hard disk space, thereby slowing down the computer.

Trojan – Trojan is entirely different from viruses and worms. The name Trojan was derived from the 'Trojan Horse' tale in Greek mythology, which describes how the Greeks were able to reach the protected city of Troy by hiding their soldiers in a large wooden horse given as a gift to the Trojans. The Trojans really loved horses and blindly trusted the gift. At night, the soldiers came out and invaded the city from the inside.

Their aim is to hide inside software that seems legitimate, and when that software is executed, they will either steal information or any other reason for which they are built.

They also provide backdoor gateways for malicious programs or malicious users to access your system and steal valuable information without your awareness and permission. Examples include Proxy Trojans, FTP Trojans, Remote Access Trojans, etc. Bots –: can be seen as advanced worms. These are automated systems designed to communicate over the Internet without need for human interaction. They could be good or bad. A malicious bot may infect one host and, after infecting it, it will establish a connection to the central server that will provide commands to all infected hosts connected to the network called Botnet.

Malware based on Actions:

Adware – Adware is not necessarily malicious, but it infringes the privacy of users. They project ads on a computer screen or inside individual programs. They come with software that are free to use, which is the key source of revenue for these developers. They will track your interests and show targeted ads. An attacker can attach malicious codes within the program, and adware can track your device activities and even compromise your computer.

Spyware – It's a program or a software application that tracks the actions on a device and exposes the information gathered to the interested party. Spyware is usually dropped by Viruses, worms or trojans. When released, they mount themselves and sit quietly to avoid detection.

KEYLOGGER is one of the most popular examples of spyware. The keylogger's basic job is to record keystrokes of the user with a timestamp. It collects sensitive information such as username, passwords, credit card numbers, etc. Ransomware – is a type of malware that either encrypts your files or locks your device, making it either partially or entirely unavailable. Then the screen will be display asking for money, i.e. ransom in exchange.

Scareware – It disguises as a tool to help repair your system; however, while the program is running, it can corrupt or fully destroy your system. The app will show a message that will scare you and compel you to do something like pay them to repair your device.

Rootkits – are built to gain root access or administrative opportunities in the user system. When root access has been obtained, the user can do everything from stealing private files to private data.

Zombies – They are similar to Spyware. Infection method is the same, except they don't spy and steal information; instead, they wait for the hacker orders.

Intellectual property theft involves violation of intellectual property rights such as patents, copyright, etc. Identity theft involves acting on behalf of someone else to gain personal information or to access sensitive information such as access to a person's computer or social media account by signing in to the account using their login credentials.

Theft of equipment and information is on the rise these days due to the mobile nature of most devices and the growth in information efficiency.

Sabotage means the destruction of a company's website to cause a loss of trust on the part of its clients.

Information extortion means theft of the properties or information of a company to receive payment in return. For example, ransomware will lock victims file rendering them unavailable and thus forcing the victim to make payment in return. Only after payment will victim's files will be released.

Those are the assaults of the old century, which continue to advance with technological advancement every year. Besides these, there are also other threats. Below is a brief overview of the threats faced by the new generation.

Technology with poor protection – With the advent of technology, a new gadget is introduced on the market every day. But very few are completely protected and follow the principles of information security. Because the market is very competitive, the safety aspect is compromised to make the product more up-to-date. This leads to the theft of data/information from computers.

Social media attacks – cybercriminals locate and manipulate a network of websites accessed by individuals in a specific organization, to steal information.

Mobile Malware – There's a theory that when there's internet access, there's a security risk. Same goes to cell phones where gaming apps are built to lure the consumer into downloading the game and unintentionally installing malware or viruses in the computer.

Outdated Security Software – With new threats arising every day, security software updates are a requirement for a completely protected environment.

Corporate data on personal devices – Nowadays, every company follows the BYOD rule. BYOD means Bring Your Own Device, such as laptops, tablets, to the office. It is clear that BYOD presents a significant threat to data protection, but because of efficiency concerns, companies are arguing that it should be adopted.

Social Engineering – is the practice of manipulating people to give up sensitive information such as account details, passwords, etc. These criminals will trick you into giving your private and sensitive information, or they can gain your trust in getting access to your computer to install malicious software-which will give them control of your computer. For example, an e-mail or a message from your friend's address which may not have been sent by your friend. Criminals may access your friends' computer and then, by accessing the contact list, send infected e-mails and messages to all contacts. Since the message/e-mail is from a known source, the attachment or link in the message would undoubtedly be checked, thus infecting the device unintentionally.

Ways To Prevent Network Security Threats

Proactively Detect Out-of-Date Software and Patch it

Several cyber-attacks seek to exploit a known security vulnerability or flaw in a software system. Software developers, in effect, constantly release new patches and updates to their software systems to remove these vulnerabilities. However, despite the simple availability of free security patches, several individuals have refused to implement them. Alternatively, they tend to use the unpatched version of the software program as it's easier to use than to take the software down for a while and upgrade it. They may not even be aware that the patch is available and needs to be adopted because they do not have a detailed inventory of all the applications they use on their network.

This is where the audit and evaluation of security policy will prove to be significant. Through running such an evaluation, you can build a map of what's on your network, inventory all the software programs there, and whether those programs are up to date with their security patches. It can be invaluable to proactively mitigate network security concerns — closing vulnerabilities before they can be manipulated.

Using Strong Passwords

Password is the most common line of protection against cyber attacks. But too many people struggle to protect these Passwords with due care. When you actually add your pet's name to all your accounts as a password, your online protection is not guaranteed. Strong passwords will make your data safer.

Don't use personal information when you add a password to an account. It's easy for hackers and viruses to find details like your hometown or address, and they can guess the passwords that use this data with relative ease. Your passwords should include letters, numbers and symbols, and should be unique to each account. Don't reuse old passwords on different accounts, even if you change a couple of details.

Using Two-Factor Authentication Before mobile phones became so popular, your password was the only thing between your account and a bunch of hackers. Fortunately, companies like Google now use two-factor authentication for added security. They normally send a text message that contains a code which allows you to log in to your accounts. Hackers would not be able to break in without this series, placing an extra barrier between them and your confidential information.

Update Your Software Regularly Software Updates include patches that fix conspicuous security vulnerabilities. If you ignore these updates, it will make it easier for hackers to exploit these vulnerabilities. Updates can be inconvenient, but the security they provide makes them less annoying.

Be careful with Mobile Devices

Users are not always conscious of their mobile protection. You may think the software you just downloaded is harmless, but it can access anything from your contact list to your photos and much more. When an application requires permission to access your details, weigh the possible risks against the benefits. For example, it might make sense for you to connect your contact list to a social networking app like Facebook, but it wouldn't be wise to offer that information to a cheap mobile game.

Don't open Suspicious E-mails or Attachments

Chain letters and money scams clog spam folders every day. Even the most malicious e-mails may look fairly credible. A friend might ask for help in a foreign country, but as soon as you open a message, your device may be locked. Hackers can hack other people's accounts and use them to send you malware and other security threats. If your e-mail appears odd, don't open it. Never download unusual attachments, either.

- Use Efficient Anti-Virus Software (and Complement It with Malware Software) Anti-Virus Software is essential, but not enough. If you want effective security, you do need to use malware software. Malware-specific software offers an additional degree of security to keep you protected from threats.
- Using a VPN to Encrypt Your Public Network Activities

If you've ever used the Internet in a café or library, you've used an unsecured network. Other users can see your activities and even steal your passwords from these connections, so you need to invest in a virtual private network (VPN) to remain secure. These tools provide you with added privacy and protection on public networks, ensuring that you stay secure wherever you are.

The Internet

The Internet is a global system comprised of interconnected computer networks that employ the Internet Protocol (TCP / IP) suite to communicate between networks and devices. It's a network of networks consisting of private, public, academic, business and government networks of local to global scale, interconnected by a wide variety of electronic, wireless and optical networking technologies. The Internet provides a wide variety of information tools and facilities, such as interlinked hypertext documents and the World Wide Web (WWW) applications, telephony, electronic mail, and file sharing.

The origin of the Internet dates back to the introduction of packet switching and research commissioned in the 1960s by the United States Department of Defense to facilitate computer time-sharing. The primary precursor network,

ARPANET, initially served as a backbone for linking regional academic and military networks in the 1970s. National Science Foundation Network financing as a virtual backbone in the 1980s, as well as private support for other commercial extensions, led to worldwide involvement in the creation of new networking technologies and the convergence of several networks. The connecting of commercial networks and companies in the early 1990s marked the start of the transition to the digital Internet. While the Internet was primarily used by academia in the 1980s, commercialization introduced its services and technology into almost every area of modern life.

Many conventional communication media, such as telephony, television, radio, paper mail and newspapers, are reshaped, redefined or even overridden by the Internet, giving rise to new technologies such as e-mail, Internet television, Internet telephony, digital newspapers, online music, and video streaming websites.

Newspaper, book and other print publications are adapted to internet technologies or are reshaped into blogs, video feeds and online news aggregators. The Internet has allowed and promoted new forms of personal interaction through instant messaging, Internet forums and social networking. Internet shopping has expanded rapidly, both for big retailers and small companies and entrepreneurs, as it allows firms to broaden their "brick and mortar" footprint to reach a wider audience or even to offer products and services entirely online. Internet business-to-business and financial services impact supply chains across industries.

The web has no centralized control in either technological implementation or access and uses policies; each network sets its own policies. The overall meanings of the two key namespaces on the Internet, the Domain Name System (DNS) and Internet Protocol address (IP address) space are regulated by the organization in charge of maintenance, the Internet Corporation for

Assigned Names and Numbers (ICANN). The technological underpinning and standardization of core protocols is an initiative of the Internet Engineering Task Force (IETF), a non-profit group of loosely aligned international members that anyone may connect with by offering technological expertise.

Origin Of The Internet

The origin of the Internet is grounded in attempts to create and interconnect computer networks that originated from research and development in the United States and included international collaboration, in particular with researchers in the United Kingdom and France. In the late 1950s, computer science was a nascent discipline that started to consider time-sharing between computer users and, later, the feasibility of achieving this over wide area networks. Autonomously, Paul Baran proposed a distributed network based on message block data in the early 1960s, and Donald Davies conceived packet switching in 1965 at the National Physics Laboratory (NPL) in the United Kingdom, which had been a research testbed for two decades. In 1969, the U.S. Department of Defense awarded contracts for the creation of the ARPANET project, headed by Robert Taylor. ARPANET implemented the packet switching technology suggested by Davies and Baran, supported by Leonard Kleinrock's mathematical work in the early 1970s. The network was constructed by Bolt, Beranek, and Newman. Early packet switching networks, such as the ARPANET, NPL, Merit Network, and CYCLADES, researched and provided data networking in the early 1970s. The ARPANET project and the international working groups contributed to the creation of protocols for internet work, in which several separate networks could be merged into a network of networks that created different standards. Vint Cerf, Stanford University, and Bob Kahn, ARPA, published work in 1973 that developed into the Transmission Control Protocol (TCP) and the

Internet Protocol (IP), the two protocols of the Internet Protocol series. The design included ideas from the French CYCLADES project led by Louis Pouzin.

In the early 1980s, National supercomputing centres were funded by the National Science Foundation (NSF) at several universities in the United States, providing interconnectivity in 1986 with the NSFNET project, which offered network access to such supercomputing sites for research and academic organizations in the United States. International connections to NSFNET, the introduction of technologies such as the Domain Name System and the implementation of TCP / IP marked the origins of the Internet internationally. Commercial Internet Service Providers (ISPs) started to appear in the late 1980s. In 1990, the ARPANET was decommissioned. By late 1989 and 1990, limited private links to parts of the Internet by officially commercial companies came up in several American cities. The NSFNET was decommissioned in 1995, lifting the last restrictions on the use of the Internet for commercial traffic.

The research at CERN in Switzerland by British computer scientist Tim Berners-Lee in 1989-90 culminated in the World Wide Web connecting hypertext documents to an information system accessible from any node on the network. Since the middle of the 1990s, the Internet has had a dynamic influence on culture, commerce and technology, including the rise of near-instant e-mail communications, voice over Internet Protocol (VoIP) telephone calls, instant messaging, two-way interactive video calls, and the World Wide Web with its discussion forums, blogs, social networking, and online shopping sites. Growing volumes of data are transmitted at higher and higher rates over fibre optic networks running at 1 Gbit/s, 10 Gbit/s and more. In historical terms, the Internet's overtake of the global communications landscape was dramatic: it registered just 1% of the information flowing across two-way telecommunications networks in 1993, 51% in 2000, and more than 97% of telecommunications information in 2007. Today, the Internet keeps expanding, powered by ever-increasing volumes of online content, commerce, entertainment and social networking. However, regional disparities can shape the future of the global network.

Internet Terminologies

Address: location of an Internet resource. The form barbarajon@mycompany.com can be used for an e-mail address. A domain address, however, would look like http://www.mycompany.com.

Bandwidth: it's a measurement of the capacity of a telecommunication line. Higher bandwidth means it is capable of handling more data.

Blog: (from the Web Log), it's an online journal with brief entries containing links to websites, news reports or images. It is revised on a daily basis with posts usually enlisted in reverse chronological order.

Broadband: fast Internet connection, using a cable modem, DSL or other high-speed Mobile connection

Browser: it's a software that enables you to view web pages. Firefox and Microsoft's Internet Explorer are two common browsers.

Cache: part of the memory of a machine where previously accessed data can be stored for fast retrieval.

Cookies: files that your browser collects that carry information about the sites you've visited.

Domain: the Internet is split into smaller sets known as domains, such as the gmail.com domain. Domain endings tells you something about the owner of the site: .com (business), .org (non-profit organizations), .edu (educational), .gov (government), and country codes such as .tw (Taiwan) or .ca (Canada).

Download: it's the process of copying files from a remote computer (server) to a local server (client). The reverse is upload, where a digital file is sent from a local computer to a server.

DSL: (Digital Subscriber Line) is an internet connection with high-speed that makes use of a traditional telephone line.

E-mail: means electronic mail.

FAQ: Frequently Asked Questions — a set of frequently asked questions and answers on a specific subject.

Favourite: a browser feature that remembers your web addresses. If you find a fascinating website, you can add it to your favourites list so that you can quickly find it again later. It's sometimes called a Bookmark.

Home Page: it's the first page of your website—also, the website you set as your start point every time you use your browser.

HTML: Hypertext Markup Language — a programming code that shows a browser how to display a web page.

Hyperlink: an underlined word, phrase or an image on a web page that, when selected, connects you to another document or to another part of the same document.

Internet: it's a worldwide network of computers that can communicate with each other through telecommunications.

ISP: Internet Service Provider — a company that provides you with an Internet connection.

LAN: Local Area Network — a network of computers within a small region, such as an office building.

Multimedia: a combination of different types of media on a computer, including text, animation, graphics, video and audio.

Netiquette: Internet etiquette-an informal set of rules for the use of the Internet and e-mail. E.g.

using ALL CAPS in an e-mail is similar to shouting at others and should be avoided.

Online Database: a web-based set of information which a library subscribes to and makes accessible to its users, including business directories, magazine article databases, etc. PDF (portable document format): a file that preserves the original document format.

RSS: it means Really Simple Syndication, a feed that informs the user about new content on a blog or website. It helps you to monitor a lot of resources without having to visit each of them separately.

Search Engine: a tool for searching for information by keyword or phrase on the Internet.

SPAM: unsolicited e-mails, often sent to thousands of users. It also includes viruses or other malware.

Subject Directories: They are lists of websites compiled by individuals who list and categorize them. Such directories do not categorize the entire Web, but merely provide links to what each directory considers to be important or the best Web sites.

URL: Uniform Resource Locator — a standard format for Internet addresses, including a protocol www.gmail.com is an address; the complete URL is http://www.gmail.com.

Virus: a malicious computer program that can reproduce itself, causing harm to the hardware or software of a computer.

Wi-Fi: (Wireless Fidelity) is a common term for wireless networks.

WWW: World Wide Web, or just the Web. A part of the Internet that makes use of hyperlinks and has a multimedia capacity.

How does the Internet work?

The Internet works based on the principle of a client-server relationship between computers, often referred to as the client/server architecture.

Some computers operate as information providers (servers) in the client/server architecture, while other computers operate as receivers of information (clients). The client/server architecture is not one-to-one, this means that a single client computer can access several different servers, and a number of different client computers can access a single server. Until the mid-1990s, servers were typically very powerful computers, such as mainframe or supercomputers, with exceptionally high processing speeds and large memory capacity. Nevertheless, personal computers and workstations are now capable of functioning as Internet servers due to developments in computing technology. Any computer that collects information from a server is a client computer. A client computer can be a personal computer, a web appliance or a wireless device, such as a portable computer or a mobile phone.

To access information on the Internet, the user must first log in or connect to the host network of the client computer. The host network is a network that is part of the client device and is typically a local area network (LAN). When a connection has been created, the user can request information from a remote server. If the information requested by the user exists on one of the computers on the host network, the information is easily retrieved and sent to the terminal of the user. When the information requested by the user is on a server that does not belong to the host LAN, the host network must connect to other networks until it connects to the network that contains the requested data. In the process of connecting to other networks, the host will need to have access to a router, a system that decides the best communication path between the networks and allows the networks to make connections.

When the client computer connects to the server containing the requested information, the server sends the information to the client in the form of a file. A special computer program called a browser helps the user to access the file. Examples of Internet browsers include Netscape, Internet Explorer, and Mosaic. Multimedia files can only be accessed by a browser. Their pared-down equivalents, text-only documents, can be accessed without a browser. There are several files available in both multimedia and text-only versions. The method of accessing files from a remote server to the terminal of the user is called downloading.

One of the strengths of the Internet is that it's built around the idea of hypertext. The word hypertext is used to describe an interlinked document system in which a user can move from one document to another in a nonlinear, associative manner. The ability to jump from one document to another is made possible by using hyperlinks – portions of the hypertext document linked to other related documents on the Internet. By clicking the hyperlink, the user is immediately connected to the document defined by the link. Multimedia files available on the Internet are known as hypermedia files.

Internet facilities The Internet is similar in some ways to the global telephone system: it enables 2-way links between locations anywhere in the world to be created almost instantly. Nevertheless, unlike telephone calls, the Internet helps people to connect in a number of ways. Perhaps significantly, we are not limited to verbal communication with other people — in certain situations, access to knowledge stored on the computer is possible. The basic facilities available on the Internet are listed below and include e-mail, list servers, USNET / Newsgroups, Internet Relay Chat, File Transfer Protocol, Gopher and WWW.

E-mail

E-mail, the Internet counterpart of postal mail, is the most commonly used service on the Internet. E-mail messages routed through the Internet can reach an overseas destination in seconds. You never receive a busy signal, and you never play a "telephone tag." Various e-mail programs offer features that allow you to print, forward, save, and/or reply to other messages. Some of them have advanced features that allow you to add a word processing document, software program, spreadsheet, video, or image file.

List Servers

The List Server facility allows the formation of discussion groups to exchange information about shared interests. LISTSERV, the most popular list server program, copies incoming messages sent to the list and forwards them to everyone whose e-mail address is on the list (subscribers). Only subscribers can submit messages to a group that is monitored by a list manager. Usually, the user (the initiator) joins the list by sending an appropriately worded e-mail message, which automatically triggers the LISTSERV program to extract the e-mail address of the initiator, add it to the list, and send the initiator an e-mail confirmation and information concerning the use of the list.

USENET / Newsgroup

Internet newsgroup servers typically offer links to groups that are far less selective than those offered by list servers. Free and unrestricted access to thousands of topic-based newsgroups can be acquired by using specific newsreader software to contact a local computer that acts as a news server. This app allows users to post messages or posts to any newsgroup so that other users can read and potentially add their comments.

File Transfer Protocol

The File Transfer Protocol facility allows Internet users to transfer software programs, product upgrades, and other computer files between computer systems connected to the Internet.

Internet Relay Chat

With Internet Relay Chat, a limited number of users meet in online chat groups and communicate with each other by typing messages on their keyboards.

Gopher

The Gopher facility, established at the University of Minnesota and named after its golden gopher mascot, is one of the first "user-friendly" Internet facilities used to obtain information over the network. Using Gopher, users can connect to thousands of different devices, known as information servers or "gopher holes," via a menu-driven "point and click" program. At every gopher hole, hierarchically ordered information is processed. Users click on a drop-down list of individual topics to retrieve information that might include text, sound, or images.

World Wide Web

The WWW is such a popular Internet facility that it has become synonymous with the Internet for many users. Developed in 1992 at the European Particle Physics Laboratory in Cern, Switzerland, WWW links users to websites. The basic unit of WWW communication is a page similar to a printed page. There are "links" on the web page that users can click on and automatically connect to similar pages on the same or other Internet sites. With its ease of use and multimedia capabilities to transfer text, images, audio and video, and to retrieve comprehensive information from anywhere in the world within seconds, the Site has rapidly become an interface of choice for Internet users.

The components of the WWW Key to WWW's success are its effective connection mechanism, which allows users to access similar data sets stored on various computers on the Internet. This link embedding scheme in the text of a web page, called "hypertext," enables any kind of data to be accessed from a web page by clicking on the highlighted and/or highlighted links that lead to other sites. Users are automatically redirected to the selected Web page even if they are on a distant computer. This web of interconnected pages gives rise to the name of the WWW.

Every web page has its unique title, known as the Uniform Resource Locator (URL The URL includes both the Internet address of the device where the web page is stored and the name of the data file that actually contains the page. There are over 1/2 million WWW sites on the Internet, each of which can contain multiple URLs. The result is tens of millions of web pages!

In order for users to access and retrieve web pages without having to learn and type the URL each time, a special form of program known as a "browser" has been created. The browser program operates on a personal computer, interfaces it with the Internet and allows users to "surf" the WWW. Browsers are affordable and generally available free of charge to educators. All browsers allow Internet users:

1) To retrieve web pages from other computers;
2) To display those pages on the user's screen using the formatting commands specified by the author of the page; and
3) To activate the web pages, to progress to the referenced file or URL by pointing and clicking on a hyperlink embedded in the page.

Browsers are very easy to use, and even a computer novice can get adapted to browsing the Internet within minutes. The new user will soon realize, however, that navigating effectively through millions of web pages requires the ability to search. To cope with this abundance of knowledge, users of the Internet use WWW software tools known as search engines. A search engine is a powerful program for locating Websites that contains keyword information. Search engines scan web pages, File Transfer Protocol sites, newsgroup posts, Gopher sites, and so on. Many of these programs are presently available, and their designs differ in little ways. Readers can select from the popular search engines offered by their web browser by simply clicking the appropriate button on the opening page of the browser. Users usually try a few before they find those that seem to be easier to use and more successful. Skilled Web surfers usually use a search engine to initiate a search, and then use hyperlinks embedded in the Web pages found by search engines to move from page to page across the Internet.

Uses Of The Internet

1) E-mail: using the internet, we can connect with a person who is on the other side of the world in a matter of seconds. We can use the facilities of e-mail today for better communication. We can talk with our loved ones for hours. There are plenty of postal companies and e-mail providers providing this service free of charge. With

the aid of these services, it has become very easy to build a kind of global relationship where you can share your thoughts and explore other cultures of different ethnicities.

2) Information: The greatest benefit provided by the Internet is information. The Internet and the World Wide Web have made it possible for everyone to access information, and it can be of any sort because the Internet is filled with information.
3) Business: World trade has seen a massive boom with the aid of the Internet because it has become very easy for buyers and sellers to connect and advertise their websites. Nowadays, most people use online classified sites to buy or sell or advertise their goods or services. Classified sites save you a lot of money and time so that most people want to advertise their goods as a platform. We have many

classified websites on the web, such as craigslist, Adsglobe.com, Kijiji etc.

4) Social networking: social networking sites have become a crucial part of the online community. Almost all users are members of a social networking site who use it for personal and business purposes. It's a great place to network with many entrepreneurs who come here to start creating their own personal and business brand.
5) Shopping: In every day's busy life, most of us are involved in shopping online. Now, almost everything can be purchased with the use of the Internet. In countries like the USA, most customers tend to shop from home. There are lots of shopping sites on the internet, like amazon.com, Dealsglobe.com, etc. Users are now using the internet to sell items. There are many online auction sites where anything can be sold.

6) Entertainment: On the internet, we can find several kinds of entertainment, from watching movies to playing games online. Almost everybody in any age group will find the right kind of entertainment for themselves. There are many items that can be found as people browse the internet. You can find and share news, music, hobbies, and more on the Internet. There are a variety of games that can be downloaded from the Internet for free.
7) E-Commerce: e-commerce is a term used for any sort of commercial manoeuvring or business transactions involving the transfer of information across the globe through the Internet. It's become a phenomenon associated with any kind of shopping, almost anything. It's got a truly impressive selection of items from household needs, electronics to entertainment.

8) Services: Many services are now available on the Internet, such as online banking, job search, ticket purchases for your favourite movies, and guidance on a variety of topics in every aspect of life, and hotel reservations and bills payments. These programs are often not available offline and can cost you more.
9) Work Search: The Internet makes life easier for employers and work-seekers since there are a number of job pages linking employers and job-seekers.
10) Dating / Personal: People communicate with others via the internet and find their life partners. The Internet helps not only to find the right person but also to continue the relationship.

How To Connect To The Internet

The two components for connecting to the Internet

Connecting to the Internet need two main components:

- A computer capable of connecting to the Internet.
- Connection to an internet service that will allow the computer to be connected.

Basically, there are a number of different forms of each of these components.

In other words, an ever-increasing number of devices can be connected to the Internet. Plus, there are also quite a few different types of services that make it possible for these devices to get online.

People's choice over different devices and means of getting online differs according to many factors, including lifestyles (whether at home or out and about), how often they need to access the internet (every day for a number of hours or just occasionally), the types of things they want to use the internet for (retrieve e-mail or download and watch movies and TV programs), and budget (internet access companies usually charge for using their services).

Let's unpack the above in a little more detail.

Devices that can connect to the Internet

The most common devices used today to get online include: smartphones, desktop computers, Laptop computers, Mobile phones, Tablets, E-readers. However, the range of devices that can connect to the Internet is expanding and shifting our understanding of what "online" means.

In recent times, we have witnessed the advent of refrigerators, central heating systems and even smartwatches that can perform all kinds of enhanced and useful functions by connecting to the Internet.

Currently, the most "traditional" machines used to access and browse the Internet are smartphones, desktop computers, laptop computers, and tablets.

Types Of Internet Connection Services

There are two major types of services that can provide you with access to the internet. They are:

- Fixed Internet
- Mobile Internet

Fixed Internet

As the name implies, this is an internet link that is fixed to a particular location (such as a house, office or shop)—meaning that the internet connection is exclusive to that property, hence, you can only access it when you are physically located there.

Nowadays, the three most popular forms of fixed internet connections are:

ADSL broadband

The most commonly used form of internet access and ADSL uses an existing phone line property to get online.

This particular form of broadband has been available for some time, often making it the most cost-effective way to get online — but not the fastest (average download speed of 8.4 Mb) when compared to the two other available forms of internet access.

Cable broadband

Instead of using a telephone line as ADSL does, cable broadband offers an Internet link via a special cable that uses the same line as your TV service.

Cable broadband generally provides higher speeds than ADSL connections (average download speeds of 50.5 Mb), but as cable broadband connections are often shared with many other users, speeds may suffer from congestion from time to time.

Fibre broadband

Fibre broadband offers more reliable and consistent speeds than cable and ADSL (average download speed of 59.4mb)—allowing multiple devices to perform high-capacity tasks at the same time, without any slowdowns or interruptions, making it an appealing proposition for busy family homes or office environments.

Mobile Internet

Mobile Internet is a way to get anywhere online without relying on a fixed-location connection — as the name suggests — by using your mobile device.

Mobile phone operators have access to this alternative form of use of the Internet. When you sign up for the services of a cell phone operator — either on a contract basis or on a pay-as-you-go basis — you will have access to a certain amount of data (measured in megabytes), enabling you to use your mobile device to link to the Internet under that limited usage limit.

Mobile internet currently runs at two different speeds and capabilities: 3G mobile internet: it has been around for several years and typically offers basic access and download speeds that enable users to complete basic tasks such as loading a web page or accessing an e-mail.

4G mobile internet: it offers much higher speeds than 3G. In fact, due to excellent connectivity and download speeds, 4G has potentially replaced fixed internet connections in more remote areas of the world that struggle to gain access to faster networks.

5G mobile internet: the initial next standard for telecommunications above the existing advanced 4G requirements.

How To Get Internet Connectivity Using Dial-Up

- Open the Settings app.
- Press Win+I.
- Select network and the Internet.
- Select Dial-Up on the left side of the screen.
- Select Set up a new connection on the right side of the device.
- The Network Connection Wizard will appear.
- Select Connect to the Internet and then press the Next button.
- If your laptop is already connected to the Internet, select New Connection.
- Click Dialup.
- This feature does not appear if your laptop does not have a dial-up modem.
- Fill in the connection information.

Wifi Internet Connectivity

- Position yourself in a property or public area that has a wireless router. I.e. Somewhere, a WiFi signal is being transmitted.
- Make sure that the computer you are going to use is a.) Able to connect to the internet and b.) Able to connect to the WiFi.
- Identify the name of the WiFi network that the router transmits to your location. Every WiFi network has its own unique name. Sometimes it can be a sequence of random numbers and letters if the router is set by default — but people often customize the name of a WiFi network to help users identify their owners. E.g. "Jones WiFi" or "Jim's Cafe"
- Once you've known the name of the WiFi network, use your device to find it. It can differ between computers (depending on

whether you are making use of a mobile device, Windows or Mac computer). However, the process for connecting to a WiFi is generally similar, following something along this line:

- Move to WiFi settings > turn WiFi on > click on the name of the WiFi network > click on connect.
- Many WiFi networks are made private, with password-restricted access. If your chosen WiFi network is password-protected, you will be prompted to enter the password at this stage. Make sure you have a password in your hand and enter it. You're meant to be connected to the WiFi now!

Ip Addressing

The Internet Protocol (IP) address is a numeric label assigned to every device connected to a computer network that utilizes the Internet Protocol for communication purposes. The IP address has two main functions: host or network interface identification and location address.

Internet Protocol version 4 (IPv4) points an IP address as a 32-bit number. However, due to the growth of the Internet and the shortage of usable IPv4 addresses, a new IP version (IPv6) using 128 bits for an IP address was introduced in 1998. The implementation of IPv6 has been ongoing since the mid-2000s.

IP addresses are written and displayed in notations readable to humans, like 172.16.254.1 in IPv4, as well as 2001:db8:0:1234:0:567:8:1 in IPv6. The routing prefix size of the address is indicated in the CIDR notation by suffixing the address with the number of important bits, e.g. 192.168.1.15/24, which is equal to the traditionally used subnet mask 255.255.255.0.

The IP address space is regulated worldwide by the Internet Assigned Numbers Authority (IANA) and by five regional Internet registries (RIRs) responsible for assignment to local Internet registries in their designated territories, such as Internet service providers and other end-users. IPv4 addresses have been distributed by IANA to RIRs in blocks of roughly 16.8 million addresses each, but have been depleted at IANA level since 2011. Just one of the RIRs still has a supply of local assignments in Africa. Certain IPv4 addresses are reserved for private networks and are not globally special.

Network administrators allocate an IP address to each computer that is connected to a network. These allocations may be on a static (fixed or permanent) or dynamic basis, depending on the network activities and features of the program.

Types Of Ip Address

IP version 4 (IPv4)

The Internet Protocol version 4 or IPv4 consists of a 32-bit version and can host more than 4,294,967,296 hosts worldwide.

IP version 6 (IPv6)

IPv6 was designed to address concerns about the capacity of IPv4 to use only 32 bits to handle IP addresses in the world, and an increasing number of network users worldwide from day to day IPv4 would exceed the maximum limit. Due to the reason, IPv6 version 128 bits was created. With its capacity much greater than IPv4 measured, it is increasingly capable of providing an IP address to all Internet users around the world.

The Internet Protocol version 6 or IPv6 is made up of 128 bits.

FUNCTIONS OF IP ADDRESS

• IP Address is used as a way of identifying the host or network interface. This feature is shown as the name of the user as a form of identifying who the user is. The same thing also applies to a computer network that uses a unique IP address to identify a computer or device on a network.

• IP address is used as a network location address. This feature is displayed as our home address, which means where we are located. In order to facilitate the delivery of data packets, the IP address contains information about its existence. There is a path to be followed so that the data can be moved to the destination device.

NOTE: The IP address is a thirty-two-bit binary number. The thirty-two bits are divided into octets which are four classes of eight bits. However, an IP address is displayed as a dotted-decimal number (e.g., 205.57.32.9). Since the IP address is a binary number represented in dotted decimal format, a review of the binary numbering system is required.

Subnet Masks

A Subnet mask is a 32-bit number which masks an IP address and divides it into a network address and a host address. Subnet Mask is done by setting the network bits to all "1"s and setting the host bits to all" 0"s. Inside a given network, two host addresses are specially kept for a specific purpose and can not be assigned to hosts. The "0" address is allocated to the network address, and the "255" is allocated to the broadcast address and can not be assigned to the hosts.

The subnet mask, in this example, is 255.255.255.0. It's not obvious what this number means unless you know that 255 is equal to 11111111 in binary notation; therefore, the subnet mask is: 11111111.11111111.11111111.00000000 Linking together the IP address and subnet mask, the network and host portions of the address can be separated: 11000000.10101000.01111011.10000100—IP address (192.168.123.132) 11111111.11111111.11111111.00000000 — Subnet mask (255.255.255.0)

The very first 24 bits (i.e., the number of ones in the subnet mask) are the network address, and the last 8 bits (the number of remaining zeros in the subnet mask) are known as the host address, which gives you the following: 11000000.10101000.01111011.00000000—Network address (192.168.123.0)

00000000.00000000.00000000.10000100—Host address (000.000.000.132)

So now you know, that the network ID is 192.168.123.0, and the host address is 0.0.0.132 using a subnet mask of 255.255.255.0. When a packet reaches the 192.168.123.0 subnet (from the local subnet or remote network) and has a destination address of 192.168.123.132, your computer receives it from the network and processes it.

Almost all subnet decimal masks convert to binary numbers that are all on the left and all zeros on the right. Many specific subnet masks are: Decimal Binary 255.255.255.192- 11111111.11111111.11111111.11000000

255.255.255.224- 111111111.11111111.11111111.11100000

Binary Numbering System

Base numbers show how many unique numbers they have. For example, humans make use of the Decimal Numbering System, which is the Basic Ten Numbering System. There are only ten basic numbers in the decimal numbering system-zero to nine. All other numbers are derived from these ten numbers. The location of a number shall decide its meaning. For instance, the number 2,534 means two thousand; five hundred; three tens; and four units.

Computers, routers, and switches make use of the binary numbering system. The binary numbering system is the base two numbering system, which means that there are only two base numbers-zero and one. All other numbers are generated from these two numbers. As in the decimal numbering system, the number location determines its value. For exponents above 7, double the value of the previous place. For instance, 28 = 256, 29 = 512, 210 = 1,024, and so on.

Decimal to Binary Conversion

Because the IP address is a binary number expressed in dotted decimal format, it is always important to convert a decimal number to a binary number.

For example, 35 is equivalent to 00100011 in binary number. The measures below are used to perform this conversion.

1. Determine the decimal number. It's 35 in this case.

2. Write down the base number and its exponent. Since the IP address uses groups of eight binary bits, eight base two exponents are listed.
3. Write the position value below the base number and its exponent. For examples, 20 has a value of 1; 22 has a value of 4; 23 has a value of 8; etc. 4. Compare the value of the decimal number with the value of the highest bit position. If the value of the highest bit position is higher than the decimal number, place 0 below the position of the bit. A 0 below the position of the bit indicates that the position is not used.

But, if the value of the highest bit position is less than or equal to the decimal number, place 1 below the position of the bit. A 1 below the position of the bit indicates the position is used.

Hexadecimal Numbering System

Hexadecimal Number System (Base-16)

The scheme of hexadecimal numbers uses SIXTEEN values to represent numbers. The values are 0 1 2 3 4 5 6 7 8 9 A B C D E F, where 0 is the lowest value and F being the highest value. Columns are used in the same way as in the decimal system, except that the leftmost column is used to denote the highest value.

Hexadecimal is also used to represent values (numbers and memory addresses) on computer systems.

Decimal value (base 10): 0, 1, 2, 3, 4, 5, 6, 7, 8, 9, 10, 11, 12, 13, 14, 15.

Hexadecimal equivalent (base 16): 0, 1, 2, 3, 4, 5, 6, 7, 8, 9, A, B, C, D, E, F.

Binary equivalent (base 2): 0000, 0001, 0010, 0011, 0100, 0101, 0110, 0111, 1000, 1001, 1010, 1011, 1100, 1101, 1110, 1111.

Binary to hexadecimal

Converting a number from binary to hex uses a grouping system. The binary number is divided into groups of four digits starting from the right. These groups are then translated to hexadecimal digits as seen above. To transition from hexadecimal, the reverse is done. Each hex digit is converted to binary, and the grouping is normally eliminated.

When the number of bits in binary numbers is not a multiple of 4, it is filled with zeros to make it up.

Example:

Binary 110 = 0110, which is 6 hex.

Binary 010010 = 00010010, which is 12 hex.

Hexadecimal to decimal conversion

There are two common methods to convert a number from hexadecimal to decimal.

The first approach is more widely used when translating it manually:

1. Using the decimal value for each hex digit. It is the same for 0-9, but A = 10, B = 11, C = 12, D = 13, E = 14, and F = 15.
2. Keep the sum of the number converted at each step below.
3. Start with the least hexadecimal digit. That's the digit on the right end of it. This is going to be the first thing in the sum.
4. Take the second least digit. It's next to the digit on the right end. Multiply by the decimal value of the digit by 16. Add this to the sum.
5. Do the same for the third least digit, but multiply by 162 (i.e., 16 squared, or 256). Then add it to the sum.
6. Continue for each digit, multiplying each digit by another 16 digit power. (4096, 65536, etc.) The next approach is more widely used when translating a number in a software. It does not have to know how

many digits the number has before it starts, so it never multiplies by more than 16, although it looks longer on paper.

7. Using the decimal value for each hex digit. It is the same for 0-9, but A = 10, B = 11, C = 12, D = 13, E = 14, and F = 15.
8. Keep the sum of the number converted at each step below.
9. Start with the highest digit (the digit on the far left side). This is the first element in the sum.
10. If there is another digit, multiply the sum by 16 and add the decimal value of the next digit.
11. Repeat the step above until there are no digits left.

How To Find Your Ip Address

For Windows XP

Step 1 Click Start->Control Panel->Select and then choose Network and Internet Connections

(If you can't find it, please go next)->Select and double-click Network Connections.

Step 2 Highlight and right-click the Local Area Connection icon; click Status and go to Support. The IP address will be shown.

Windows 7

Step 1 Click on Start->Control Panel->Network and Internet->Network and Sharing Center.

Step 2 In the task list, click Change Adapter Settings. Right-click the Local Area Connection icon; press Status and go to Details. The IP address will be shown.

For Windows Vista

Step 1 Click Start->Control Panel->Network and Internet->Network and Sharing Center.

Step 2 In the task list, select Manage Network Connections. Right-click the Local Area Connection icon; click Status and go to Info. The IP address will be shown .

For Windows 8

Step 1 Go to Control Panel.

There are various ways to locate a control panel on Windows 8.

1) Press "Windows key+F" and the search box will appear, type control panel and press enter;
2) Press "Windows key+R", and there will be a "run" box, type the control panel and press enter;
3) Press "Windows key + X" and click "control panel";
4) You can also enter "control panel" in the search bar on the right side of the screen.

Step 2 Select Network and Internet- > Network and Sharing Hub Center, then Change Adapter Settings on the left.

Step 3 Highlight and right-click Ethernet, go to Status- > Details. The IP address will be shown.

For Windows 10

Method 1

Step 1 Go to Control Panel. Click Windows + X at the same time and choose Control Panel.

Step 2 Select Network and Internet- > Network and Sharing Center, then Change Adapter Settings on the left.

Step 3 Highlight and right-click Ethernet, go to Status- > Details. The IP address will be shown.

Method 2

In the task tray, select the network icon (may look like a computer or WiFi signal). Go to the Network Settings area.

Click Ethernet > Edit Adapter Options. Or select Status > Change Adapter Options.

Highlight and right-click Ethernet, go to Status- > Details. The IP address will be shown.

Note: If your device is linked to a wireless network, click the Wireless Network Connection icon.

For MAC OS

Step 1

Click the Apple icon, pick Device Preferences from the Apple drop-down list.

Step 2 Select the Network button.

Step 3 In the left column, pick either Ethernet (for wired connection) or WiFi (for wireless connection). Your IP address will be displayed directly below the status of your link, in a smaller print.

Method 2:

Using Windows OS command

Step 1 Open Command Prompt

Solution 1 Press Windows and R key on your keyboard at the same time, you will see a small window that pops up below, and then enter "cmd" in the field. Press enter to open the prompt for the command.

Solution 2 Click on the Windows button at the bottom left of your screen, then start typing "cmd" in the "Start Search" column at the bottom of the page, click on "cmd" under programs to open the command prompt.

Step2 Type "ipconfig" and click enter

This will cause a list of your network link information to be displayed. Look near the top of the list for "IPv4 Address" under either Wireless Network Connection or Local Area Connection (depending on whether or not your device is using WiFi).

For MAC OS

Step 1 Open the terminal.

Type Terminal in the search bar, and pick Terminal in the list.

Step 2 Use the ifconfig command.

Click on the Return key on your keyboard after selecting Terminal. Enter ifconfig in the command window and press the Return button again. Your IP address will be shown next to the "inet" entry in eto or Wi-Fi1.

Ip Address Configuration

For Windows XP:

Step 1 Click Start->Control Panel->Select and double click Network and Internet connections->Select and double-click Network Connections.

Step 2 Double click the Local Area Connection icon; highlight the Internet Protocol (TCP / IP) tab in the window of the Local Area Connection Properties that shows up.

Step 3 Double click or click Properties. The TCP / IP Properties window will be displayed.

Step 4 You now have two ways to configure the TCP / IP protocol below:

1. Assigned by DHCP Server

Select obtain an IP address automatically and automatically obtain a DNS server address as shown in the figure below. These can be selected by default. Then select OK to save the settings.

2. Manually assigned

i. Select Use the following IP address.

If the LAN IP address of the router is 192.168.1.1, enter IP address 192.168.1.x (x ranges from 2 to 253), subnet mask 255.255.255.0, and the default gateway 192.168.1.1.

ii. Choose Use the following DNS server addresses as shown in the figure below. Then type the IP address of the DNS server, which should be given by your ISP. Finally, remember to select OK to save your settings.

Note: In most cases, enter the IP addresses of your local DNS server area.

The Recommended DNS server is the same as the default gateway. For a secondary DNS server, you may leave it blank or type 8.8.8.8.

Step 5 Click OK to save and utilize your settings.

For Windows 7 & Windows Vista

Step 1 Press the Windows key+R key on the keyboard at the same time.

Step 2 Type in ncpa.cpl, then press OK.

Step 3 Choose a local area connection, right-click it, and then select Properties.

Step 4 Choose Internet Protocol Version 4(TCP / IPv4), double-click it or select Properties.

Step 5 There are two methods to configure the TCP/IP Properties allocated to the DHCP server automatically or manually.

1. Assigned by DHCP server

Select obtain an IP address automatically and automatically receive a DNS server address. If required, click OK to save the settings.

2. Manually assigned

i. Choose Use the following IP address, enter IP address, the subnet mask, and IP address of the default gateway.

If the LAN IP address of the router is 192.168.1.1, enter IP address 192.168.1.x (x is from 2 to 253), the subnet mask 255.255.255.0, and default gateway 192.168.1.1.

ii. Choose Use the following DNS server addresses. Then type the IP address of the DNS server, which should be given by your ISP. If required, click OK to save the settings.

Note: In most cases, enter the IP addresses of your local DNS server area. The Recommended DNS server is the same as the default DNS gateway. For a secondary DNS server, you may leave it blank or type 8.8.8.8.

Step 6 Select OK to save and add your settings.

For Windows 8, 8.1

Step1 Click the Windows Key on your Keyboard and Press X. Click the Control Panel on the screen that appears.

Step 2 In Category View, click Network and Internet

Step 3 Click Network and Sharing Center

Step 4 Click Change Adapter Settings

Step 5 Right-click Local Area Connection and click on Properties

Step 6 Select Internet Protocol Version 4 (TCP/IP) then click on Properties.

Step 7 Exchange 'Dot' to use the following IP address and enter your IP and DNS information.

Step 8: To save and apply your settings, click OK.

For Windows 10:

Step 1 Right-click the Internet icon in the Task Tray, pick Open Network and Sharing Center.

Step 2 Select Switch Adapter Settings.

Step 3 Highlight and right-click Ethernet, then choose Properties.

Step 4 Click Internet Protocol Version 4

Step 5 To automatically allocate IP settings, choose Automatically Get IP Address and Automatically Get DNS Server Address.

Note: To get fixed IP settings, choose Use the following IP address and use the following DNS server addresses, then manually enter the IP address, subnet mask, default gateway and DNS server.

For MAC OS:

Step 1 Click on the Apple icon after which you click System Preferences

Step 2 Select Network

Step 3 Click on Configure IPv4 field and select 'Manually' Step 4 Enter your IP details (Router is the default gateway address) and select Apply

Note: 1.DNS server will be provided by your ISP. Please contact your ISP to check it out.

2. In most cases, it may be possible for you to enter the IP addresses of your local area DNS server. The DNS server is the same as the IP address of the router LAN. You may also leave it blank or type in 8.8.8.8 in some cases.

Dhcp

DHCP means dynamic host configuration protocol which is a network protocol used on IP networks where the DHCP server automatically assigns an IP address and other information to each host on the network so that they can interact effectively with other endpoints.

In addition to the IP address, DHCP also assigns a subnet mask, default gateway address, the domain name server (DNS) address and other related configuration parameters. Request for Comments (RFC) 2131 and 2132 describe DHCP as an Internet Engineering Task Force (IETF) – a standard specified by the BOOTP protocol.

The Internet Protocol (IP) describes how computers interact on the Internet inside and through local networks. The DHCP server can control IP settings for devices on its local network, e.g. by automatically and dynamically assigning IP addresses to those devices.

DHCP is based on the client-server model. When a computer or any other device is connected to a network, the DHCP client program sends a DHCP broadcast question asking for the necessary information. The request can be supported by any DHCP server on the network. The DHCP server maintains a list of IP addresses and client configuration parameters information such as the default gateway, domain name, time servers, and name servers. Upon receipt of a DHCP request, the DHCP server may reply with specific information for each client, as previously configured by the administrator, or with a particular address and any other information relevant for the entire network and for the duration for which the allocation (lease) is valid. The DHCP client normally queries this information immediately after booting, and regularly thereafter until the information expires. When the DHCP client refreshes the assignment, it initially requests same parameter values, but the DHCP server may allocate a new address based on the assignment policies laid by the administrators.

A single DHCP server can serve the entire network on large networks consisting of multiple links when assisted by DHCP relay agents located on interconnecting routers. These agents relay messages between DHCP clients and DHCP servers located on various subnets.

Depending on the implementation, the DHCP server can have three methods of assigning IP addresses: dynamic allocation A network administrator reserves a variety of IP addresses for DHCP, and each DHCP client on the LAN is configured to request for an IP address from the

DHCP server during network initialization. The request-and-grant mechanism uses a lease model with a controllable time limit, allowing the DHCP server to collect and reallocate IP addresses which are not renewed.

Automatic Allocation

The DHCP server permanently allocates an IP address to the requesting client within the range specified by the administrator. It is like dynamic allocation, except the DHCP server maintains a table of past IP address allocations so that it can preferably allocate the same IP address to the client that he previously had.

Manual Allocation

Often generally referred to as static Allocation and Reservation. The DHCP server gives a private IP address that is dependent on the client Id (or, usually, the MAC client address) of each client, based on the administrator's predefined mapping. This function is called static DHCP assignment by DD-WRT. If no match can be found for the client ID (if given) or MAC address (if no client ID is given), the server may or may not fall back to either Dynamic or Automatic Allocation.

DHCP is used for version 4 (IPv4) and IPv6 of the Internet Protocol. Although both versions serve the same purpose, the protocol specifics for IPv4 and IPv6 vary enough that they can be considered separate protocols. Instead, devices may use stateless address autoconfiguration for IPv6 operation. IPv6 hosts can also use a local link address to conduct operations restricted to a local network connection.

Operation

An example of a standard non-renewing DHCP session; each message may be either broadcast or unicast, depending on the capabilities of the DHCP client. The DHCP uses the User Datagram Protocol (UDP), connectionless service model. It is incorporated with two UDP port numbers for its operations which are just the same as the bootstrap protocol (BOOTP). UDP port number 67 is the server's destination port, and UDP port number 68 is for the client.

DHCP operations are in four phases: server discovery, IP lease offer, IP lease request, and IP lease acknowledgement. These steps are also shortened as DORA for discovery, offer, request, and acknowledgement.

The DHCP operation starts with a request from clients. When the client and the server are on separate subnets, the DHCP Helper or the DHCP Relay Agent may be used. Clients applying for renewal of an existing lease can communicate directly through UDP unicast, as the client already has an IP address at that stage. In addition, there is a BROADCAST flag (1 bit in the 2 byte flag zone, while every other bits are reserved and are set to 0) that the client can use to indicate how (broadcast or unicast) DHCPOFFER can be received: 0x8000 for broadcast, 0x0000 for unicast. Normally, DHCPOFFER is sent through unicast. For hosts that can not accept unicast packets before the IP addresses are configured, this flag can be used to work around this problem.

How DHCP functions

DHCP offers an automated way of distributing and updating IP addresses and other network configuration information. The DHCP server sends this information to the DHCP client by exchanging a sequence of messages known as DHCP transactions or DHCP conversations.

DHCP Discovery

Client computers send messages to the physical subnet to discover the available DHCP servers. This client-computer generates a User Datagram Protocol (UDP) packet with a default broadcast destination of 255.255.255.255 or a specific broadcast subnet address if configured.

DHCP Offer

When a DHCP server detects an IP lease request from a client, it reserves the client's IP address and expands the IP lease offer by sending a DHCPOFFER message to the client. This message includes the MAC address of the client, the IP address provided by the user, the subnet mask, the length of the lease and the IP address of the DHCP user making the request.

DHCP request

In most organizations, two DHCP servers have an IP address fault tolerance if one server fails or needs to be removed for maintenance. So the client may receive DHCP offers from multiple servers, but only one DHCP offer will be accepted. The client requests the server in response to the offer. The client responds to the DHCP request, which is unicast to the server, requesting for the address offered. Based on the Transaction ID portion in the request, the servers whose offer the client has accepted are notified. When other DHCP servers receive this letter, they will withdraw any offers they may have made to the client and turn back the offered address to the pile of available addresses. In certain cases, the DHCP request message is broadcast and not unicast to a different DHCP server because the DHCP client has not yet received an IP address. Additionally, this way, one message will let the other DHCP servers know that another server will supply the IP address without missing a server with a series of unicast messages.

DHCP acknowledgement

The configuration process reaches its final phase when the DHCP server receives the DHCPREQUEST message from the client.

The acknowledgement phase involves sending the client a DHCPACK packet. This packet contains the duration of the lease and any other details about the setup that the client may have asked for. The process of configuring an IP is completed at this stage.

IP ADDRESS CLASSES

Internet Protocol hierarchy includes many classes of IP addresses that can be used effectively in various circumstances, depending on the host requirement per network. The body in charge of assigning the IP addresses is the Internet Corporation for Assigned Names and Numbers. The IPv4 Addressing Scheme is widely divided into five IP Address Classes. The first octet of the IP Address identifies all of the five classes. The first octet referred to here is the leftmost one. The octets numbered as follows representing dotted decimal notation of IP Address – IP Decimal Notation This formula will derive the number of networks and the number of hosts per class – Number of networks 2 IP addresses are decreased when calculating hosts' IP addresses as they can not be allocated to hosts, i.e. the first IP of a network is network number and the last IP is reserved for broadcast IP.

Class A Address

Always set the first bit of the first octet to 0 (zero). Hence, the first octet ranges from 1 to 127, i.e. Class A addresses include only IP addresses beginning from only 1.x.x.x to 126.x.x.x. The 127.x.x.x.x IP range is reserved for loopback IP addresses.

The default Class A IP address subnet mask is 255.0.0.0, which means that Class A addressing may have 126 networks (27-2) and 16777214 hosts (224-2).

Class A IP address format is thus:

0NNNNNNN.HHHHHHHH.HHHHHHHH.HHHHHHHH

Class B Address

An IP address which belongs to class B has the first two bits in the first octet set to 10, i.e.

Class B IP Addresses range from 128.0.x.x to 191.255.x.x. The default Class B Subnet mask is 255.255.x.x.

Class B has network addresses 16384 (214), and host addresses 65534 (216-2).

Class B IP address format is:

10NNNNNN.NNNNNNNN.HHHHHHHH.HH HHHHHH

Class C Address

The first octet of Class C IP address has its first 3 bits set to 110, that is –

Class C IP addresses range from 192.0.0.x to 223.255.255.x. In Class C the default subnet mask is 255.255.255.x.

Class C gives network addresses 2097152 (221) and host addresses 254 (28-2).

Class C IP address format is:

110NNNNN.NNNNNNNN.NNNNNNNN.HHH HHHHH

Class D Address

The first four bits of the first octet of Class D IP addresses are set to 1110, ranging from 224.0.0.0 to 239.255.255.255. Class D is reserved for Multicasting. Multi-casting data is not intended for a specific host, so there is no need to extract host address from the IP address, and there is no subnet mask for Class D.

Class E Address

This IP class is reserved for R&D or Study or for experimental purposes. Within this class, the IP addresses range from 240.0.0.0 to 255.255.255.254. Like Class D, this class doesn't have any subnet mask, either.

Subnetting

A system administrator can further divide or subnet a Class A, B, or C TCP / IP network. This is important when you reconcile the logical Internet address scheme (the abstract realm of IP addresses and subnets) with the real-world physical networks in use.

A system administrator assigned a block of IP addresses can manage networks that are not organized in such a way that match such addresses easily. For instance, you have a wide area network with 150 hosts linked via a TCP / IP router on three networks (in separate cities). There are 50 hosts in each of these three networks. You are assigned the 192.168.123.0 Class C network. This means you will use the 192.168.123.1 to 192.168.123.254 addresses for your 150 hosts.

Two addresses which cannot be used in your example are 192.168.123.0 and 192.168.123.255 due to the invalidity of binary addresses with a host portion of all ones and all zeros. The zero address is invalid since it is used without specifying a host to specify a network. The 255 address (a host address of all ones in binary notation) is used to broadcast a message on a network to every host. Note that no individual host can be allocated the first and the last address in any network or subnet.

You should now be able to give 254 hosts IP addresses. That works well when all 150 computers are on one network. Your 150 computers are, however, on three distinct physical networks. Instead of requesting additional address blocks for each network, you split the network into subnetworks that allow you to use several physical networks with one block of addresses.

In this case, by using a subnet mask, you split the network into four subnets, making the network address larger, and the potential range of host addresses smaller. In other words, you 'borrow' some of the bits that are usually used for the host address, and use them for the address network portion. The 255.255.255.192 subnet mask gives you four networks, each with 62 hosts. This works since 255.255.255.192 is the same as 11111111.11111111.11111111.11000000 in binary notation. The network addresses are the first two digits of the last octet, and you get 00000000- (0), 01000000- (64), 10000000- (128) and 11000000- (192) as additional networks. (Some administrators only use two of the subnetworks using 255.255.255.192 as a subnet mask.) The last six binary digits will be used for host addresses in these four networks.

Using the 255.255.255.192 subnet mask, the 192.168.123.0 network will then become the four networks 192.168.123.0, 192.168.123.64, 192.168.123.128 and 192.168.123.192. These four networks will have these valid host addresses:

192.168.123.1-62

192.168.123.65-126

192.168.123.129-190

192.168.123.193-254

Note, again, that any or all of the binary host addresses with all ones or all zeros are invalid, and you can not use addresses with the last octet of 0, 63, 64, 127, 128, 191, 192 or 255.

Looking at these two host addresses, 192.168.123.71 and 192.168.123.133, you can see how this works. If you used the default 255.255.255.0 Class C subnet mask, the two addresses are located on the 192.168.123.0 network. When you use the 255.255.255.192 subnet mask, however, they are on separate networks; 192.168.123.71 IP address is on the 192.168.123.64 network, and 192.168.123.133 IP address is on the 192.168.123.128 network.

Cloud Computing And Virtualization

Cloud computing is the availableness of computer system services, particularly in data storage and computing power, without the user having direct active management. This term is generally used to describe data centres which are accessible over the Internet to many users.

Large clouds, which are predominant today, often have functions dispersed from central servers over multiple locations. If the user's connection is relatively close, an edge server may be designated.

Clouds may be restricted to a single organization (enterprise clouds) or open to many (public cloud) organizations.

Cloud computing depends on resource sharing to achieve efficiency and economies of scale.

Cloud providers usually use a "pay-as-you-go" model which can result in unforeseen operating expenses unless administrators are familiar with cloud-pricing models.

The accessibility of high-capacity networks, low-cost computers and storage devices, as well as the widespread adoption of hardware virtualization, service-oriented architecture, autonomic and utility computing and service-oriented architecture, have contributed to the development in cloud computing. By 2019, Linux was the most widely utilized operating system, including in the offerings of Microsoft, and is therefore described as dominant. The Cloud Service Provider (CSP) will screen, maintain and collect data about the firewalls, identification of intrusion or/and counteractive action frameworks and information streams within the network.

History Of Cloud Computing

Large mainframe computers were developed in the 1950s and used in schools, large corporations, and even governmental organizations. Because of the size and cost of owning one of those computers, businesses needed a way to allow access to more than one user. The beginning of modern-day virtualization was the invention of "dumb terminals" so that multiple people could access the giant mainframe computer, and thus the beginning of cloud computing.

As technology improved in the 1970s and mainframes became a thing of the past, people were able to have their own separate computers but were still linked through a network. IBM introduced this sharing of some of the resources while also being able to have each machine containing its own memory, and processor as an operating system called VM. It took the idea of obtaining access to a mainframe to a new level and allowed more than one computing environment to exist in one physical environment.

In the 1990s came the next major jump in cloud computing. Through internet commercialization, online resources were managed and used by the average user. As machines became more available to the average consumer, more and more people started to have computers in their homes, but it wasn't until the mid-1990s that technology became sufficiently advanced and rendered accessible enough for the masses. Sufficient bandwidth was eventually able to link companies with their employees.

The year 1999 saw several developments, including the introduction of the idea of enterprise applications across the internet. Amazon began offering many cloud-based services in 2002 and provided the first publicly available cloud computing network by 2006.

Cloud computing quickly developed from grid to utility computing, to SaaS and eventually to cloud computing. In 2009 Google and other organizations started offering browser-based web applications with the advent of Web 2.0.

Cloud computing, as it is today, provides businesses with environments that enable them to employ their own clouds effectively, either private or hybrid. They are no longer dependent on public clouds and can improve overall efficiency. IT departments now have greater insight at their system's back-end. Cloud computing has undergone and will continue to develop tremendous changes throughout history.

Characteristics Of Cloud Computing

Agility for organizations can be strengthened, as cloud computing may increase the versatility of users to re-provide, incorporate or extend technological infrastructure services.

A public-cloud distribution model turns capital expenditure (e.g. purchasing servers) into operational expenditure. This allegedly lowers entry barriers because infrastructure is usually operated by a third party and is not expected to be purchased for one-time or infrequent intensive computing tasks. Pricing on a utility computing basis is "fine-grained," with billing options based on use. In addition, the implementation of projects using cloud computing needs less in-house IT skills.

Device and location independence allow users to access web browser systems irrespective of where they are located or what device they use (e.g. Laptop, mobile phone). Since infrastructure is off-site (normally provided by a third party) and accessible through the Internet, users can connect to it from anywhere. Management of cloud computing systems is simpler as they do not need to be installed on the device of each user and can be accessed from various locations (e.g., various offices, during travel, etc.).

Multitenancy enables the distribution of resources and expenses through a wide pool of users, thus allowing for centralization of facilities at lower-cost locations (such as real estate, power, etc.) peak load capacity increases (users do not need to design and pay for services and equipment to reach their maximum possible load levels) network performance efficiency. Time can be saved because information does not need to be re-entered when fields match, nor do users need to install application software updates on their computer. Availability increases with the use of many redundant sites, which allows well-designed cloud storage ideal for business continuity and disaster recovery. Safety is often as good or better than many traditional programs, partially because service providers may dedicate resources to addressing security issues that other customers can not afford to solve or lack the technical expertise they need to fix. However, as data is spread over a wider region or among a greater number of devices, as well as in multi-tenant networks shared by different users, the safety complexity is greatly increased. Additionally, it may be difficult or impossible for users to access security audit logs. Private cloud installations are motivated in part by the desire of users to maintain control over the network and avoid losing control over the protection of information.

Virtualization Of Cloud Computing

Virtualization of cloud computing is rendering server operating system and storage devices a virtual platform. This would support the user by having several devices at the same time as it also enables several users to share a single physical device instance of resource or application. Cloud Virtualizations often handle the workload by transforming conventional computing and making it more flexible, cost-efficient and effective.

Cloud Computing virtualizations quickly incorporate the basic way of computing. One of the major advantages of virtualization is that it allows many customers and businesses to share applications.

To support the virtualized world, cloud computing may also be known as services and application delivered. This could be a public or private environment. The customer could maximize resources with the aid of virtualization and reduce the physical device that is in need.

Types of Virtualization in Cloud Computing

- Virtualization of the operating system
- Virtualization of the hardware
- Virtualization of the server
- Virtualization of Storage

Operating system

Virtualization In the virtualization of the operating system in Cloud Computing, the virtual computer program installs in the host's operating system rather than directly on the hardware. The most critical use of virtualization of the operating system is to test the program on multiple devices or operating system. Here the program is present in the hardware, enabling the running of various applications.

Server Virtualization

In virtualization of the server in cloud computing, the program runs directly on the server system, and the use of a single physical server will divide and distribute the load across multiple servers on the basis of demand. It can also be claimed that the server virtualization masks the number and identity of the server resources. The server administrator splits one physical server into multiple servers with the help of a software.

Hardware Virtualization

In the Virtualization of Hardware, cloud computing is used in server platforms because it is more versatile using Virtual Machine instead of physical machines. In hardware virtualizations, virtual machine software is installed in the hardware system and is then known as hardware virtualization. It consists of a hypervisor used to manage and track operation, memory, and other hardware resources. After completion of the hardware virtualization process, the user can install a different operating system and use a different application on this platform.

Storage Virtualization

In virtualization of storage in Cloud Computing, physical storage pooling is achieved from multiple network storage devices, so it appears like a single storage unit. It can be implemented with the aid of software applications, and storage virtualization is carried out for the backup and recovery process. It is the physical storage sharing from multiple storage devices.

How does Virtualization work?

Cloud Computing Virtualization is a mechanism in which cloud users share data present in the cloud, which can be application software, etc. It offers a virtual cloud environment that can be hardware or anything else. In virtualization, the software application and the server provided by the cloud providers are managed by a third party and, in this case, the cloud provider may request a certain amount from a third party. This is done because it would be expensive if a new version of the application is launched and the customer has to be updated.

It can also be described in such a way that the cloud client can access the server with the aid of Hypervisor, which is the program. A hypervisor is the connection between the server and the virtual environment and the distribution of resources between different virtual environments.

Benefits Of Virtualization

i. Security

One of the most critical issues is security during the virtualization process. Security can be established with the aid of firewalls, which will help avoid unauthorized access and keep the data confidential. In addition, with the aid of firewalls and encryption, data can be defended against harmful malware viruses and other cyber threats. The encryption process often takes place with protocols that shield data from other threats. As a consequence, the customer can virtualize all data stores and create a backup on a server where the data can be stored.

ii. Flexible operations The work of an IT professional is becoming more productive and efficient with the aid of a virtual network. The network switch introduced today is very simple to use, versatile and time-saving. With the support of cloud computing virtualization, technical issues can be solved in physical systems. This alleviates the issue of recovering data from wrecked or corrupted computers and therefore saves time.

iii. Economical Virtualization in Cloud Computing saves costs for a physical device such as hardware and servers. It stores all the data on the virtual server, which is quite economical. It reduces wastage, lowers electricity bills as well as maintenance costs. As a consequence, an organization will run several operating systems and applications on a single server.

iv. Eliminates the possibility of device failure When performing certain tasks, there are chances that the device may crash at the wrong time. This failure can cause harm to the business, but virtualizations help you perform the same task on multiple devices at the same time. Data can be stored in a cloud that can be accessed at any time and with the aid of any computer. In addition, there are two servers running side by side that make the data available at all times. And if the server fails with the help of the second server, the data can be accessed by the client.

v. Flexible data transfer Data can be transferred to a virtual server and recovered at any time. Customers or cloud providers don't have to waste time searching hard drives to find data. With the aid of virtualization, it will be very easy to locate and move the required data to the assigned authorities. The transfer of data does not have a limit and can be carried over to a long distance with the lowest possible fee. Additional storage can also be offered, and the cost would be as minimal as possible.

Network Troubleshooting

Network Troubleshooting is a common method and mechanism used to locate, diagnose and address problems and issues within a computer network. It is a systematic process aimed at solving problems and restoring regular network operations within the network.

Troubleshooting Process

- Identify the problem.
- Establish a theory of possible cause.
- examine the theory to determine the cause.
- Establish an action plan to solve the problem and execute the solution.
- Check the full functionality of the program and, where necessary, enforce preventive measures.

- Document observations, actions and outcomes.

Troubleshooting Hardware Issues

Hardware Troubleshooting is a method for evaluating, diagnosing and resolving operating or technological issues within a hardware system or computer. It is intended to solve physical and/or logical problems and problems within computer hardware. Hardware troubleshooting is done by a hardware or technical support technician.

Hardware troubleshooting methods are specifically designed to address computer hardware issues using a systematic approach.

The process begins with the first identification of the problem and then finding various issues that may trigger such a problem and eventually contribute to the implementation of a solution or alternative.

Hardware troubleshooting is generally done on hardware devices mounted on a computer, server, laptop or similar devices.

Some hardware troubleshooting processes include:

- Removal, repair and replacement of faulty RAM, hard disk or video/graphic card.
- Cleaning dust from RAM and video card slots/ports and cooling fans.
- Tightening of cables and jumpers on the motherboard and/or components.
- Software related hardware issues, such as device driver update or installation.

Troubleshooting Software Issues

Software troubleshooting is the method of scanning, detecting, diagnosing and fixing problems, errors and software bugs.

It is a systematic method that aims to root out and solve problems and return the program to normal operation. It's an IT troubleshooting subcategory.

Software troubleshooting is usually done to fix technical or source-code related issues in software. This may be both functional and non-functional in nature. The software troubleshooting process starts by identifying the problem, checking possible issues that could cause these problems, and then working on interventions and alternatives to find a solution.

Usually, issues are resolved by a software developer or tester who reviews and optimizes software, removes bugs and errors from the source code. Software vendors also aid in troubleshooting software by releasing regular software updates/patches that can help ensure smooth software operation. Computer troubleshooting can also be achieved when software needs to be installed properly, such as troubleshooting problems due to incorrect installation or device recovery after infection or virus-related file deletion.

Networking From Beginners To Advance

Networking is a common term in the information technology industry. It has two meanings to it: The process of connecting computers and other devices so that they can communicate, and the process of meeting and talking to other people to help you in your IT career.

What is the network?

Networking is the process of meeting, talking and meeting with people with the long-term goal of helping you in your career. Many people do it, and it is good to know what it is about and why you should do it.

Networking is more than a "chat" for those who take the proverbial career path. Instead, networking helps to open doors for growth and the exchange of ideas. You may have asked yourself: How do professionals refine their networking skills and become even more effective? Are relationship building skills relevant to both new and experienced professionals? Why is networking so important?

Networking is the exchange of ideas, in which people exchange and convey technical concepts and connect to convey a better understanding. It can be summarized as small talk and includes determining who can be helpful. The key to an effective network is to build and build relationships and manage shared information. The first part includes maintaining existing relationships and acquaintance. For example, collect business cards and develop a contact tracking system. The relevant information of mutual interest is also listed.

In addition, networking occurs as a communication process when you exchange information, but it also expands your personal ties and affiliations. Some considerations for building these connections include:

Reaching new contacts isn't aggressive or scary; it's a refined skill.

Establish industrial connections to expand possible connections

Use innovative technology after building a personal relationship.

Discover resources with acquaintances instead of keeping a short-sighted perspective

Establish trust and connections between people in matters of mutual interest.

Roles and rules change regularly, so you often expand your circle of contacts.

Networking includes useful skills, even for experienced professionals. Keeping in touch with new allies gives people with years of experience the opportunity to stay connected and give unique insights. Networking for a seasoned veteran could even be an opportunity to act as a mentor or advisor.

Networking skills are essential to maximizing a strategic focus. The exchange of ideas, contacts and resources has a lot to do with it. Trust that you can get out there and start.

A network is a collection of cable-connected computers, printers, and other devices — the sharing of data and resources. Information is transmitted over cables so that network users can share documents and data, print to the same printer, and generally share hardware or software that is connected to the network. Any computer, printer, or other peripheral devices that are connected to the network is called a node. Networks can have tens of thousands, thousands, or even millions of nodes.

Cabling:

The two most popular types of network cabling are twisted-pair (also known as 10BaseT) and thin coaxial cable (also known as 10Base2). The 10BaseT cabling looks like a normal telephone cable, only that there are 8 instead of 4 cables.

The thin coaxial cable looks like a copper coaxial cable that is often used to connect a VCR to a television.

Network adapter:

A network computer is linked via a network card to the network cabling (also known as a "NIC", "Nick" or network adapter). Some network cards are installed in a computer: the PC is opened, and a network card is connected directly to one of the internal expansion slots of the computer. 286, 386 and many 486 computers have 16-bit slots, so a 16-bit network card is required. Faster computers like high-speed 486s and Pentiums often have PCI or 32-bit slots. These PCs require 32-bit network cards to achieve the fastest possible network speeds for speed-critical applications such as desktop video, multimedia, publishing and databases. If you want to use a computer with a Fast Ethernet network, you also need a network adapter that supports data rates of 100 Mbit / s.

Hubs

The last part of the network puzzle is called the centre. A hub is a box for gathering groups of PCs with 10BaseT cording at a single spot. If you are networking a small group of computers, you may be able to work with a hub, some 10BaseT cables, and a handful of network adapters. Larger networks often use a thin coaxial backbone that connects a series of 10BaseT hubs. Each hub, in turn, can connect a handful of computers using 10BaseT cables so that you can build networks with tens, hundreds, or thousands of nodes.

Hubs are available like network cards in standard versions (10 Mbit / s) and Fast Ethernet (100 Mbit / s).

LAN (local area networks)

A network is a collection of independent computers that communicate with each other over a shared network medium. LANs are networks that are generally restricted to a geographic area, e.g. B. a single building or a university campus. LANs can be small and connect only three computers, but they often connect hundreds of computers that are used by thousands of people. The development of standard network media and protocols has led to the worldwide distribution of LANs in all business and educational organizations.

WAN (WAN)

A network is often located in several physical locations. The wide area network combines several geographically separated LANs. This is achieved by connecting the various LANs using services such as rented dedicated telephone lines, dial-up telephone lines (synchronous and asynchronous), satellite connections and packet data carrier services. Wide area networks can be as simple as a modem and a remote access server for employees, or they can be as complex as hundreds of globally connected branches that use special routing protocols and filters to minimize the cost of sending large amounts of data Distances sent.

Internet

The Internet is a system of interconnected networks of global scope that provides data communication services such as remote login, file transfer, email, the World Wide Web and newsgroups.

With the rapid growth in demand for connectivity, the Internet has become a communications highway for millions of users. The Internet was originally limited to academic and military institutions, but today it is a complete channel for all forms of information and commerce. Internet websites now offer personal, educational, political and economic resources for all corners of the world.

Intranet

With the advances made in browser-based software for the Internet, many private organizations are implementing intranets. An intranet is a private network that uses Internet-type instruments but can only be found in the business. For large companies, an intranet gives workers quick access to company information.

The most common physical layer LAN technology in use at the moment is Ethernet Ethernet. The Token Ring, Fast Ethernet, FDDI, the Asynchronous Transfer Mode (ATM), as well as LocalTalk are also LANs. Ethernet is common because it strikes a good balance between deployment speed, cost and ease. Combined with the wide adoption of the computing industry as well as the ability to adopt virtually all common network protocols, Ethernet is today the ideal network technology for most computer users. The IEEE describes the IEEE standard as IEEE 802.3. IT Electric and electronic engineers (IEEE). This specification specifies the rules for the network configuration and the interaction of the elements in an Ethernet network. Network devices and network protocols can interact effectively by complying with the IEEE standard.

Network Protocols are protocols for the coordination of computers. A protocol specifies how computers classify each other within a network, how data is to be interpreted when it hits its final goal and how this information can be transported. The protocols often set out procedures to deal with transmission or 'packets' lost or damaged. The major network types of protocols currently in use are TCP / IP (for UNIX, Windows NT, Windows 95 and other platforms), IPX (for Novell NetWare), DECnet (for Computer Equipment Corp.), AppleTalk (for MacintoSh computers).

Each of the network protocols is different, but the physical wiring is the same. A common physical network access approach makes possible the peaceful coexistence of many protocols via the media and allows the network constructors to use specific hardware for a variety of protocols. This principle is called "Protocol Independence," which allows the user to run a variety of different protocols on the same media using devices that support the physical and data connecting layers.

Topologies A Network topology is used in two general configurations-the spatial arrangement of nodes and cable connections on a LAN: Bus and Star. Both topologies describe how nodes interconnect. An active unit, such as a computer or printer, connected to the network, is a node. A network machine like a hub, a switch or a router, may also be a node. A bus topology involves the nodes connected to the long cable or bus in series with each node. Many nodes will link to the bus in this cable segment and start communication with all of the other nodes. A disconnection in any part of the cable usually leaves the entire part inoperative before the break is repaired. Examples of bus topology are 10BASE2 and 10BASE5.

10BASE-T Ethernet and Fast Ethernet use a star topology, where a central computer controls the connection. A machine is normally located at one end of the line, and in a central position with a hub the other terminates. Since UTP also operates with telephone wire, this central location may be a telephone cabinet or another place in which a UTP section can be conveniently linked to a backbone. The key advantages of this form of network are redundancy and when one component breaks down, only both nodes on the link will be affected. Many network device users tend to run as if it did not exist.

Peer-to-peer networks Two or more PCs will pool their resources in a peer-to-peer network. The general and specialized resources that are available from any machine are converted into individual resources such as disks, CD-ROM drives, or even printers.Contrary to customer-data-networks where network information is processed and transmitted to tens, hundreds, or thousands of customer PCs on centralized file server PCs, information stored in pair to pair networks is particularly decentralized. Since peer-to-peer PCs have their own hard drives that can be accessed by all computers, each PC functions as a client (information requestor) and server (information provider). A point-to-point network can be built with 10BaseT cables and a hub or with a thin coaxial backbone. 10BaseT is best for small workgroups with 16 or fewer users who don't travel long distances, or for workgroups with one or more laptops that can be disconnected from the network from time to time.

After installing the network hardware, a peer-to-peer network software package must be installed on all PCs. This package allows information to be transferred between PCs, hard drives and other devices when users request it. Popular NOS peer-to-peer software includes

With most NOS, each end-to-end user can determine which resources are available to other users. You can connect or disconnect certain hard drives and floppy drives, directories or files, printers, and other network resources through the software. When a user's hard drive is configured as "shared", it generally appears as a new drive for other users. In other words, if user A has drives A and C on his computer and user B sets his entire drive C to be shared, user A suddenly has drives A, C and D (drive D of user A) is actually the user -BC drive). Directories work similarly. If user A has drives A and C and user B sets the "C: WINDOWS" and "C: DOS" directories as shared, user A may suddenly have A, C, D, and E.

Drive (D from user A is C: WINDOWS from user B and E are C: DOS from user B). Did you understand all this

Since drives can be easily shared between PCs, applications should only be installed on one computer, not on two or three. For example, if users have a copy of Microsoft Word, it can be installed on User A's computer and still be used by User B.

The advantages of peer-to-peer NOS over client-server include:

- No network administrator required
- The network can be configured and maintained quickly / inexpensively

- For security reasons, each PC can save your data on other PCs. Peer-to-peer is by far the easiest type of network to set up and is suitable for both home and office use.

Client-server networks

In a client-server environment such as Windows NT or Novell NetWare, files are stored on a central high-speed file server PC that is available to client PCs. Network access speeds are typically higher than in peer-to-peer networks. This is appropriate given the large number of clients that this architecture can support. Almost all network services such as printing and email are routed through the file server, so you can track network tasks. Inefficient network segments can be changed to make them faster, and user activity can be closely monitored. Public data and applications are stored on the file server, where they are run from the locations of the client PCs. This makes updating software an easy task: network administrators can easily update applications stored on the computer, rather than physically updating everyone.

Client PC.

The following client-server diagram shows that client PCs are separate and subordinate to the file server. Applications and core client files are stored in a common location. File servers are often configured so that everyone on the network has access to their "own" directory and a number of "public" directories in which applications are stored. If the following two clients want to communicate with each other, they have to go through the file server. A message is first sent from one client to another to the file server, where it is then forwarded to its destination. With tens or hundreds of client PCs, a file server is the only way to manage the often complex and concurrent operations that large networks require.

Computer networks are very important and essential part of information technology.

Millions of computers are connected to form the Internet. Networks play an important role in all types of organizations, from small to medium-sized, in banks, multinationals, stock exchanges, airports, hospitals, police stations, post offices, schools, universities and even at home summary. Networks play an important role wherever computers are used. This article is interesting for students, network professionals and people interested in computer networks.

Why Should I Network?

One of the most popular idioms at work (which you've probably heard before) is "It's not what you know, it's who you know." This means meeting and partnering with the right people can be more important than what you know or do. Your goal is to remind you of the importance of people's skills and networking.

There are many reasons why networking is a good idea:

- Stay up to date on career opportunities in your industry.
- Know the ideas and trends in the industry.
- Meet new people
- Understand more about other areas
- Develop your communication and listening skills.

If you are thinking about changing careers or are looking for new opportunities for promotion, you should contact a network whenever and wherever possible. You will not always receive a promotion or change that has just been delivered to you. You should be able to find out where they are and follow your own steps to get there.

How can I network?

Well, the answer to that is to go out and talk to people. You can do this at work, at social events, at various meetings, wherever people are in your industry or at work. You don't even have to be in a group situation. You could talk to one person.

In essence, you talk to people, and you know them. It doesn't always have to be work or business. It can be a personal conversation. However, you need to understand why you are online and why you are there to have a proper conversation.

How can I improve the networks?

There are a few things you can do to be more effective when talking to your peers. Some of these could be:

- Think about the reason why you meet people. Does it find out what's going on in your company? Are you looking for new job offers? Or something else? Knowing why you are, there will help your discussions.
- Networking is about being mutually beneficial for both people. Realizing what you have to offer is a good thing.
- Get a business card if you don't have one yet. At a minimum, it should include your name, email address, and phone number.
- Practice your "soft skills", including listening, body language and conversation skills. These come with practice and experience.

Networking is a core business and life skill. It is the continuous process of building and developing an interconnected network of mutually beneficial relationships. In other words, you meet people and build relationships with them, be it a deep friendship or occasional business contact. Strengthens relationships by communicating with people, giving them the things they need, finding common interests, and doing things together. The relationship is consolidated when the other person finds a way to help you in the form of information, support, or business recommendations. It is a cycle of actions, interactions and surveillance.

If you repeat this process with more and more people, you will have a growing group of contacts that you know, know, and can count on to help you in return. You will be in different stages with different people. Relationships will strengthen, diminish, and perhaps end, but an experienced networker will have a net growth in his base of close "friends" and the large number of people he has interacted with.

Not all contacts will be friends, but most should be friendly. You may have members of your network that you are not friends with and that you may not even like, but because you have done something for them, they are ready to reciprocate. The bond becomes stronger and more reliable when you have a personal relationship. An unfriendly relationship only exists as long as they can do something for each other.

This process is called "networking". The result is his "network", a group of people with whom he interacts to some extent.

It is a very simple set of activities. Go to places, meet people, interact with them and keep track of who, what, where and when. That's it. Simple things Why is it so difficult for us to build a network or do it consistently? Because it's easy not to do that. The current business environment is complicated, and our daily life is overworked, stressed and over-analyzed. We oppose networks because we are overwhelmed. We have thought too much about the process until it appears to be a desperate complication, not a meaningful activity that is now benefiting us and worsening over time.

If we go back to the foundation of networking, a simple process of building relationships, we will be more ready to start and move on. Take a few minutes each day to find a way to move forward in a relationship you currently have. Find a way to expand your current contacts to just one person at a time. By not overwhelming ourselves with a complicated process, we can expand our network and build our business.

To know where to begin, you first need to understand what networking is and why it is important to grow your business. Networking in its purest form simply means speaking to people, making connections and building relationships to expand our sphere of influence. Corporate networks are essentially the same, except that our main goal in corporate networks is to help us grow our business. Creating a network is our primary aim for most of us, meeting people who can or should be doing business with us, or suggesting people who do business with us.

In reality, some of the best networks are made up of people who own and run their businesses. When building valuable network relationships, build them based on mutual trust and share knowledge, experience, and resources to help each other grow their business by referencing each other or doing business directly with each other.

This works like this: if you do a good job, a client will say 3 to 5 of his colleagues, family and friends.If you build a network of 10 to 20 strong supporters, everyone can tell a single person about you, but your "exposure" has more than doubled: With the right network, the ultimate "word of mouth". Mouth "Marketing is done. You are supporting and growing the network.

Have you ever taken part in a BNI or Le Tip or in any other types of network structures? Maybe you're in a similar party already.Otherwise, you could choose one of the fastest-growing business network concepts. These groups invite business people to join exclusively. This means that if you are a chiropractor and become a member of one of these groups, no other chiropractor will be invited or can join.

These groups have scheduled regular meetings (from monthly to weekly) with a list of rules and goals that need to be achieved. In some cases, a minimum number of recommendations are required to participate. In other cases, members only need to do business with one or more online companies. However, keep in mind that everyone must do their best to do business with other group members so that this type of network pays off for everyone involved.

If this form of structured networking is not suitable for you, there are other ways to find potential network sites and partners.

Here are few ideas to assist you on your way to network success.

a. Develop an attachment. By that I mean, don't just log in to list our names. REALLY JOIN. Take part. Take part in discussions, events and be visible. The saying "out of sight, out of mind" is true when it comes to networking. I was involved in groups and decided to take a break for 2-3 months (and sometimes longer) to get people to tell me that they forgot my company name, so they had to find someone. Through a friend or through the local phone book. SHANK!

Yes, Participate in network functions. These can include Chamber of Commerce meetings, social events outside of business hours, ad hoc committees and working groups for special events.

C. Participate in a nonprofit group such as Kiwanis, Lions, Jaycees, etc.

Re. Volunteering with a nonprofit organization whose mission you love and believe in. People with similar passions will want to do business with you.

Organize my events: I started an event called Goddess Gatherings in my house over 2 years ago. It is an intimate gathering of women (max. 8) who share a common interest and / or want to expand their own circles. I invite women who don't know each other yet, although they may be familiar with their names. These women are women in my sphere of influence, either directly or indirectly (they are members of the 22 groups I belong to and which I visit regularly, or they are part of a circle within these groups). You can invite a "surprise" guest who can entertain women like a masseuse or a tarot card reader, or present a company like a jeweller or makeup artist. This helps create an unforgettable evening, and the women start their own meeting or wait to be invited to another meeting organized by one of the women present.

F. Find ways to cross-promote with companies that complement yours. For example, a spa can join a health food store or restaurant and advertise its products and services to stay healthy. A salon can join a florist to promote weddings or graduation parties, and a real estate agent can join a mortgage broker to promote a unique experience for home buyers.

Sun. Question others. An excellent way to access the network is to interview women for projects I'm working on. Since most people are flattered when you ask for their opinion on something or life experiences, this has been a great way to expand my own circle for various reasons. I could interview a woman (or even a man) about an article or book that I am writing, or a seminar that I am developing. People love to share their stories. I record the interview (with your permission, of course) and then give them a copy. Before the interview, it is beneficial to list the questions. However, if you don't insist, I won't give you the questions in advance. I conducted these interviews by phone, email and in person. Many of the women have since.

H. Join an online business or social media community like MeetUp, Ryze, Max-in-Common, Linkd In, and Open BC to name a few. These groups have sub-groups of people with a specific focus and similar interests. Or you can join an unspecific group to get more knowledge, contact and contacts.

Attend a new networking event every month to watch it. Make a list of the people you know, the organizations that you have heard and read, and the companies that are currently doing business with you. These are all great resources to use and find new networks. Get the local newspaper and find out about the organizations and companies that organize events that the public is invited to. Take care of them.

The best networking starts with planning and action. Being strategic in your planning is important for your ultimate success as an effective and caring networker.

The U.S. Army's semi-automatic terrestrial environment (SAGE) was one of the first computer networks in the late 1950s. The USA And the reservation system for commercial airlines are called the semi-automatic business research environment (SABER).

The Advanced Research Projects Agency Network was established in 1969 with the goal of improving projects initiated in the 1960s. The Defense Department focused on the circuit switching concept that the two-piece telephone connection of a certain circuit is sufficient for a single communication line. This basic network has become the Internet today.

Some of the basic components that can be used in networks include: Interface Card-Enables the communication between computers across the network by using Media Access Control (MAC) adresses to differentiate between one device and another with a low-level addressing scheme.

Repeater: These are electronic devices that amplify signal communication as well as filtering noise, which interfere with signaling.

Hubs: They contain several ports so that you can copy an unchanged information/data packet and send it to all computers in the network.

Bridges - Connect network segments so that information can only flow to specific destinations.

Switches: These are devices that forward, make forwarding decisions and filter fragments of data communication between ports according to the MAC addresses in the information packets.

Routers: are devices that forward packets between networks that process the information in the packet.

Firewalls - Deny network access requests from insecure sources, but allow requests from secure sources.

Different types of networks are classified according to certain characteristics, e.g. B. the type of wired or wireless connection, the size of the network and its architecture and topology.

Network types include local area networks, wide area networks, metropolitan area networks and backbone networks.

Network Hardware Guide For Beginners

Do you want to configure your home network? Setting up your home network is very easy if you are familiar with the technical language for the hardware required for a computer network. However, if you don't know her and have no experience, it can lead to disaster. For computer repairs, it's also a good option to turn to an expert.

Network hardware plays a crucial role in building the home network. These are used to reduce network traffic congestion. Hubs, switches and routers are used for data transmission to the network. A firewall is also used to protect the network from intruders.

Let's start the discussion with hubs. This device is used for networking a group of computers in a LAN. The centres are usually very inexpensive. A hub's job is to push a broadcast to any other computer or device in a network cluster. All computers are connected to a hub via a network cable. You can use a hub to connect 4 to 64 computers. It depends on the quality of the centre.

Another jargon is changed. Switches are used to expand the existing network or to connect more computers to the network. Like hubs, switches are used to transmit a signal from one computer or device to another. These smart devices are more expensive than hubs.

Routers are very important for managing network traffic. These tools can be likened to switches, but are more advanced. In fact, they are more powerful than switches. To monitor data transmission over different LANs and WANs, e.g. B. Internet routers, these are used. In addition, the management of databases with information about networks and computers in networks is the responsibility of the router. They examine the transmitted data packets and transmit the data to their corresponding computers. Routers are important for receiving packets of data that are transferred from one network to another using the IP protocol.

The previous part of our discussion mentions the work of firewalls. Simply put, this is a security tool. It can be a hardware or software device, or it can be a fusion of the two. By establishing a connection between a private and a public network, firewalls filter out all incoming and outgoing transmissions that pass through this network. To protect the network, security criteria are set and transmissions that do not meet these criteria are blocked. It also blocks any unauthorized inbound transmission from outside the network that can be harmful to the network.

For home and office networks, network maintenance is necessaryHaving a computer at home is no longer a luxury. Having one in a house is more a necessity than a social status like a few years ago. In fact, the need has grown so large that people have a computer for every family member. In the offices, too, each employee is assigned a computer to carry out their daily activities. As the number of computers per home or office increases, these computers clearly need to be connected to each other for greater efficiency and faster task completion. There are professional companies that offer services such as installing networks in households and offices. However, some of them do not promise or may promise network support to their customers, but do not keep their promises.

Network maintenance is very important for any computer network after configuration, regardless of how small or large it is or how many computers and users are on the network. The reason for the maintenance is to ensure that network security is maintained without the user's private information being lost, and that network computers are accessible to authorized and authenticated users on the network. Hackers are constantly working on hacking and accessing the main companies' internal networks to steal data and then sell information from those companies. The security professional or the company that provides network maintenance and support should ensure that all such attacks are detected and mitigated as quickly as possible before damage occurs.

The idea of network support can be summed up in one word: FCAPS (F for errors, C for configuration, A for accounting, P for performance, S for security). The technician should respond to network hardware or software problems as soon as possible. Any delay in classifying such errors can mean a tremendous loss for the customer because most of his work is done digitally. Likewise, the specialist has to work hard to keep the server operational at all times and to keep it running smoothly for the users. If necessary, hardware and software updates should be carried out as part of network maintenance. Network support is also responsible for adding new users to the network and including their computer on the main server.

Network support begins after you configure the base network. The technician must install enough antivirus software to prevent viruses from entering. We recommend using more than two of these programs to ensure maximum security of customer information. In addition, facilities must be created to validate network users when they log on to the network. Use of passwords, retina scans, fingerprint scans, passwords, etc. this reduces the likelihood of unauthorized entry.

When choosing an agency to build a network at home or in the office, the company's reputation for network support should be taken very seriously. Since this depends on them for future changes, the agency must be reliable and fast in its service.

How To Fix Network Problems

Network problems are often a reason for a lot of frustration. They can involve hardware and software problems and sometimes require a considerable amount of experience and / or money to deal with them. In addition to the desperation of the situation, the Internet is a good source for troubleshooting information to fix network problems. However, if there is a network problem, the Internet is often no longer accessible.

The common problem is that the computer cannot reach the network. This can occur for several reasons. In such a situation, it is most obvious to check the connectivity of the network cable.

If everything is OK with the cable, you should check the installation of your network hardware. This can be done via the Device Manager: Click on "Device Manager" to open it. Look for "Network Adapters" and click the plus sign next to it. If you see an exclamation mark or a red X, this indicates a problem with your network card. Also check your network settings: Right-click on "Network Locations" on your desktop. Select "Properties" from the menu. Look for the Local Area Connection icon. Right-click and go to "Properties". Click on "TCP / IP". If nothing works, write down the details of the error and look for a solution from a working terminal on the Internet.

Another common problem is that computers on the network cannot recognize each other. You can first check that the necessary precautions have been taken: Right-click the "Network Locations" icon on your desktop. Click on "Properties". On the General tab, make sure that Client for Microsoft Windows and File and Print Sharing for Microsoft Networks and Internet Protocol (TCP / IP) is installed. Also, check other computers and make sure they are all in the same workgroup or domain. You can also try turning off the firewall to find out if this is causing the problem.

Network Administrator's roles and obligations

The responsibilities of network administrators vary depending on the size of the company and the infrastructure. Generally, a network administrator needs two to four years of training and work experience. The most important basic tasks during work are:

Network installation / configuration

Security and stability monitoring.

Regular updates and tests.

Expand network

Breaking down these points will give you a better idea of what a network administrator is doing.

Network installation and configuration:

One of the first steps is to know the requirements of your network. You don't want to waste unnecessary resources or create a network that is too large. Worse, you don't want to end up with a network that is too small. Find out how many users will be online, what software they are using and what kind of work they are doing. If your company has other networks, you probably want to follow the same network design with updates and improvements. Avoid unnecessary changes or completely different things. This will solve headaches in the future.

Consider more in the company's best interests. Try to minimize costs while maximizing network efficiency, stability, and speed. Get it right the first time, so you don't have to come back later and do what you already did.

After completing the design, start building the network. It will manage everything from ordering components to wiring. Use industry standards for cables and other components to ensure compatibility with network devices.

Security and stability monitoring

After configuring the network, installing and updating all security software should be a top priority. Set up the firewall and make sure the network is stable. Check the connection speed and make sure that all connected devices are working properly.

Regular updates and reviews

Make sure you update important updates as soon as possible. Check for security updates weekly or enable automatic updates if possible—test small updates before installing them on the network. Unfortunately, an update from time to time causes random problems and requires a patch before the errors stop. Stay up to date on hardware manufacturers' websites to make sure you're doing the best for your network.

Expand network

When hiring new people and buying new computers and technologies, you are responsible for installing and managing the network to take these types of things into account. You can need a fast update to upgrade and extend your network depending on how long it took after you implemented what you learned during training. Personally, I've found that when you expand your network, you need to make sure you take your time and get it right the first time. As with designing the network, it is important to follow the design of current and other networks in the company. When working with other network administrators, you can ask for ideas or suggestions.

Network hardware

Both large and small computer networks require critical network hardware to take advantage of computer networks. A list of the same is given below:

Computer networks cannot work without a router. A router is network hardware that unites all computers and also facilitates communication between all devices. You can use a WiFi router for home use.

Another important network hardware is cable. These cables are used to connect a computer's network card to a router. For home use, the cables are connected to the router, and for office networks, the cables are attached to a wall and connected to the data centre.

Wireless connections are also important for a computer network and are being used more and more. They help to minimize cable consumption.

Servers are devices that manage the authorization part of a network. They can allow and even prohibit a user from accessing information and software. For an office network, a server would be a machine with large storage space, so that all user requirements can be comfortably met.

Network cards or network cards are also an essential part of computer networks. The installation of these cards in computers and servers is required. All of these cards have a unique MAC address.

If you now get to know all types of network hardware, I would like to give you some helpful tips for buying good network hardware:

When buying a router, look for Wi-Fi-protected access and standard advanced encryption keys.

If you want all computers to use a single printer, choose a router with a server.

When you buy a router, also consider various configuration alternatives.

Be sure to check the interface before you get a network card.

The company where you buy your network card should offer 24-hour support.

Hardware: A look at the problems

When choosing a provider to deploy your IT network hardware, you often want to try to buy a used car in another country. The hardest part can be choosing a brand from an unrecognizable group of manufacturers. There are many options, and although the usual response is to find the lowest price, we all know that there are many other factors that are important for good decision-making.

Choosing a hardware provider

Most major hardware vendors base their prices not only on the first purchase but also on possible future purchases. It is often possible to get better deals on today's sales if the provider can count on future sales and account growth. For this reason, it is a good idea to let the provider know your long-term goals.

Your subscription service and repair guarantees are also important when choosing hardware for your network. Were you aware of the services provided at your place by your provider? What is the maximum distance that technical support must travel for the service at your location? Are there any additional costs and do you outsource these services to another company? Telephone technical support and guarantees are also important. What can you rely on for firmware, updates and support after your first purchase? Find out in advance and put it on paper.

Our practise was selected by Dell. For a good price, a life cycle for your product that takes longer than we want to maintain our hardware, this is a good combination. In addition, Dell offers a four-hour on-site service for server and switch problems. Volume discounts are offered. The more we buy from them, the better our discount.

After selecting a specific hardware provider, your core decisions form several core components.

Switches: As with the spinal cord of the network, you will connect all cables here.

Choosing the right switch for your practice depends on the expected traffic capacity and media used, either fibre or cable. A network often has copper and fibre optic cables. In this case, the switch must be configured to support both functions.

Server - Pay attention to redundancy when selecting the server. Will one redundant machine exchange power if the other fails? Are there sets of RAID drives to prevent the system from crashing when the hard drive does so? How much RAM and how many processors does the server system have? More is better. Make sure you select a backup tape drive that is large enough to store your information and fast enough to back it up during nightly system outages. Try not to look beyond the physical configuration of your hardware on the network. A special housing unit or secure rack may be needed to contain the machines. This applies especially to a number of servers, as with other EMR system solutions.

End-user devices: Are you using real client terminals or computers? Can the firmware be updated? If you choose thin client terminals, do they need a legacy port? Do you use an articulated arm for examination rooms? Our practices use all of the above. As a result, we have agreed on the minimum hardware configuration per device, be it desktop, laptop, server, printer or thin client. These decisions are based on our performance expectations. A doctor should check with the IT department before buying a fancy laptop to make sure it works well online. We check the network every few months to stay in sync with changes in our system and technology. This continuous maintenance and upgrade system ensures optimal performance and optimizes the need for technical support.

Network hardware: various types and functions

A Network Computer consists of different hardware types that operate across various network protocols. Some of these hardware styles are easy to install and maintain, while others are highly complex and need installation and maintenance experience.Check out some of the new or used network hardware types that are used in different network scenarios.

Modem The term "modem" is a short name for modulator-demodulator. It enables the transfer and conversion of data between digital form such as in computers and analogue form as in telephone lines. In order for the Internet connection to be shared, the modem must be connected to a router. The Internet Service Provider (ISP) can provide modems or buy from network hardware providers.

Routers If modems act as converters, routers act as gateways. A router is used to send data packets to the corresponding computers and to manage the traffic between computers connected to the network. You can implement security protocols, assign static or dynamic IP addresses, and work both wirelessly and by cable. Routers can be small routers that are used in private households or business routers that are used in large companies.

Network interface card A network interface card or network card installed on PCs and laptops enables the motherboard of a computer to access the LAN. A very common form of network card is the ethernet card, which allows users to access broadband internet via a wired connection. Other forms of network cards include wireless network interface cards, fibre optic network interface cards and Token Ring network interface cards. These cards are classified according to their speed and connection to the computer.

Switches

On multiple ports you can easily detect this form of network hardware. It can be used to redirect traffic between computers on a regional grids, because data packets are copied via the MAC address of the attached devices from one port to another. Switches can be seen as hubs descending easier and less smartly. It also is one of the most popular network devices sold by approved distributors.

While everything today can be Wireless, at least 2-3 cable connections must be available on a computer network. Cables and wires Category 5 or CAT5 cables, for example, are a popular way to make cable connections. A. Ethernet cables connecting the modem to the router. Cables and wires can also be purchased in any hardware store in the form of network equipment.

5 S for corporate network hardware

There are several major network hardware vendors, and choosing a brand can often be confusing. Do you want a Cisco router, Juniper router, or Nortel router? Which brand network switch or server should your company buy? Each specific company offers a wealth of details/information about why you should choose your solution. I decided to hide some of these product details and provide a general list of features your company should look for in your corporate network hardware.

Regardless of what type of vertical business you are in or where you do business, network hardware is a critical aspect of your business. The five main functions that your network hardware and network infrastructure must provide are:

* Simplicity: An extremely simple, logical and easy to use network product and operating system makes everyone's life easier. Network hardware that is easy to install and run, but that provides the infrastructure for the company's complex communications is a must.

* Security: Your company data is your company's most valuable resource. Regardless of whether it is customer data, financial data or intellectual property data, it is extremely important that your network offers protection and access control for this data. The brand of your network hardware can make the difference between an occasional security breach and a perfect protection record.

* Speed: It is important that your company network works at the speed of your company. You should never interfere with your company's workflow, whether it is accessing data on your company's network or at a global access level. The network equipment you use is the engine that runs the network infrastructure of your entire company.

* Scalability: It is very important that your network is scalable with the growth and reduction of personnel in your company. A network that is not scalable can cause unnecessary costs for your company and undesirable difficulties for business efficiency. Scalability means a network infrastructure that offers open-source flexibility: the ability of your company not to be tied to a specific solution, but the ability to use the best technology available on the market.

* Savings: Maintaining a network infrastructure can often be a very expensive process and can drive a company's profits in one direction or another. It is quite difficult to find network hardware that is cheap and reliable. Depending on where you look, buying a used Cisco router or an overhauled Cisco switch can sometimes make the difference in terms of simplicity, security, speed, and scalability. However, it is equally important that you do not break the bank that builds your company's network infrastructure.

The key is to find a reliable network hardware provider, be it a used network hardware dealer or a direct seller. Make sure they are clear and reliable.

In addition to this list, there are basic guidelines that consumers must follow when purchasing network hardware. One of these components is the manufacturer's guarantee. Make sure there is a guarantee on your network hardware purchase, so you don't pay the cost if your requirements change.

The most important hardware problems to consider when choosing a provider

The hardest part about choosing a hardware brand could be the lack of familiarity between the options. For this reason, choosing an IT network hardware provider can be similar to buying a used car abroad. With several options, our first reaction is to choose the cheapest option. However, this is not always the best option as there are several important factors to consider when making smart purchases.

Service and repair guarantees play an important role in the selection of network hardware. For example, how far do technicians travel to maintain your network on-site? Which services are included and what additional costs? What can you expect after choosing the hardware in terms of ongoing support and upgrade options? Before proceeding with the purchase, you should understand the terms of these types of services and their relationship to your network and location.

Many of the larger hardware vendors set their pricing structure for future purchases. Often, a customer can get discounts on the initial sale if the seller expects the account to generate future sales as well. For this reason, it is a good idea to communicate your long-term technology goals to the supplier.

There are a few important factors to consider when choosing the right hardware provider:

Switches - Connect the cables, the "backbone" of the entire network. It is common for networks to contain both copper and fibre optic cables. In this case, the switch must accommodate both. Otherwise, the selection of the right switch for your office depends on the data traffic and the type of media used.

Devices: Your choice of devices should be based on performance expectations and network compatibility. Will the firmware be upgradable? Do you use normal computers or thin client terminals? What about articulated arms in examination rooms? It is important to make agreements about the device settings, whether it is a server, printer or laptop. In fact, before buying a computer, doctors should always check that the device they want works well on the network. By regularly checking the network, the entire system can be kept in sync and state of the art. This updated upgrade system will help you achieve top results and optimize your technical requirements.

Server: Take redundancy into account when choosing a server. Does one machine cover the performance of another that fails? If the hard drive fails, will a number of RAID drives take over? How many processors are there and how much RAM? Choose a backup tape drive that is large enough to store all of your data, but fast enough to back up everything overnight. What about the physical configuration of the network equipment? A custom rack or secure chassis unit might protect the servers, especially if there are multiple servers, as in many EMR system configurations.

Build A Better Business With Network Hardware

Consider the importance of network hardware as your business grows. You will increase productivity according to the number of workers and the type of work you do. Small businesses may be able to meet their network needs with relatively inexpensive devices. Depending on how the business grows, you should consider a completely new topology or a completely new design. This may require moving to a more complex system that includes a server. In this case, time is of the essence.

For small businesses

If you have a small number of employees, computer devices such as laptops, printers, personal digital assistants, and phones can communicate with each other over a local area network (LAN). This may be just a little more sophisticated than what most families use at home. In this case, the need for network hardware can cost $ 50 or less.

A network router facilitates communication between two networks. This connects the LAN to the Internet. Using a WLAN router and equipping each individual's computer with a WLAN card opens up more flexibility. All of these devices can, therefore, communicate with each other remotely. Employees can move around the work area and bring their laptops to meetings. In the meantime, they can also maintain access to the Internet and local printers. This improves the opportunities for creative interaction.

Do We Need A Server?

Too often, small businesses waste thousands of dollars on a server. Often they only need a peer-to-peer network like the one already described. This is usually sufficient if 10 or fewer employees need network access. If you have more than 12 users or if you expect rapid growth in the future, invest in a server.

Topology needs to be planned.

The topology relates to the design of the local network. Typically, workstations in each department must communicate as a layer, with each layer connected to the entire network. However, the simpler the topology, the more efficiently it works. You can make the mistake of adding switches with a small number of ports as the network grows. If growth is expected, the system must be designed to take it into account. Replacing multiple small switches with a 16-port switch can significantly improve performance.

Buy the best hardware

All of these routers, hubs, and switches are kept in a closet where no one will ever see them. The temptation to cut costs can be huge. However, you can save more by buying devices that survive. The cheapest hardware is malfunctioning. Instead, buy the best quality that fits your budget.

This saves expensive maintenance costs until you are ready for the next general overhaul in three to five years. synchronization

Plan the right downtime for maintenance and upgrades. Checking switches and routers takes a few hours. A new network with hundreds of computers will take several days.

In the early stages, postponing network hardware questions can be tempting. However, this will be critical to the company's growth over time. Careful planning at the beginning can save considerable time and money.

Network hardware that you need in your organization

It doesn't matter whether you are connected to the government or the education sector. You need to get important equipment to do your job as well as possible. For example, there are many areas where things are not possible without the right type of printer and scanner. Here people think of an HP ScanJet N7710 network printer.

However, when it comes to networks, there should be plenty of hardware. This is one of the main reasons why finding the right location is extremely important. In fact, there are many devices and gadgets that are used in an organization, and then a site that sells network hardware will help. But do you really know what kind of network hardware is important to you? Here are some popular options you should consider.

o Ask someone about important network hardware and the answer is "network camera". Without using the right type of network camera, many different tasks cannot be done. When buying one of these cameras, however, you must pay attention to the technical data and functions. Always make sure that your camera has features like digital zoom with presets, full-screen monitoring, built-in microphone, remote monitoring from your phone, plug and play installation and image timestamp.

o Another important thing that is extremely important for all organizations involved in the network is a firewall. It is extremely important to consider this particular aspect. Fortunately, you can now find some options in this regard. There are websites that sell network security and firewalls to prevent intruders from entering your network. Be sure to buy this special network hardware after paying attention to its functions. When you buy one, you need to make sure you get features like maximum global VPN clients, Green Compliance certification, 10 or more ports, 128 MB or more storage, and 30Mbps encryption performance.

o Routers and gateways are also important for networking. They offer you several advantages. However, if you want to get the maximum benefit, you should choose a router for integrated services. It has 2 ports, a data transfer rate of 10 Mbit / s, an intrusion prevention system, a network access controller, a controller with four interface cards, expansion slots and a 256 MB

DRAM memory. o In addition to these types of network hardware, there should be a few others in your organization. For example, POE injectors and splitters, consoles and extenders, network and interface modules, print servers, USB hubs, host bus adapters, and network adapters are some of the most popular network hardware options.

So these are the popular options for those who don't know much about network hardware. You need all of this and to get it you need to find a better site. Just go online and look for the best place to make a purchase.

How To Buy Network Hardware

Buying network hardware can be difficult because it requires a lot of technical knowledge. Therefore, before you meet your network requirements, it is important to familiarize yourself with the basic network hardware. The following information can help you.

Wireless access points are hardware devices that act as central transmitters and receivers for WLAN and radio signals. They are supplied with integrated network adapters, antennas and radio transmitters.

Wireless Ethernet bridges convert a wired Ethernet device for use in a wireless computer network. However, for larger LAN segments and better manageability, you should buy switches.

SFP transceiver modules facilitate the upgrade or maintenance of the fibre optic network or the fibre optic Ethernet network

Network drivers are required for the application software to communicate with the adapter hardware.

Print servers or print servers can accept print jobs from computers and send the jobs to the appropriate printer. This is a particularly useful device for large networks with high printing requirements.

A WLAN router is a router and an access point in one. It allows wireless access to the Internet or a computer network.

Internet security devices are small boxes that serve as security guards for all systems in the network. These devices generally have important security features such as network protection, firewall protection, virus protection, spyware protection, spam blockers, identity theft protection, etc.

Digital media receivers transmit HD media directly from your PC to your television. This instrument is particularly suitable for people working in the fields of production, design, animation, etc.

You can choose the network hardware you want to buy based on your needs and budget.

Network racks: Choose a network rack for your hardware

There are many factors to consider when considering a network rack. The equipment in these racks is, after all, inexpensive, and the data in your network hardware can be invaluable. Therefore, choose a network rack that is functional, durable and of high quality. You can't save it in this area. On a practical standpoint, when we pick network racks, we must take into account five items.

The first thing you want to see is the real dimensions and weight of your network equipment. Weight and height of your network hardware You can look for a server cabinet once you have defined the physical measurements. To manage the biggest hardware you need a cabinet.

You may also want to allow expansion and growth. Do you expect more servers, network hardware or devices in the future? In this case, you should consider a network storage solution that is suitable for these future hardware purchases. Doing so now can save you time and money in the future.

There are generally three types of network racks and cabinets:

Independent racks

Closets

Versatile (can be used as a wall, desk or stand-alone)

Usable space for rack mounting

The usable installation space or the usable dimensions differ from the dimensions of the network rack or the cabinets. The dimensions in the mounting area of the server racks refer to this.

It is a good idea to leave extra space in front of and behind the network, cabinet-mounted devices, cables, and accessories. When the hardware has power cables, network cables, etc. and most of them have, simplifies installation. You can also provide additional space for equipment maintenance.

Access to your network hardware

You should also consider how your devices are accessed and whether you need a server rack to accommodate these access areas. Most hardware only requires front access. However, some devices may require side or rear access. Therefore, take hardware accessibility into account if you want to purchase server racks.

Accessories for network devices

Think about what kind of accessories your network hardware needs. Servers generate a lot of heat, and many cabinet and rack systems require cooling systems as a precaution. Other common accessories for server racks are:

Hardware shelves

Cable management systems

Power distribution systems

Solid panel shelves

Earthing systems

Again, when considering the value of your network data, it makes sense to consider all suitable server rack accessories as well as a network cabinet system that can accommodate these accessories.

Special requirements

The above four considerations apply to most network racks or cabinets. However, certain types of network devices may require special consideration when choosing a network storage option. It is best to carefully read any restrictions that the device manufacturer specifies for special accommodations.

Choosing The Right Network Rack For Your Needs

Hopefully, the points above will help you choose a network rack or cabinet for your servers and hardware.

Optimize your server rack for network hardware

Server racks are used to conserve space by installing multiple devices or defending against various threats and natural disasters, such as earthquakes and overheating. Server racks have several uses. In other applications the sound is reduced by sound proof housing, or as several server racks have space for cable management the working atmosphere is made more organized and professional.

When it comes to network hardware, a server rack is critical as it ensures smooth operation of the system by maintaining a cool temperature, preventing overheating that in effect reduces downtime. A server and ensures that it runs smoothly. There are many special types of accessories and housings with which the temperature can be kept at a certain value.

Another important aspect in order to purchase a server rack is providing additional space for all cables. This is especially important in crowded environments as too many cables on the floor can cause people to trip and cause personal injury and damage to the hardware itself, which would be worse with network hardware as you could miss a valuable date. The ability to manage your cables in the rack prevents cables from spreading, which is much more attractive in a work environment.

Server racks not only make your work environment much safer and more professional, but they also simplify the use of your hardware. Without a large number of tangled cables that need to be constantly classified, or without the ability to easily assemble your hardware without worrying about space or overheating, as the airflow design of a server rack forces hot air and ensures that the temperature is kept cool at all times.

Another important factor is the various accessories that you can use for your server rack to accommodate the hardware. As wall brackets with which you can save space or if you need hardware for mounting at a certain point on the wall. There are also additional fans if your hardware generates a very large amount of heat. Finally, there are many accessories to prevent damage to valuable data in the event of earthquakes, accidents or fires, which is particularly important for the network hardware.

A custom server rack may be the best choice for your network hardware.

Using a network rack or IT cabinet offers many advantages. For one, you get what you need to host your network hardware. You can also benefit from greater effectiveness, comfort, stability and lower costs. When you customize your network or server rack, you can set certain options, such as:

Wall, desk, shelf or free-standing cabinet bracket

Types of the locking mechanism with key or combination lock

Built-in accessories that consist of cooling systems, shelves, cable management, etc.

Any other requirements you may have for your specific equipment colour

Specify a non-standard height or depth size.

Access points especially for devices for rack or cabinet mounting

Levelling system

Solid or perforated metal or glass door

Solid or perforated sidewalls. Often the need for a designed rack or cabinet is the result of a non-standard size requirement that is not available on the market. For example, if your equipment requires a 17U rack or cabinet with a 16 " depth, but you can only find that the market offers 20U racks with 20 " depths as standard, you may need to develop a custom rack. Keep in mind that if you only have a few racks, you may be able to survive. But if you are a manufacturer, distributor, or installer who sells in bulk, you might seriously consider hosting your equipment in a custom server rack.

Network rack design requires prototyping, engineering, and design work, so additional R&D costs will be incurred, but typically, if 100 or more server racks are ordered, it will be better than create a custom network rack.

When selecting a partner to develop your network cabinet, take note of a few things. Does the company specialize in developing custom network racks? Will they work with you to develop your ideas, explore your reasons for developing a custom network cabinet, and offer ideas to improve the design of your custom network cabinet?

You should wait for the company that builds your server racks to develop a prototype for approval, before full-scale production.

Used network hardware: a solution forced by the economy

Many companies are feeling the effects of the economy going down. The great successes in the economy can be contributed to gas prices up to the real estate sector. What will large and small companies do with their increasingly thin budgets to keep their networks running and continue to do business with their customer base? There are solutions out there that many people don't realize. Businesses can save a large amount of money that could contribute to other areas to overcome growth by searching the secondary market for network hardware.

As reported from the Bloomberg site in an article titled "Cisco Profit Disappoints Some Investors; Shares Fall", many companies are feeling the effects of current conditions in our American economy.

"They feel the effects of the United States economy, it is difficult to escape it," said Shaw Wu.

Shaw Wu is an analyst at American Technology Research in San Francisco, California. Nor did I fully understand the immediate price cut for used network equipment; Before entering this industry, I assumed that used equipment could only be obtained from auction sites such as eBay or Yahoo (Yahoo auctions recently ended in the

US market). It has even been reported that the Canadian dollar is worth more than a US dollar. As of Wednesday, November 7, 2007, the value of the Canadian dollar was close to the value of $ 1.09 for every US dollar. This is clearly a sign of a market crash and a troubled economy in the United States.

A solution must be presented to all companies that want to maintain Internet communications. New network equipment for a company serving thousands of employees within its infrastructure may be looking to spend $ 100,000, where choosing the secondary market could save more than half the cost on your bill.

Leading network hardware vendor Cisco Systems, Inc. seems to frown on the aftermarket as if it were doing something illegal. Of course, this is not the case. Secondary markets are being confused with the black market. Quite often, China is a major source of counterfeit equipment that ends up even in the hands of legitimate resellers. However, legitimate vendors have established practices for detecting fake network hardware and informing the vendor of where imitation equipment was purchased from UNEDA.

Look at your spending budgets and really soak up the fact that you are not required to directly buy new equipment and waste money that could be invested in other areas. This industry is what I am fully aware of, and I will continue to share my thoughts and research to save large and small businesses the money they deserve to invest in other businesses. A company has the option to buy new or used equipment if it supports a business technology infrastructure. Organizations use a local area network or high-bandwidth LAN to share Internet connections, applications, devices, and data storage with users. The hardware-implemented for a LAN can be simple or extensive, depending on the number of users and the number of processes that are processed. A basic configuration often includes computing devices, peripherals, switches, and workstations to filter multiple requests over a local area network (LAN). Redundant components are common throughout the LAN configuration to ensure that the error does not significantly affect business processes. Large companies can use multiple LANs in conjunction with a wide area network (WAN) for extended connectivity in a large geographic region. With the network hardware used, any company can buy what is needed without spending too much on useful technologies.

Refurbished servers: where do they fit in the network image?

A LAN connects PCs or devices to other components in order to share them between users. They can include a combination of workstations, laptops, computers and peripherals, printers, and other resources. Some companies configure a system for data security reasons only, while others want these components to perform certain tasks, such as B. the management of web services. In general, a

LAN or WAN is a tool to facilitate communication between users and devices. The individual company must define the precise purposes for this type of infrastructure setup. Renewed units are a method of controlling the expenditure that companies have on their procurement. Every company can benefit from the price reductions of the resellers, as long as the available devices meet the exact requirements for the functionality of the organizational processes.

Various system components are used to establish a secure connection to overhauled units or components that are shared across the system. Cables or wireless antennas must be available to manage each connection. While implementing wireless methods is cheaper, using many connections will result in slower speeds. A wireless configuration can pose security risks and is most commonly used for restricted laptop connections. The cabling of connected computers is connected to switches that consist of one or more NIC cards in order to quickly forward the data traffic. An administrator can log in to these components if they need to manage connections or change settings. The designs determine the number of manageable connections across each switch. They can be interconnected and arranged to support a large number of work stations.

A router can then be implemented to connect one or more LANs to a WAN or other type of larger network. Other components, such as Load balancers can be used to manage traffic further when resources are shared for the service, e.g. B. a website. Proxies, firewalls and routers are all components that a company can use to increase security. The number of workstations, external connections, managed services, and many other factors determines what a company needs to build reliable network infrastructure. A large amount of computer equipment and peripherals may be required to meet the organization's requirements. The network hardware used reduces the total investment a company must make to account for the processes and users managed by this configuration.

The components used are one of the most cost-effective ways for a company to get the supporting technology needed for a well-organized infrastructure. Network devices include a conglomerate of elements such as routers, switches, and computers that are arranged to share applications or complete certain processes. The hardware provided affects consistent system collaboration, but can also add up to a company's total technology cost. Not all companies are vulnerable to buying used network hardware. However, the selection offers considerable cost savings compared to new devices. In addition to reduced costs, restored components offer several advantages. The decision to use new equipment The decision to buy new devices can lead to loss of functionality and missed networking opportunities.

What are the positive aspects of buying used servers?

Servers are a purchase of devices that companies can use to save a lot of money. Refurbished IT or network components offer the same functions with comparable service and comparable guarantee. Resellers of used servers follow the test procedures of the same manufacturer, check the component quality, make the necessary configurations and sell the device for fifty per cent less than the new recommended retail price. Depending on the brand and model selected, the cost savings can be up to ninety per cent. Manufacturers offer customer service but are often difficult to deal with when a problem occurs with a particular component. Solving compatibility problems between different brands is almost impossible by a single manufacturer.

A reliable reseller generally offers better customer service and is able to solve problems regardless of the brands involved. The reseller guarantees the support of the purchased equipment for the duration of the property. An organization receives the necessary advice without having to pay extensive technical support costs. These advantages make it important for companies to consider used servers or devices without having staff available to troubleshoot the system. They also provide additional help by limiting the amount of time it takes for an in-house employee to solve a problem. Refurbished or used devices are considered used after opening the packaging. This factor is important because most resold devices have never been operated. Models are discontinued by the manufacturer, have surface defects or are returned by the customer without prior use. Companies have the opportunity to purchase components that are essentially new at a reduced cost.

The new devices are subjected to rigorous manufacturer tests before they leave the warehouse for sale. Even after completing these tests, many companies experience errors after receiving the devices. A reseller thoroughly tests each device in the second round before marking the product as reconditioned. Items that fail in this process are marked as used but must meet the reseller's specific standards before they are offered for sale. The network hardware used is also an ecological approach that the company can take to avoid landfill dumping and environmental damage. Resellers offer several solutions to help you find the best option for your business needs. There are many other reasons to buy used or refurbished equipment. An organization can apply the savings it makes to the additional equipment required or return the money for the unexpected without removing or limiting the technology implemented.

The Advantages Of Using Used Network Hardware

Information technology has expanded its reach in recent decades. This explains a lot about the failure of dot.com, the time when a multitude of IT tools and device types, especially server routers, were used. Server routers can perform a variety of business functions, such as B. High-speed data transport, virtual private network services, improving broadband usage, downloading large amounts of data from network connection resources, etc.

However, the trend has slowed somewhat, and the excitement has subsided. Now the market, especially those involved in starting small businesses, is no longer ready to invest money in new capacitive hardware like this. In fact, hardware vendors and distributors are now exerting pressure on customers to focus more on the resale aspect of hardware: how can the budget be reduced, how can environmental problems such as global warming be protected, and how can this be done to monitor market trends.

Buy Used Network Hardware To Cut The Budget

The budget constraint is one of the most important reasons for investing in outdated IT devices such as used juniper routers. However, the decision largely depends on the needs of the buyer and the business goals to be achieved using the network hardware used. The network hardware used is preferable for the following reasons:

When performing test methods

Delivers development projects

Can be used as a backup for older systems

Simplify employers' workload with familiar work tools and settings

How can the hardware network use to protect the environment?

The use of used routers can help contain production waste and thus protect the environment by eliminating the possibility of electronic waste. Using available resources can help conserve energy and contribute to a greener environment.

How Can You React To Sharp Market Trends?

A smart business person will always invest in a tool that will boost their trade credits and ensure the company's progress. Routers serve as an excellent technical support system and are therefore classified as an indispensable part of information technology. A network server/hardware router is, therefore, a must for entrepreneurs who want to simplify and organize business data. Investing in used hardware not only enables the use of innovative technological advances, but it is also the smartest and most profitable investment policy for the buyer.

Refurbished devices can be the perfect foundation for a flexible and intellectual network system that includes high-tech programs that can protect investments and reduce operating costs.

For any small or large business, network hardware can generate a very large invoice relatively quickly when purchased directly from a supplier. Secondary markets offer customers the opportunity to save money and generally get a more direct form of customer service. If you're a small business, buying new network devices can be a daunting task. You need to figure out your budget and know what to do with the right network device without paying more than you have to pay for the bill.

The undeniable advantage of buying used and refurbished network products is the cost savings for the items. You can save more than half even if you buy from a secondary retailer in the market, especially from Cisco devices. Just make sure the company has a good reputation and is legitimate. eBay has a large number of network resellers, but you need to make sure that seller feedback is checked. There are many resellers selling counterfeit devices claiming to be owned by a manufacturer, although these devices may have been made in overseas markets that look like the original.

Regarding the above, Uneda (Unite Network Equipment Distributors Association) was founded to raise awareness among consumers and to fight fraud and counterfeit resellers. Other members certify the Uneda organization's network resellers as legitimate resellers. Contact Uneda for a list of legitimate resellers.

Buying a failover device is also a great benefit when buying a refurbished device. This way, you don't have to pay the full cost of a network device that is saved until the time has come if the device is currently down—being a smart and smart consumer who does your research at full price before buying will pay off in the end. You can use the extra money you save for other business opportunities. You should increase your marketing budget.

Update your network hardware infrastructure

As technology evolves rapidly, it is inevitable (and recommendable) that you want to strengthen your company's network infrastructure with the best and latest technologies. Getting the best possible network hardware and technology means stronger infrastructure, better security, and foster collaboration. Although the best practice is to update your network hardware and software, the process must be done correctly so that your expensive network does not freeze and burn when you need it most.

Although it is very likely that you will experience network outages (depending on how complex it is) throughout the life of your setup, there are several things you can do to minimize this. Especially today, when capital savings are of the utmost importance for companies, avoiding network outages saves your company headaches and the loss of valuable income. Below is a list of steps you could trust to reduce the risk that a full power failure would blind you to:

1. Plan Compatibility: As you want to know a date's likes and dislikes to determine if there is a possibility of long-term compatibility, you should

also carefully plan to incorporate new and updated network hardware into your older structures. This could be done simply by searching for network hardware products with a good Google search.

2. Testing is the most important thing: Create an almost identical test environment that mimics the network environment to be run before you put it into operation. Running new network hardware without beta testing for potential problems and outages can be very dangerous. Although it is very difficult to create a live test environment without real stress, it is important to try this as carefully as possible.

3. Change your version: As with any experiment with control variables, it is important that each addition is installed and tested individually and one after the other. If you add multiple variables at the same time and something goes wrong, you can't determine what caused the problem. If each step is implemented and tested with a controller,

it is easy to determine what works and what does not in each interval.

4. Prepare for the worst-case scenario: Expect downtime to deploy your new network hardware. Prepare for this by creating a quick restart log, a plan you can follow to make the network work as quickly as possible. Also, plan your deployments for downtime when it doesn't have a big impact on your business users.

5. Quit twice: if you think everything is OK and working well, return to the drawing board and try again. There are usually one or two components that you have not predicted, and that will cause a problem in the future. Your due diligence during installation can prevent future capital losses and problems.

Hope that helps. As you can see, the important part is preparation, and how everything applies: the more, the better. Another important part of the equation of success is ensuring that your network hardware products are the best on the market. This is easier said than done, especially when small businesses are trying to save every penny available due to the economic downturn. I recommend using a reputable reseller for used network hardware, where you can purchase the devices at a fraction of the cost. Make sure they offer a good guarantee and make sure customer support is online to answer your questions before proceeding with the purchase.

Steps To Properly Restore Network Equipment

Many companies that resell network devices state that they test their products extensively. If you are going through a secondary market for buying used network hardware, make sure that your products have gone through the following steps, which are comparable to those of Network Liquidators:

When network devices are first received at the facility, they must first be physically inspected to ensure that no damage has occurred during shipping and handling.

All internal and external serial numbers must match, and all manufacturer labels and markings are intact. All devices with these defects must be returned to the seller.

All devices whose tamper-evident labels are not intact or defective should be opened and carefully examined. If the hardware is missing on the motherboard or other internal components, the device must be returned to the manufacturer or fully restored by certified technical engineers.

If a network device has minor, repairable damage to the box or missing screws or mounting brackets, we will repair and / or replace these parts or parts.

All network devices must be powered and operated with all input voltage capabilities that the device can maintain.

All network products should be updated to the latest diagnostic software and tested to the highest possible standard.

The entire network hardware should be warmed up to normal operating temperature before further diagnosis. This helps in the search for thermal problems that the device may have. If the network device can perform internal diagnostics, these must be performed. It is advantageous for a customer if all internal diagnostic results are recorded, and a copy is included in the scope of delivery of the device when the device is purchased.

Every empty box we buy has to be filled with known function knives to ensure that all of the slots, plugs and connectors work.

All cards, power supplies and hot-swap modules should be tested to ensure that you have no downtime in case you ever need to replace a faulty component. A faulty device must also be tested.

With all network switches, each port must be tested individually to ensure that they operate at maximum and optimal performance.

All redundant systems must undergo a failover test to check reliability.

All network devices must be configured and tested under real conditions to ensure proper operation. This includes all Layer 2, 3 and 4 protocols supported by the device.

Once the network hardware has completed all of the diagnostic steps, it must be thoroughly cleaned and packaged for inventory.

For greater accuracy, any device in stock should be re-checked before shipping, if selected, to complete an order.

If a standard network drive is upgraded to another operating system, additional diagnostic tests must be performed to include the new test results that are included in the device.

All products must be packaged professionally in the manufacturer's original packaging or with our state-of-the-art packaging system when sensitive systems are being transported.

Given these important steps, there is no reason to believe that a device will malfunction or be damaged during the shipping process. Nobody wants to bother to make a profit in any industry. Therefore, buying equipment from reputable resellers is much more important.

What To Look For In A Restored Network Computer

If you're looking for a way to lower your business costs, there are many approaches you can take. You can reduce overtime, opt for a cheaper cleaning service, or switch to more efficient lights. However, it is another option that you can overlook, which can actually save a significant amount of money. This budget-saving option is to choose outdated network devices instead of buying new ones.

Nowadays, there are many companies that use and recover used network devices so that they can be used for many years. You shouldn't always buy new devices for your computer network. Now you can spend less and still do more. Regardless of whether you are looking for switches, routers, gateways, or servers, there are many companies that have learned how to remove, update, and repair (if necessary) these elements from network devices and then use them at a reduced cost. "But," you might ask, "how do you make sure the repair is the answer?" Don't worry If you want to determine whether the restored network equipment is the answer to your business, don't worry.

What type of warranty does the reconditioned network device come with? If the company is not ready to give you a guarantee, it means that it is not very convinced of the performance/capabilities of the parts. Choose a catering company that is ready to offer an extended warranty.

Does your network hardware have a reliability rating that supports this? If the provider refuses to take a position and tells you how often his team works correctly or incorrectly, they are poor record managers or know the numbers but do not want to share the information.

What type of network hardware exchange program do you offer your customers? If this option is activated, the network provider is not ready to offer replacements for defective parts and then looks for another provider. As a buyer, you need to know that the part works. If not, it will be saved and replaced. Again, failure to do so is an indication that the company does not believe in the quality of its work.

Does your cost compare to other companies you have considered working with? Beware of any company that is significantly below the market. The lowest price is not necessarily the best decision.

Are your parts reviewed by an external source? This shows that the company is willing to have someone else verify their work and is willing to share that review. This indicates a desire to meet high-quality standards, which means you will get ahead.

Wireless Networks

A Brief History Of Wireless Networks

ALOHAnet, established within the University of Hawaii in the early 1970s, was the first true wireless network. This has contributed to the development of wireless networks which are widely used today, such as WLAN standards 802.11 and Bluetooth PAN standards 802.15. ALOHA used a random access method for UHF frequency data packets, and this data packet delivery system became known as the ALOHA Channel Method. ALOHAnet was used to link multiple computers across 4 of the Hawaiian Islands. The adoption of this method of communication spread to the satellite world and was even used in some first and second-generation mobile phone systems.

The ALOHA experiment sparked a lot of research in packet radio networks using spread spectrum techniques, and in 1985 the FCC assigned experimental frequency bands for the use of spread spectrum techniques for commercial purposes. These bands were known as the ISM (Industrial, Scientific, and Medical) bands, originally for use with non-communication devices, such as microwave ovens and hospital equipment, such as diathermy machines used as muscle relaxants when creating heat.

Such ISM bands can be used by devices used for communications, but with the understanding that ISM equipment may be a source of interference. For this reason, the communications equipment working in these bands had to be built to operate in conditions that are vulnerable to error. Effective methods for detecting errors had to be established to ensure, for example, that a nearby diathermy machine did not disrupt the conversation.

The first wireless LAN standards were born from meetings and seminars that took place in the early 1990s, and the IEEE eventually introduced the first 802.11 Standards. The 802.11b standard operates at speeds of up to 11Mbps within the 2.4Ghz band, while the 802.11a and 802.11 g protocols operate at 54Mbps for the 2.4Ghz and 5Ghz bands respectively.I n 2008, the 802.11 committees approved a draft of the 802.11n standard with data rates of 300Mbps. This draft standard used MIMO (multiple inputs, multiple outputs) by using multiple transmit and receive antennas and a technique called spatial diversity. Some modern wireless networking equipment may use two separate bands (2.4Ghz and 5Ghz) to increase reliability and performance.

The modulation techniques used for WiFi should include methods to combat interference in the error-prone ISM bands. IEEE 802.11b uses a modulation technique called Direct Sequence Spread Spectrum with Complementary Code Key (CCK), which uses 64 eight-bit code words to encode the data at 5.5 and 11Mbps and finally modulated using QPSK (Quadrature Phase Shift Keying). The IEEE 802.11a and 802.11g standards use OFDM (Orthogonal Frequency Division Multiplexing) where the radio band is divided into 64 subchannels that run in parallel. Each subcarrier is modulated using BPSK, QPSK, or Quadrature Amplitude Modulation. Some of the subcarriers carry redundant and duplicate information, so if the interference affects multiple subcarriers, the data can usually still be received and rebuilt.

WiFi, as it is widely known, can be configured in 3 main topologies:

Ad hoc: An ad hoc network is known as IBSS (Independent Basic Service Set), where all stations communicate with each other in a point-to-point configuration. There is no need for a wireless access point, as all stations communicate directly with each other. Usually, there is no planning, and certainly, no site survey before an 'ad hoc' network is formed. Stations can only talk to other stations that are within range of each other. This is a problem known as a "hidden node" where one station can listen to two other stations, but the two stations cannot listen to each other due to their geographic location. The station in the middle has no way of transferring information between the other two. There is no access point that serves as a source of time information, so time must be reached in a distributed manner. The first station to transmit sets the "beacon interval" and creates a set of destination beacon transmission times (TBTT). Once a client has reached TBTT, a client can:

- Interrupt the delay timers pending from a previous TBTT.
- Determine a new random delay.
- If another beacon signal arrives before the random delay ends, stop the random backward timers. If a beacon does not arrive, send a beacon and continue the reverse timers that were stopped.

There is an integrated timer synchronization function (TSF) within the beacon, in which each client compares the TSF on a received beacon with its own timer. If the received value is higher, it updates its own timer. As a result, every client ultimately synchronizes with the station that has the fastest timer. The time required for the distribution time depends on the number of clients in the network.

BSS (Basic Service Set) - All stations communicate via a wireless access point and must be assigned to this wireless access point using an SSID (Service Set Identifier). Within a BSS, an access point acts as a central point for all communication within the BSS network. The AP actually forwards frames between clients and therefore receives all data and management traffic. In addition, the AP can be connected to a wired network, giving clients access to communication across a wider audience.

ESS (Extended Service Set) - A series of BSSs that are connected via their uplink interfaces via a wired or wireless connection. The BSS is connected to the so-called Distribution System (DS), which in most cases is wired networks. An

ESS is sometimes referred to as a multi-infrastructure BSS because multiple BSSs are used to build it. Again, clients must communicate with an AP to route traffic to other clients within a BSS or to a neighbouring BSS that is connected to the same DS.

Wireless networks have become increasingly popular for both business and home users, largely due to the mobility they allow. Less cabling infrastructure is required, and users can move within the area covered by the WiFi. Many devices are now wirelessly activated, including wireless access points, wireless adapters, wireless routers, and of course, many laptops have built-in wireless connectivity.

Understand the difference between a wired and a wireless network

The wireless network has become increasingly popular in recent years. As technology advances, wireless speeds are approaching those of wired, and many households and businesses are implementing them on their networks.

While wireless technology certainly offers flexibility and convenience, there are many other important factors to consider when using wired networks instead.

Speed: We are becoming much more impatient when it comes to data transmission, and speed is certainly crucial in networks. Many wired networks are upgraded to gigabit, as much hardware is gigabit-capable these days and many cables support gigabit. On the other hand, wireless is unlikely to reach the speeds offered by cables. Wireless N has speeds of 300 Mbit / s. In a typical setting, of course, you'll probably only get about a third of it.

Another point that needs to be considered at speeds is fluctuation. When you transmit over a cable, you usually get a constant and constant speed. The same is not always true for the wireless connection. Interference and signal drops can cause the transfer rates on the wireless connection to rise and fall significantly.

Reliability: The transition from the previous point to wireless networks is much more susceptible to reliability issues. As there is no physical medium, the data must be transmitted through the air and through every surface on its way. This means that the signals can be blocked and redirected, and your connection may suffer or even be broken.

Even large distributed wireless networks can have these problems, and without careful planning of where the wireless access points are, this can be a nightmare for connection problems. On the other hand, hand-wired networks depend on physical cables that remain in the same location and have a long lifespan. Cables rarely fail in networks, and this means that you can achieve the same speed and performance every day for many years.

Security: The biggest problems with the wireless network is proper security practices. Since the data is transmitted wirelessly, it can easily be intercepted. Secure encryption (WPA / WPA2) means that the data can only be read if you have the correct key. However, many wireless networks remain insecure or have poor WEP encryption and are vulnerable to security breaches.

Wired networks are not faced with this problem. The physical access can only be done by someone who has access to the infrastructure. On the other hand, a wireless network can be accessed from outside a building, for example, in a parking lot.

As you can see, when choosing whether to use wired or wireless networks there are a number of factors to consider. A combination of both can be very effective with the right security procedures. It would be foolish enough for any company to replace their wired network with a wireless one completely.

Network Authentication Process

Linking and authenticating an access point by a client is standard. If authentication for shared keys is selected on the client, additional packets are sent that confirm the authenticity of the keys.

EAP network authentication is described below.

1. The client sends a probe to all access points.
2. The access point sends an information frame with data rate etc.
3. The customer selects the most suitable access point.
4. The client scans the access point in the order of 802.11a, 802.11b and then 802.11g
5. The data rate is selected
6. The client is assigned to the access point with the SSID
7. The client authenticates with a RADIUS server with EAP Network authentication

Open authentication

This type of security assigns a chain to one or more access points that define a logically segmented wireless network called a Service Set Identifier (SSID). The client cannot be assigned to an access point unless it is configured with this SSID. The assignment to the network is as simple as determining the SSID of a client in the network. The access point can be configured so that the SSID is not broadcast, which improves security somewhat. Most companies implement static or dynamic keys to complement the security of the SSID.

Static WEP keys

Using a static WEP (Public Wireless Equivalency Public Key) to configure your network adapter increases the reliability of your wireless transmission. The access point is equipped with the same 40- or 128-bit WEP key and is compared during an assignment with these encrypted keys. The problem is that hackers can intercept wireless packets and decode your WEP key.

Dynamic WEP keys (WPA)

The provision of encrypted dynamic WEP keys per session increases security through a hashing algorithm that generates new key pairs at certain intervals, which makes phishing considerably more difficult. The standard protocol contains 802.1x authentication methods with TKIP and MIC encryption. Authentication between the wireless client and the RADIUS authentication server enables dynamic security management. It is worth noting that any type of authentication indicates the support of the Windows platform. An example is PEAP, which allows each client to have Windows XP with Service Pack 2, Windows 2000 with SP4, or Windows 2003.

The 802.1x protocol is a protocol for encryption authentication with these approved types of EAPs per client and device: EAP-TLS, LEAP, PEAP, EAP-FAST, EAP-TTLS and EAP-SIM. The network authentication information received by the user has little to do with the client device configuration. Losing computer equipment has no impact on health. The encryption method is done with TKIP, an improved norm for encryption that improves WEP encryption by packet key hashing (PPK), message integrity testing (MIC), and key rotation broadcast. The protocol uses 128-bit keys to encrypt the authentication data and 64-bit keys. The sender adds a few bytes or MIC to a packet before encrypting it, and the receiver decrypts and checks the MIC. By turning the broadcast button, the broadcast single and broadcast buttons are rotated at certain intervals. Quick Reconnect is an available WPA function that allows employees to move around without having to authenticate themselves to the RADIUS server again if they change floors or rooms. The client user name and password are temporarily stored with the RADIUS server.

EAP-FAST

Implement an asymmetric key algorithm to create a secure tunnel

Mutual authentication of client and RADIUS server

The client transmits the user name and password in a secure tunnel

EAP-TLS

SSL v3 creates an encrypted tunnel

PKI certificates assign client-side and server-side RADIUS with mutual authentication

Dynamic keys per client and session to encrypt data

Protected EAP (PEAP)

Implemented on Windows clients using any EAP authentication method

Server-side RADIUS server authentication with digital root certification authority certificate

Client-side authentication with Microsoft MS-CHAP v2 client RADIUS server with the encrypted user name and password credentials

EAP network authentication process for wireless clients

1. The client is assigned to the access point
2. The access point enables 802.1x traffic
3. The client authenticates the RADIUS server certificate
4. The RADIUS server sends a user name with an encrypted password request to a client
5. The client sends a user name with an encrypted password to a RADIUS server
6. The RADIUS server and the client receive a WEP key. The RADIUS server sends the WEP key to the access point
7. The access point encrypts the 128-bit broadcast key with this dynamic session key. Send to customers.
8. Client and access point use the session key to encrypt/decrypt packets

PSK WPA

Pre-shared keys use some functions of static WEP keys and dynamic key protocols. Each client and an access point are configured with a specific static access code. The access code generates keys with which TKIP encrypts data per session. The access code must be at least 27 characters long to protect against dictionary attacks.

WPA2

The WPA2 standard implements WPA authentication methods with the Advanced Encryption Standard (AES). This encryption method is implemented in government deployments, etc., where the strictest security must be implemented.

Application-level access code

SSG uses an access code at the application level. The client can only authenticate if it knows the password. SSG is introduced in public locations, such as hotels, where the customer pays the password allowing network access.

VLAN assignments

As previously mentioned, companies provide access points with SSID assignments that define logical wireless networks. The SSID of the access point is assigned to a VLAN in the wired network, which segments the traffic of certain groups as in the conventional wired network. Wireless implementations with multiple VLANs configure 802.1q or ISL trunking between an access point and an Ethernet switch.

Other options

Disable Microsoft file sharing

Deploy antivirus and firewall software

Install your company's VPN client

Turn off the automatic connection to a wireless network

Never use AdHoc mode. This allows unknown laptops to connect

Avoid signal saturation with a good site survey

Use a minimum transmit power setting

Anti-theft device

Some access points have an anti-theft device, which is available via a padlock and wiring to secure the equipment during use in public places. This is an important feature in public deployments where access points can be stolen, or there is a reason why they should be mounted under the roof.

Security attacks

Wireless packet trackers capture, decode and analyze packets sent between the client computer and the AP. The purpose is to decode security information.

Dictionary attacks try to use a list or dictionary of thousands of standard passcode phrases to evaluate the decryption key installed on the wireless network. The hacker gathers authentication information and checks every dictionary word based on the password until a match is found.

The specific mode which each wireless client is assigned affects security. Ad hoc mode is the least secure non-AP authentication method. Any computer on the network will forward information to a neighboring ad hoc computer. If available, select Infrastructure mode.

IP spoofing is a popular network attack which falsifies or replaces the source IP address of that packet. The network system is of the opinion that it interacts with an authorised computer.

Often SNMP is a source of security which is compromised. Implement SNMP v3 with complex strings for the Group. The information age was revolutionized not only by the ability of computers to process data but also by the power of communication between computers. This communication is responsible for the spread of computer networks. Sharing information, sharing resources (both software and hardware) and sharing processing load are some of the main goals of a computer network. One of the latest trends in the computer and communications industry is wireless communication. A wireless network does not use cables but radio waves. Such networks improve the functionality of computing devices by freeing them from the location restrictions of a wired network. Although wireless networks are very useful for laptop users who move from one place to another all day, there are also benefits for fixed users. Many schools and companies have an architecture that is unsuitable for a wired network. Wired networks are very inexpensive in such environments.

Wireless networks can generally be classified as fixed wireless systems and mobile wireless systems. A fixed wireless system supports little or no mobility of the devices connected to the wireless network. For example, a local area network can be set up using a wireless network to eliminate the hassle of laying cables. The mobile wireless systems support the mobility of the devices and enable the user to access information from anywhere and at any time. The devices used in the mobile wireless systems include personal digital assistants (PDAs), smartphones and pagers with Internet access.

Wireless networks communicate by modulating radio waves or pulsating infrared light. A wireless network router is connected to the wired network infrastructure via stationary transceivers. Wireless communication technologies used in wireless networks include analogue cellular, digital cellular, cellular digital packet data (CDPD), cellular networks, personal communication services (PCS), satellite, microwave, and local multipoint distribution (LMDS) systems. Although the data rates supported by analogue cellular technology are low, it is the most popular method for wireless data communication due to the wide availability of modems and analogue cellular services. Commonly used wireless technologies include 2G and 3G technologies, wireless LANs, wireless local loops (WLLs), radio router technology, wireless multihop networks, and wireless application protocol (WAP).

A step-by-step guide to setting up a wireless network

Wireless networks are becoming increasingly popular over time. They are easy to install and practical to use when you want to surf the World Wide Web from anywhere in the house. For this reason, wireless networks are attractive in the eyes of Internet users. It is easy to set up a wireless network. However, you need to know some simple things before you can start setting up. To get a better understanding of wireless networks, you can read protocols from wireless networks.

To set up your wireless network, you need an online broadband connection with a DSL modem or cable. Typically, the normal home setup includes a desktop computer that is directly connected to a modem. If you are reading this, we may presume that you already have a laptop that you want to connect to a Computer with an internet connection wirelessly. For this, you need hardware, e.g. B. a WLAN router, a WLAN-USB network adapter for your desktop computer and a card-based PC network adapter for the laptop. It is, of course, recommended to choose the same vendor as any additional hardware you buy. For installation information, see the documentation that comes with the hardware.

After you have installed all the necessary hardware, you can start with the setup. You must first switch off or disconnect your DSL modem before connecting your WLAN router to the modem. If you need help, just check your hardware documentation. After this is configured, your computer will connect to the router wirelessly. Next, you need to configure the WiFi router. With Internet Explorer, you can go to your router's configuration page.

Most of the default settings are safer if left alone. Some stuff have to be programmed, however. You need to choose an SSID or a unique name for your wireless network, which is also the name of your network. Make sure no one around you uses the exact same name. If the router needs this, enter a unique access code that generates several keys. Before you have finished configuring your router, the last thing you need to do is set an administrator password. Choose a password that is long and difficult to guess for security reasons. Make sure that you save every configured configuration. The actual steps to configure the settings may vary depending on the router type.

Next, configure your laptop's network adapter. Follow the instructions in Windows XP on-screen for this. Right-click the wireless network icon in your system tray and go to "View available wireless networks" after the menu appears. The Wireless Network Connections window is displayed. The selected name for the wireless network should be displayed here. Click Refresh Network List if the network is not shown. The password which you entered in the key fields Confirm network password will be requested.

Select to connect. You will then see the progress of your connection while connecting to the network. Once the connection is established, you can close this window. Your wireless connection is already configured.

Wireless networks are new for about a decade and the extent to which they have spread today clearly shows the benefits and potential they have for the future. In the beginning, networking computers in various government organizations and agencies were common in the last century. However, this was a wired network and had several difficulties when adding the new systems to an existing network.

Several new topologies were later introduced, and some of them were successfully implemented in real-time on stage. Although this has been widespread for several decades, technological change has highlighted the limitations of wired networks, and most organizations, research laboratories, universities, and public places are switching to wireless networks with their technology for continuous benefits.

So if you've chosen a wireless network, you need to know something about setting up a wireless network. First, consider how many computers are connecting to the network, where the entire network is located, and which operating system you want to use on the systems. Once they are fixed, the first step is to install a WiFi router. If you plan to build a new network and not develop/update an existing one, place the WiFi router in a central location, so that network coverage is good everywhere. Note that computers closest to the router get faster speeds than computers farther away. Therefore, the location of the router is critical. The next step is to repair the access points on the router. The location of the access points is also important because they also affect the speed and connectivity of computers on wireless networks. The next move is to configure the router and access points for your WiFi adapter. This can be achieved by first installing TCP / IP on the host computer and attaching the adapter to computers that are explained in the object documents. All of the following settings can be configured manually. However, all wireless adapters must use the same parameter settings for the wireless network to function properly.

The final step is to install the ad hoc network on the Home LAN or on all computers for wireless network access. If you connect the WLAN adapter to ad hoc mode and not to infrastructure mode, you can do this if you want to set up a home LAN with restricted users. Otherwise, set the infrastructure mode in which the router detects new computers and the settings are adjusted accordingly. There is a security aspect to consider when setting up a wireless network. If you want to keep your network away, just set a security password and disable the SSID so that your network is not recognized during a random search. Other problems associated with setting up a wireless network can be easily understood while working. If you think you can't do the work yourself, ask a technician or company to set up a wireless network.

Types Of Wireless Networks

In the early days of computers, networks were reserved for technophiles. The houses rarely had more than one. Nowadays, however, home computers are used for everything from email and schoolwork to television, games, and social media. The increasing popularity of portable devices makes the wireless network even more important. When consumers are aware of the different types of connections that are possible, they can better choose the type of network that suits them.

The Wireless Personal Area Network (WPAN) is the first form of wireless network. A WPAN is created by connecting two devices that are relatively close to each other. The two tools are normally within one arm's reach. The contact between the TV and its remote control is a perfect example of this.An infrared light connects the two so that the remote control can change the channel. Other examples are the connection between a keyboard and a computer and the connection between Bluetooth and a mobile phone.

Wireless local area network (LAN) is another type of wireless network that is widely used. A LAN may be connected to two or more computers by means of an access point. A strong example of LAN is wireless domestic networks (HAN). If a LAN is connected to the Internet, the same connection is between the two computers. If a larger area than a LAN needs to be covered, a wireless Metropolitan Area Network (MAN) is created. A MAN connects several locations in a general area. A university campus generally has a LAN for each branch called the University Area Network (CAN). The branches combine to form a MAN.

A WAN (Wide Area Wireless Network) is even larger than a wireless network in the metropolitan region. A WAN is a network that connects devices in a large geographic area and transmits data over common points such as telephone lines and satellite dishes. The best example of a WAN is the Internet. The Internet connects local and urban networks worldwide.

Another type of wireless network is the ad hoc network. An ad hoc network is a decentralized wireless network. It enables multiple devices to communicate without using a router or other access point. Instead, an ad hoc network enables data flow through each node by forwarding data from the other nodes. As a rule, ad hoc networks are created during operation for a specific purpose. Most ad hoc networks are closed, which means that they have no access to the Internet. An example of an ad hoc network is the connection between two portable video game systems. A connection is made, data is exchanged, and then the connection is broken, and the network is destroyed.

A particular type of ad hoc network is the Wireless Mesh Network (WMN). A wireless mesh network connects the access points at every location of the user. Each user acts as a node for passing data across the network. A good example of a WMN is Voice over Internet Protocol (VoIP). VoIP picks up analogue voice signals and converts them into digital signals that can then be transmitted over the Internet.

Information about different types of networks can make a difference in how difficult it is to build a wireless network. The local network, the metropolitan area network, the wide-area network, the ad hoc network and the wireless mesh network have advantages and disadvantages. End-user requirements should determine the type of network that the user should choose.

The Advantages Of A Wireless Network

Have you used the WIFI connectivity available at prime post locations around the world such as the airport, five-star hotels and many others? Have you thought about how your internet works, even if it is not connected via a wired medium? When we talk about a network, we actually call it the collection of devices and computers that are connected through communication channels, which not only allows users to communicate, but also to share and share resources, hardware, files and software, and many more. When it comes to categorization, The wired and wireless network is usually categorized and each has its own advantages and drawbacks, including the benefits of a wireless network over a wired network.

In terms of networks, the real difference between wireless and wired technology is that the end nodes are connected without cables or physical media, making it a completely virtual experience. Information travels through electromagnetic waves and is carried out on the physical level of the OSI model. The IEEE 802.11 standard is the basis for most wireless networks.This gives us the flexibility to contact the Internet or intranet without having to intervene or use a physical medium. Excessive stray cables can be avoided by using a wireless network.

There are many advantages to a wireless network. If you plan to make data use portable, a wireless network is your ultimate answer. This type of system is less prone to system failure, which is a very important case when wiring. Some of the other benefits of the Wireless networks include wireless Internet in public areas like airport, train station, library, university campus and hotels. So your system and network card can be modified easily and your system is ready here with full network connectivity and no cables.If you think from an installation and maintenance perspective, a wired network costs more than a wireless one. This also means that the time spent on installation and maintenance is also on the top. Who wants to get into this complexity and pay more for a wired network connection? In addition, the overall possibility of system failures is much greater in the case of a wired network. In an organization where profits depend on data availability, the wireless network plays a critical role.

The prices for WLAN routers are certainly below the total cost of an Ethernet cable. It is actively investigating that the use of a wireless network can damage health and lead to memory loss and premature senility. However, the advantages of a wireless network are far more valuable than the possible disadvantages. This will surely make the wireless system a network of the future. For anyone in the decision phase of the router or cable, wireless or wired, flexible or rigid, the wireless network is the answer to all your questions.

WiFi storage adapter - Please check two warnings before purchasing

If you are looking for network storage for your home or home office, you probably know its benefits. They know you will get a safe place to put your important files for business or personal use. It can save videos, MP3s, PDFs, documents, photos and you will never wonder what hard drive you have saved them on. They are always in your storage unit and connected to the network.

As netbooks, notebooks, and laptops are being used more and more in private households. It is tempting to think that such storage connected to the network may be available over the wireless network. As long as your laptop is on, you have instant wireless access.

While there are some network-connected storage adapter products on the market that are said to be "wireless," there are two limitations to consider before purchasing such a wireless network storage adapter, sometimes referred to as a storage cabinet.

Network are: Some "wireless" adapters are not really wireless and cost. Let's look at the two here.

Is the wireless network storage adapter really wireless?

Some companies have vendors who are a little bit enthusiastic and write that a network adapter is "wireless". Be careful with such claims, because while some network adapters are truly wireless and can transmit information with a built-in radio, others do not have these built-in radios. However, each of these network storage adapters can connect to a LAN port on a wireless home router so that your network storage can be accessed wirelessly over the air.

Is the Wireless Network Storage Cabinet Really Worth the Cost?

Some of the other benefits of the Wireless networks include wireless Internet in public areas like airport, train station, library, university campus and hotels. So your system and network card can be modified easily and your system is ready here with full network connectivity and no cables. Your network storage is wireless or wired through the router. Good performing wireless routers are common these days, and their prices have dropped significantly. However, wireless adapters are still quite expensive. So if you are looking for a "wireless" network adapter, consider a combination of a wireless router and a wired storage adapter. You will find that this combination works the same or better. You have an additional option for wired access through the router, and it will likely cost you less than a single adapter connected to the wireless network.

The Importance Of A Wireless Network

A wireless network opens up many possibilities.

Wireless networks provide an easy and inexpensive way to share a single Internet connection between multiple computers. This means that all you need is a modem and you can add additional computers to the network simply by plugging in and turning on a WiFi card. The new machines immediately connect to the Internet.

You can also access files and printers from anywhere in your home via a wireless network.

You can synchronize the files on your laptop with your home computer and easily send files between computers. It is easier to use a wireless network to forward files than to email or burn to CD! Because all computers are connected to one of the machines on that network, you can write documents in your home anywhere, click "Print" and pick up the print files from a printer on a monitor. You probably also found that your games have always the ability to play across the local area network or LAN if you are a game player. LANs are Wireless Networks! This means you can play these games together with your kids, and you don't have to sit on computers next to each other to do so. Let's face it-playing against real people is more enjoyable, and playing against people you meet, instead of strangers on the internet, is even more enjoyable. Your games will play over your LAN much faster, too. You can also connect game consoles to the Internet, and start playing these games online. Experiencing online play via an Xbox or PlayStation 2, which is linked to a wireless network is much easier than using a modem!

There are still wireless network links in. It means that anytime you want, you can connect to the Internet without waiting for your modem to dial in. Laptops can be moved from room to room, and they will still have Internet access. Because wireless networks operate without the need to sign in, no usernames or passwords need to be configured.

A wireless network's single best thing is that it's wireless! The main reason to have a wireless network is that it removes the need for costly, messy, and dangerous wires that trail across your house. You can use your machine in whatever room you choose-no longer being stuck in your home by a phone socket, or walking through the tangle of wires. The cost of having enough Ethernet cables will add up, and sometimes, to set up a wired network, you might even have to holes in your walls. Of course, if you're renting, that's unlikely. You don't have these issues with a wireless network-you can even use your machine outdoors, if you want to! And when you pass, there's no need to disconnect and pack all those wires, so when your Internet link goes down, you don't have to check all the wires for harm any more.

You can see how using a wireless network can make your life easier.

The Risks Of Unsecured Wireless Networks

An explosion of Wireless (Wi-Fi) networks has occurred in the home over the last few years. And for a good reason: they're inexpensive to introduce, to avoid the expense and labour of running cable through your walls, to allow you to walk around your house and near surroundings with a machine in tow. Plus, the setup is fairly simple. I say "relatively" because it's far from being a matter of common sense, particularly when it comes to "properly" setting up wireless home networks. You can easily access the Internet by connecting the wireless cables you have linked to with the wireless router to your home wireless network.A lot of people do this, and it typically works. Yet what many people are neglecting to do is develop wireless security, and that is an incredibly risky oversight. I'll explain why in this post.

You May Get "WarChalked" "WarChalking" is a geek-speak for someone piggybacking or freeloading on the wireless Internet connection of someone else, without the permission or consent of that person.

If you have a wireless network that's unsecured, this is the least that could happen. By connecting to your unsecured broadband router, your neighbour could be having free Internet access. If you haven't set up your wireless protection, there is nothing to stop this happening. At least this practice of leaching on the Internet connection of someone else will drain the bandwidth of the user, resulting in slow downloads or surfing. If enough people tap your wireless network, your access to the Internet could slow down to a crawl.

Getting an unsecured wireless network will also allow people to access your device and private data unauthorizedly. It opens a "backdoor" even if behind a firewall; otherwise, your network is protected. Wireless access to your Internet port of call (i.e. your Cox, Comcast, or Qwest modem), puts an unauthorized user into the "network," just as if they were popping in and connecting to the network via an Ethernet cable.

You're scared? Are you scared? It gets worse. You will give your personal details, such as credit card numbers, social security numbers, bank account numbers, usernames, passwords, etc., to the place where you sell your product or service, if you buy anything online. You could stolen your personal data.

Your Home Network Could Be Used to Hide the Criminal Behavior of Anyone Else Every wireless home network (or, more specifically, every wireless gateway device) should have a unique address traceable to its owner and to its household. It's called an "IP Address "- say 71.33.56.166. This number especially distinguishes your home network from the countless others around the world. No two are the same anyway.

For several reasons, this IP Address is special, and one reason is that it enables some authorities to track online activities back to the person, household, or company from which those activities originated. Even though when you are browsing the web, you can feel anonymous. You are not actually. Any web server or Internet service provider, among other details about your device and program, will maintain a log that records your IP address.

Now, this does not concern most people, unless they are advocates for privacy because they do nothing illegal on the internet. It is a big issue for those who commit crimes on the Web. How do they get away with this?

We will tap into the neighbourhood's unsecured wireless network. This makes it very convenient for them to get around, making the proper authorities recognise them. Why? For what? But then it will be you and your home network who are found! It is your IP address which is going to be registered.

Not many people want the FBI kicked open their doors during a predawn search because of the Internet activities of someone else. Someone could use your wireless network to access or distribute child pornography, hack in corporate networks or commit credit card fraud.

Okay, I'm scared now. What would I do to defend against this?

The fast and simple way to do this is to employ a qualified computer or network technician to protect your wireless network for you, or at least to check that you did it correctly.

When it comes to setting up its security, each wireless router or gateway system may be different. The computer will come with the manufacturer or ISP instructions.

WEP or Wireless Encryption Protocol is the most important thing to set up. WEP encrypts the data stream from your device to any Web server you have on the Internet, prevents unauthorized interlopers being detected on your online business, transactions of credit cards, etc.Perhaps as significantly, it also prevents unauthorized users from linking to your wireless network, either free-of-charge piggyback on your Internet connection or hide their identities behind your own. To link, they have to have the encryption key.

To secure the wireless network, you should take additional steps. For example, you can disable the function that broadcasts your Wireless Network ID, rendering your wireless network invisible to your neighbours for all practical purposes. This is a clever thing to do but is often ignored.

Ways To Secure Your Wireless Network

Wireless networking technologies are so popular and inexpensive that anybody can set up a wireless LAN very quickly; indeed, as part of their broadband services, many service providers are now giving wireless routers away. The through use of wireless networks has allowed network intruders to hack the home or office network.

LAN equipment is mostly insane and is often pre-configured with hardware supplied by broadband providers. And it's worth testing your wireless LAN router's protection configuration; here are some easy things you can do to secure your wireless network.

Safe the code for Administration. Wireless routers usually have an administrator password to enter before they can alter the configuration.

Some computers are preconfigured with a default password for the user, and certain computers have no password at all. You should always make sure you configure an administration password or change it if the device has a default password. When you leave the computer with no password or the password set to a default value, you run the risk that the system will be reconfigured without your knowledge; either by someone who has managed to connect to your network or by malware that you have accidentally downloaded.

It is using WPA instead of the WEP encryption. 802.11 WEP encryption (Wired Equivalent Privacy) has vulnerabilities which make it fairly easy to crack the encryption and access the wireless network. WPA (Wi-Fi Safe Access) is a better encryption standard which provides much better protection and is easier to use. Nearly all modern wireless hardware and operating systems incorporate WPA support. WPA2 is a newer version of the standard that offers even more efficient encryption. You may have some devices that don't support WPA (often devices like media players, PDAs, etc.). It's tempting to turn off encryption fully in this case, but this would really leave you wide open to attack. With all its drawbacks, WEP encryption is better than nothing and should, therefore, be used if you have devices which do not support WPA. By using WEP, make sure you don't use a simple encryption key to guess. Also, you should consider changing the encryption key for the WEP at least once a week.

Don't channel the SSID. Most wireless access points and wireless routers transmit the name of the wireless network on a continuous basis.The service set identifier or SSID is commonly known. This is intended to make wireless networks easy to configure, since wireless devices can detect the wireless media available. However, it also announces the existence of the cellular network in all wireless networks. If you turn off SSID, you'll be invisible to your neighbors and even to your intruders, but that always becomes clear to those with a wireless network sniffer.

And use MAC filters. The MAC address is a hardware address for a network adaptor which is specifically for that adapter on a global basis, unlike the IP address. By filtering MAC in your wiresless access point or router, you can track the various devices that can connect to them. Anyone with the right skills can manipulate MAC addresses so they do not provide utter assurance of protection, but they provide another impediment to the intruder.

Disable Remote Control. Many wireless LAN routers can be remotely administered over the Internet. This function can only be used any time you can also identify a particular IP address or a restricted set of IP addresses that can be used for router administration. When you can do that, they could theoretically have access to your router somewhere. It is best to disable it unless you really need this feature; Most LAN wireless routers default to deactivate this feature, although testing is still worthwhile.

Reduce the power of a Wireless LAN transmitter. This function doesn't exist on all wireless LAN routers and access points, but some will allow you to reduce the transmitter capacity, thus reducing the signal range. It is typically difficult to fine-tune the signal to the point that it does not leak outside your premises. Still, you can restrict the degree to which the signal reaches so that people outside your premises can have access to your wireless LAN.

Wireless networks Security solutions have become popular these days. Quick every home has wireless routers or wireless access points these days. The technology does have security problems, however, particularly if you don't follow safe practices. If you breach network security, you may lose your important data, such as your credit card or bank information. Wired Equivalent Privacy (WEP) and Wi-Fi Safe Access (WPA) I and II are those protocols that manage wireless network protection.

You will need to set up one of the above-mentioned wireless access authentication protocols when setting up the wireless network on your device. It will safeguard the unauthorized sharing of your device and data. To authenticate, you will need to set up a password. Make sure you just give the password to those people you want to get linked to.

Ways to protect your device inside the wireless network: Network protection passwords are not something that can be taken lightly. You can't let your access to network get into the wrong hands. Many of us don't even care about changing the default password. In reality, creating a stable, wireless network is the first step.

Some essential steps to protect your wireless networks from unauthorized access are listed below: swapping the default network password to something safer.

Please use such a good password that everybody would have trouble guessing.

Password should not be a term on a dictionary. Ideally, a long string will be with a mix of alphanumeric letters and special characters.

Often pick security protocol for WPA authentication if it is not available then using the WEP protocol at least for protection of the wireless network.

SSID (service set identifier) is the name you are creating for the network. You can block everyone's display of the SSID name. Only those individuals who know your SSID network will be able to connect to your network through this.

DHCP is the protocol for dynamic host configuration. To protect your wireless network, various users could be allocated manually to the SSID network. It's a smart way to beef up the security of your wireless network.

Next, pings that block anonymous request for network connection.

You should not allow pair-to-peer connections from your network.

You can allow MAC (Media Access Control) filtering for users for greater security. Through doing so, only those computers can connect to the network that already has a MAC address registered in your network. Only those devices which have registered MAC addresses will connect to your network.

The network router must require the features of the firewall, and must be activated.

All connected computers require a personal firewall, which is in addition to the default firewall for the network.

Complete router / access point updating process regularly as soon as new versions become available.

By implementing only one of the above mentioned security measures you might not be able to make your network fully secure. But a combination of multiple security measures can provide your networks with enhanced and unbreakable protection.

How To Make Your Wireless Network Hacker-Proof

Protection, whether it be your home, vehicle, or personal possessions, has become the second nature of people over the years. Machines are no exception as digital criminals lurk everywhere, and it is almost impossible to detect the average computer user. A very important step to prevent unauthorized access to your wireless home or business network is a hacker who doesn't need to know you personally to hurt you.Wi-Fi hackers in the communities in the homes of people who are searching for wireless networks, connect through multiple open doors in the wireless router setup and then have an informative day. Within this post, we'll step by step go through the several settings of your wireless router that vulnerable your network and adjust to make your network basically hacker-resistant.

Step 1: Login to our router's setup service is first of all required.To do this, you need to understand which IP address is your gateway. Click Start > Run and enter the CMD. You can do this. That opens a fast session for a order. Without the command prompt quotes, click 'ipconfig' and press enter. If you connect to your network, it will return several different numbers. The one we need is listed on the Automatic Gateway. Take and select the "Default Gateway" IP address, or copy the address. This is a sequence of numbers separated by intervals like this, if you are not familiar with IP addresses: 192.168.1.1 Yes, this particular IP address that is used only as an example, but can be listed as something similar to your IP address. Now open a web browser, such as the Internet explorer or Firefox, and paste or copy the IP address in the address bar and press Enter. You are pulling up the login page of your router. You will need to find user ID and password for your router from the manufacturer if you know your login information here. This can be found in the manual with the router or in the hunt for manuals under the router's model number (a sticker at the back, hand or bottom of the router is available) at the website of the supplier. Initially, you can try common ones, such as user ID administration and password, or user ID and password administrator. If these aren't operating, refer to the User ID and password manual for the maker. If you set up and forget your own User ID and password, or the default User ID and password of the manufacturer doesn't work, whether other people in your home have access to the router or have a previous owner, the default User ID and password may have been changed. In such a case, by pressing and holding the reset button on the back of the router for at least 5 seconds, you can reset them to defaults. You can now sign in using the manufacturer's default User ID and password collection.

Step 2: Change your User ID and password if set to the defaults of the fabricator. If anyone gains access to your wireless network, they can easily log into the settings of your router and change them to match their taste.

Step 3: Reset your SSID. Your SSID is the name you see for your wireless network when you use a Wi-Fi-enabled device to search for open networks. If the SSID is set to the manufacturer's default, anyone searching for a nearby open network will be able to see yours, and with a little internet search, they will be able to figure out your router's model number which will help them access your router's settings.

Step 4: Disabling your SSID broadcast. Broadcasting an SSID is simply how the names of open networks appear on your computer when you search for open networks in a region. When you disable your SSID broadcasting while people are searching for open networks, yours won't even show up, so ultimately they won't even know your wireless network exists. You can still connect to your network by manually typing your SSID into your Wi-Fi-enabled devices.

Step 5: Trigger WPA2 encryption where appropriate. If WPA2 doesn't exist, allow WPA encryption. If none is available, and only WEP is available, check the manual or website of your router for information about upgrading the firmware of your router. An upgrade to your router may provide WPA or WPA2 encryption support. If your current router is unavailable for updates, you will consider purchasing a new router as yours is possibly very outdated. WPA2 encryption is ideal, because it is much safer than WPA and particularly WEP.

Step 6: Set up a PSK or pre-shared key or network key. This is the "password" to your network, whatever your router calls it. It should not be confused for the password we changed to your router in step 2. The pre-shared key you set up should be impossible to guess and should include letters, numbers and special characters from the upper and lower case. It's really important to have all of these to make cracking virtually impossible, but don't make it so long it takes you 5 minutes to get into every system. When it's hard to recall, you can always look it up when you need to log in again to the settings of your router.

Step 7: Allow Filtering MAC Address or Authenticating MAC Address. This move is optional, and can only be taken if you don't have guests using your Wi-Fi or if the devices that use your Wi-Fi are regularly the same devices. A MAC Address is essentially an ID that any device allowed on the Internet or the network has that looks like this: 00:20:e0:00:41:00 Every computer that has ever been developed has a unique MAC address so they can be properly recognized as a person on a network. Using MAC Address Filtering or Authentication will only allow you to connect the specific devices you select to your wireless network. Some external devices won't be able to connect because their MAC address won't be in the allowable device list you make. To add a list of accesses to your Wi-Fi activated devices, you need to get the MAC address of every device first. For computers and laptops, with no quotation marks, simply go to Start > Run and type 'CMD.' That will bring up a window for the Command Prompt. Then type in 'ipconfig / all' and press enter without quotation marks. Somewhere near the top should be mentioned some saying "Email Address." Next to it, you can see the MAC Address for your device. This can be listed with hyphens in between every 2 characters instead of colons as in the above example. This is all right, just make sure that when you enter the MAC Address in the access list, you do it in the format your router needs, so you may need to turn all hyphens into colons. Do this for any device that links to your wireless network. You will most likely have to look for your system details in the Configuration menu for devices such as iPods, iPads, mobile phones, etc. (or it may be somewhere else, depending on the computer). If it is a computer enabled for Wi-Fi, you can find the MAC Address here. Do this for all non-computer devices communicating with your wireless network and adding them to your access list each. Don't forget that if you buy a new computer or visit someone, and want to use your Wi-Fi, you'll have to do this move.

Except for the optional step # 7, it is necessary to perform all steps to protect your wireless network correctly. However, the above steps are the most effective and most appropriate to avoid unauthorized access to your wireless network, there are other security measures that can be enforced. You should be confident that your wireless network is virtually impenetrable now when you have taken all the measures mentioned in this guide.

Ip Addresses

How Do IP Addresses Function?

This is an simple way to grasp IP addresses, and how validation of IP addresses will work for you. The Internet Protocol Address is a numeric label attached to each user, such as an Internet Protocol printer or device that used the Internet Protocol to communicate as part of the computer network.

An Internet Protocol address performs two key functions: naming and defining the location of the host or the network interface. It is a 32-bit number to its programmers, and the Internet Assigned Numbers Authority (IANA) controls its worldwide space allocations. It delegates regional web registries (RIRs) to allocate blocks of IP addresses to local Internet service providers.

IP addresses are allocated to a host either anew at boot time or permanently via a set software or hardware configuration. Using a "password to the static Internet Protocol" implies permanent setup. In the other hand, the use of a "dynamic Internet Protocol code" attributes the code of a device every so often.

An administrator manually assigns a static IP address to a device, and each platform has a different procedure. In the case of dynamic IP addresses allocated by the user interface or host program, or by a device using Dynamic etwork Configuration Protocol or DHCP this is done differently. These dynamic Internet Protocol addresses are most commonly allocated by DHCP servers to LANs and broadband networks, and they relieve the administrator from the additional task of assigning unique static addresses to each system on the network. They also allow for the sharing of limited network address space by increasing devices if only a certain number of them are online at once.

An operating system may allocate an Internet Protocol address to a network interface by using stateless auto-configuration methods in the event that static or stateful address configurations fail or are absent.

You can also learn about IP filtering and firewalls very often. Firewalls perform IP blocking tasks to protect networks from illegal or unwanted access, and are widely used today. The blocked address is the assignee's actual Internet Protocol address, either by the use of a blacklist or whitelist. This means that if the client uses a proxy server or network address translation, blocking of the Internet Protocol address can result in blocking of individual computers.

IP address validation services are commonly available today to validate addresses and help deter fraud by checking and geotargeting website users. For example, there is a validation service that is a programmable XML Web Service that enables businesses to incorporate IP-based location information, distance calculation, and other geographic intelligence into Web-enabled applications and business processes.

Not only does this service verify emails, but it also gathers anonymous proxy data from 165,000 computers which are distributed around the world and serve as listening posts. Those computers give access to other computers involved in malicious behaviour.

If you're new to the Internet, stuff can also sound very confusing. People throw around words such as IP addresses, name servers, hosting, FTP, etc. You'll know just what they are and how they relate to optimizing search engines (SEO).

The Internet Protocol Address is an Internet Address, typically composed of four "octets" or period-separate numbers. Each octet can be a number from 0 to 255 Some examples of valid IP addresses are-1.123.150.243, 35.35.36.10, 240.216.1.80 There is also a new IP address format, called IPV6 (IP version 6), which is gradually being introduced. IPV6 numbers look very different from our IP addresses of today.

An example of an IPv6 IP address is-2001:0db8:85a3:08d3:1319:8a2e:0370:7334

You'll find that with Several more potential variations each is much longer. The new IP system is designed to give us sufficient IP addresses to avoid running out of unique IP addresses at any time in the foreseeable future.

Why do we need IP addresses, then? Very literally, your physical home address is like an IP address. This designates a specific internet linked device. An IP address is given to each computer connected to the internet. It is essential to provide and receive information. The first "octet" is the broadest in the current collection of IP addresses, going from left to right, with each subsequent octet being ever more granular or unique.

To clarify a little better

134-Quite large 134.125-is still very wide, but becoming more precise 134.125.244-is becoming more precise and is possibly referring to a particular web host.

134.125.244.1-is as specific as you can get and refers to a specific computer, you will often hear about different classes, such as class A, class B and class C, when dealing with IP addresses. Below are some examples of what people refer to when they talk about classes.

Class A 134.XXX.XXX.XXX 240.XXX.XXX.XXX 22.XXX.XXX.XXX

Class B 134.254.XXX.XXX 36.36.XXX.XXX 36.37.XXX.XXX

Class C 254.210.135.XXX 36.36.1.XXX 36.36.2.XXX

Thinking of IP addresses as physical addresses is often easier, with the Class A octet being similar to country, Class B being a city in that country, Class C being a street in that city, and the last octet being a specific house in that street.

Looking above, you should be able to see that when some speak about an IP address of Class A they refer to the first "octet" and when they say that two IP addresses are on separate subnets of

Class A, it simply means that the first set of numbers is separate.

So for instance 255.123.124.255 34.123.124.255 Are on various Class A's. While the remaining IP addresses are the same because they are on different Class As, they are MUST far apart (remember, Class A is the broadest).

The same is true for Class B. The second octet of numbers is referred to in Class B. When someone says two IP addresses are on different Class B's it simply means that each IP is different from the second octet's. The IPs may be on the same Class A, or it may be different, but the number Octet 2 is different. To explain better. Look below.

255.123.124.255 255.34.124.255 34.34.124.255 The first two IP addresses in the above example are of the same Class A but different Class B's. The third IP address has the same Class B number (34), but because the first Octet is different, it is also on a different Class B address (as with physical addresses, two countries the have the same names of towns, but they are still different).

We are looking into the third octet for Class C.

255.123.124.255 255.123.34.255 34.42.124.255
Again, the first two above are on different Class C's, while the third has the same Class number as the first, but the first and second octets are different, and it is also on another Class C.

I hope that's sensible for you. I've tried to provide a lot of examples to make it obvious no matter what your tech experience is. The good thing is, you've never ever had to deal with IP addresses. When you obtain your domain name from a web hosting account, your host will assign an IP address to your domain name. You also HAVE not even to learn this. Your host will usually set up all this for you, without you having to grasp any of it. From that point on, when someone types in your domain name, that name will be converted to your assigned IP address and voila ... your website visitor will wind up.

IP Address Sales, Exchanges, and Rental Pricing Supply And Demand An growing market is starting to gain traction in IP address exchanges. ~decreased with a greater supply of addresses available for sale or lease. In addition, this would also provide more time for companies that are in the process of transitioning to IPv6 to do so properly and thus reduce costs.

Sale Pricing The first point to be aware of is the variation between regions in terms of IP address sale pricing, that is, buyers purchasing the right of use from sellers. The main governing body for IP addresses is the IANA (the Internet Assigned Numbers Authority) which distributes them globally across the five main RIRs. As different regions of the world have various needs, there is a related price fluctuation in demand.

Microsoft, however, set a precedent with a large purchase of IPv4 allotments that effectively set all possible purchases at the base price. In 2011, the firm bought 666,624 IP addresses for $7.5 million from bankrupt telecom Nortel. That set the price per address to $11.25 per number. Microsoft did not need to make this order, as the North American RIR, ARIN, already had addresses available for registration.

Microsoft has obviously agreed to step in to set a precedent so any other speculators can do so to inflate the price artificially. Many RIR regions have replied accordingly with the base price-per-address set at $11.25. For example, addresses transactions in the RIPE area (covering Europe, the Middle East, and parts of Central Asia), with a current price of about $12 per address. The price, however, can be pushed down to as low as $8 per address, if large bulk transfers are done.

Prices in the ARIN area, which mainly covers the United States and Canada, are lower, for now, due to the availability of legacy address blocks, plus a remaining supply of addresses available from the RIR itself. Prices in North America are expected to end at $5 per address, but for now, that is pure speculation. The bigger point is that no single fixed fee schedule has been set for final transactions across the regions yet.

Rental Pricing

Also, many companies are exploring the option of renting IPv4 addresses, while migrating systems and services to IPv6. For a number of reasons, this move can often be a more viable option. Next, IP address rentals are usually priced between $1 and $2 per IP address per annum. Second, companies that aggressively introduce IPv6 migration within a short span of time, i.e. five years, may simply consider renting IPv4 blocks simpler and more cost-effective for that duration.

These renters will simply return the addresses after completing protocol migration until they're no longer needed. If the process took five years, the total cost per address would still be lower than making a complete purchase at twice the price. Organizations such as Pub Concierge will help promote this process by bringing together partners and assisting the negotiating process.

Rentals of IP addresses have ignited a new business by renting address-requiring facilities such as host servers. Hosting companies that at one point were free to host websites or servers would now charge customers for the use of the IP address. Fees are usually set at about $1 a month. However, if a hosting company buys a block of IP addresses for server use at $11-$12 per address, and then charges customers $1 per month per address, they immediately start seeing profits after only twelve months.

Scale those numbers up on a service agreement to thousands of addresses over several years, and the opportunity for benefit is immediate. A myriad of factors needs to be weighed for companies looking into IPv4 address transfers, each containing its own level of complexity. The variables inherent in pricing alone demonstrate this point easily.

Networking Protocol

Individuals have to tap into their communications abilities to be a successful networker. A major part of networking establishes and fosters relationships. Networking depends in part on having knowledge, understanding and respect for others. That is, there's a certain social protocol involved that can decide the networking performance level.

Mentioned below are helpful tips for handling the next event or encounter.

Know-How to Communicate Be aware of the things you say while networking. You don't want to look sales-driven or willing to take on a new customer or company. You want to communicate that you are interested in that particular person, its business or its endeavours. Be also watchful of non-verbal communication signals such as body movements/gestures. Take the time to gauge the level of focus of the other person, too.

Know how to be marketable

Make sure your discussions are constructive as you dive deeper into the discussion at events. Often provide specific information while you're thinking about products, services or promotions. This could include rates, bundles, specials/sales and other logistics. Use this opportunity to send your business cards around so that people can keep in touch and get more information.

Knowhow to Be Appropriate

Be sure to always display etiquette. Whether it's enjoying a meal, having a conversation or even following up. Be aware and pay attention to access to various situations and then act accordingly. It demonstrates a high degree of professionalism to be conscious of others.

Ideally, these few tips could prompt you to make the most of your next networking effort.

Understanding how to communicate with others and conduct business properly is essential in developing quality relationships.

LAN protocols-Ethernet, STP, Fibre

Spanning Tree Protocol Spanning Tree is an algorithm operating on Layer 2 campus switches to avoid Layer 2 loops and broadcast storms over a network with at least two switches or bridges. The algorithm determines which ports are to be blocked at each switch or bridge to create a free topology for the loop. IEEE and 802.1d are key requirements. The port states of the spanning tree listen, read, block, forward or disable. For a loop-free topology, each group of switches will choose a root bridge as part of determining which switch ports must be blocked. The root bridge is selected as the lowest priority switch (MAC address), by default. The selection of root bridges can be modified with the bridge priority order. Considering your campus switch design is important, and if necessary, modify the performance selection of the root bridge.

New switches which use VLAN run one instance of spanning tree per VLAN. That is important to note as there are layer 2 loops per VLAN or section. It allows a switch with dual connections to the same switch or separate switches to load equilibrium across those links without worrying about causing a storm. This is done by assigning two VLAN's to a switch that has dual links to different core switches in the campus. Each connection is designed to forward and block traffic from one VLAN to the second link. Consider, for example, a switch assigned to VLAN 10 and 24 ports to VLAN 20 with 24 ports, and a supervisor engine with 2 Gigabit ports that connect to different core switches. Port A is assigned to VLAN 10, and port B to port B to port 20. If traffic from VLAN 10 is also enabled on port B, you will have a loop because traffic could leave on port A and return on port B provided there is a trunk connection between the core switches on the campus.

Ethernet This is the most common data link protocol currently running on the campus. Today's main standards are 10BaseT, 100BaseT, and Gigabit Ethernet. Currently, several networks consist of 10BaseT and 100BaseT, from the client and server to the campus turn. Gigabit Ethernet can be used from a switch to switch and from build to build. 10BaseT is a 10 Mbps standard for unprotected Category 3 twisted pair (UTP) cables. The distance from the screen to turn is a maximum of 100 metres. The specification 100BaseT is the same except that the speed is 100 Mbps over unshielded twisted UTP) pair category 5 cable. Gigabit is a 1000 Mbps Ethernet, STP, and UTP cabling standard. Ethernet uses CSMA / CD as a method for handling collisions when two desktops send data at the same time. Both workstations are waiting for a specified and specific length of time before retransmission attempts. An Ethernet packet has a maximum packet size or MTU of 1518 Bytes.

The Gigabit Ethernet optical fibre technology uses multi-mode fibre (MMF) and single-mode fibre (SMF) for data transmission. Single Mode Fiber requires only one light mode to travel through the fibre strand, using a laser as the source of light. Multimode allows multiple light modes to pass through the fibre strand at various angles, using an LED as a source of light. Modal dispersion results from different types of light spread through a strand of fibre. The effect is a higher bandwidth of Single-Mode Fiber, which transmits over greater distances. Supports Multi-Mode Fiber with 62.5 micron and 50-micron diameter fibres. The 50-micron fibre can carry more than 62.5-micron fibre over longer distances. For Gigabit transmission, Dual Mode Fiber uses Short Wave Lasers (SX), and Long Wave Lasers (LX). Single Mode Fiber serves a fibre core with a diameter of 9 microns. It uses lasers with long waves to send data 10 kilometres apart between buildings.

What is the Web?

The internet is the broader network that enables businesses, governments, universities and other organisations to speak to each other about computer networks around the world. The effect is a mass of cables, computers, data centres, routers, servers, repeaters, satellites and wifi towers that allow digital information to move around the world.

It's the infrastructure the helps you to order the weekly store, post your life on Facebook, stream Netflix outcast, email your aunt in Wollongong, and check the web for the smallest cat in the world.

How wide is the Web?

One measure is the amount of information it trains: about five exabytes a day. That's the equivalent of 40,000 standard two-hour definition films per second.

It takes up some wiring. Hundreds of thousands of miles of cross-country cables, and more, are laid along the seabed to connect islands and continents. The global internet is underpinned by about 300 submarine cables, the deep-sea version just as thick as a garden hose. Many are hair-thin fibre-optics packets that hold data at light speed.

How much energy is the Internet making use of?

The Chinese telecoms firm Huawei reports that the ICT industry will use 20 per cent of the world's electricity and release more than 5 per cent of the world's carbon emissions by 2025. The author of the report, Anders Andrae, said this was to blame the coming "data tsunami."

In 2016, the Lawrence Berkeley National Laboratory of the US government predicted that in 2020, American data centres – facilities where computers store, process and exchange information – will require 73bn kWh of electricity. That is the output of 10 nuclear power stations at Hinkley Point B.

What is the internet web?

Advertising The internet is a way of accessing and exchanging information online. The information is written on web pages supported by a web browser, whether it's text, music, images, or videos or whatever.

Google manages more than 40,000 searches per second, and Chrome accounts for 60 per cent of the global browser market. Almost 2bn websites exist, but the bulk is rarely visited. The top 0.1 per cent of websites (around 5 m) are involved in more than half the world's web traffice.

Among them are Google, YouTube, Facebook, Baidu, Instagram, Yahoo, Twitter, VK.com, Wikipedia, Amazon and a smattering of porn pages. The increase in apps means that many people today are less interested in searching the open web than in having more oriented information: news, notes, weather forecasts, videos and the like.

Where is the Web of Darkness?

A web search doesn't search for everything. Google will use the term "puppies", and your browser will view web pages discovered by the search engine in the hundreds of billions entered into its search database. Although the search index is huge, it only contains a fraction of what's on the web.

Therefore, maybe 95%, are not indexed and thus invisible to ordinary browsers. Find the Web to have three layers: bottom, dark and top. Default web browsers trawl the Web surface, the most available sites. Beneath the surface is the deep web: a mass of unindexed pages, which include pages that are kept behind passwords – the kind found, for example, on the office intranet, and pages that no one links to, as Google and others create their search indexes by following links from one web page to another.

The dark web, a collection of places with addresses that hide them from view, is buried in the deep web. You need special tools like Tor (The Onion Router) to access the dark web, a device originally developed by the US navy for online intelligence agents. Although the dark web has many legitimate applications, not least in protecting the privacy of journalists, activists, and whistleblowers, illegal activity drives a large portion. Illicit web marketplaces trade everything from drugs, guns, and falsified money to hackers, hitmen, and child pornography.

What are the numbers online?

It hinges on how you measure it. One metric that is common with the International Telecommunications Union (ITU), a UN organization, counts on being online in the last three months as having used the Internet.

Advertising This means that people are not expected to be using the internet merely because they live in a community with an internet cable or near a wifi tower. Using this yardstick, by the end of 2017, some 3.58 billion people were online, or 48 per cent of the global population. By the end of 2018, the number should reach 3.8 billion, or 49.2 per cent, with half the world online by May 2019.

Fixed-line Internet connections in developing countries are costly, so most people communicate through their cell phones. The phenomenon brings in a two-tier internet experience obscured by development estimates. What can be accomplished on a cell phone is a fraction of what a desktop, laptop or tablet can do, as someone who has attempted to file their tax return on their smartphone will know.

"In the debate regarding access and affordability, the distinction sometimes gets lost," says Dhanaraj Thakur, web foundation research director. "We might say 50 per cent of the world use the internet, but most do it on their tablets. This is totally different in terms of productivity from using a desktop or laptop.

Mobile internet's success leads to other issues, too. For example, in Africa, the telcos enable people to purchase 20 MB to 1 GB packages of data by offering access to key apps such as Facebook, WhatsApp, Instagram, Gmail, and Twitter, even when data runs out. The upshot is that instead of the open web, people equate the internet with certain sites. Others don't even know they use the internet.

The problem came to light after polls and focus groups in Africa, and south-east Asia showed that more people used Facebook than it was online. "Facebook is the Internet for them. They don't explore beyond that, "said Nanjira Sambuli, who leads the efforts of the Web Foundation to encourage equality in accessing the internet.

Who are they, then?

Almost everybody in certain countries is online. Over 98 per cent of Icelanders are online, with comparable figures in Denmark, Norway, Luxembourg and Bahrain, says ITU. About 95 per cent are online in Britain compared to 85 per cent in Spain, 84 per cent in Germany, 80 per cent in France and just 64 per cent in Italy.

Additionally, a Pew Research Center survey from 2018 showed 89 per cent of Americans are online. The unconnected are typically poorer, older, less educated and rural. Nevertheless, the online world isn't dominated by the West. Although the US has around 300 million internet users, China in 2018 has notched up more than 800 million, with 40% of its population remaining unconnected. India this year crossed an estimated 500 million internet users, with 60 per cent of the country still offline.

What is it they are doing? Advertisement, A minute on the internet, looks like this: 156 m emails, 29 m texts, 1.5 m Spotify albums, 4 m Google searches, 2 m Skype calls, 350,000 tweets, 243,000 pictures posted on Twitter, 87,000 Netflix hours, 65,000 pictures posted on Instagram, 25,000 posts posted on Tumblr, 18,000 matches posted on Tinder, and 400 hours of video uploaded on YouTube.

Most user internet traffic is a video: add up all of the online content viewed on blogs, Twitter, Netflix and webcams and you've got 77 per cent of the world's internet traffic, according to US tech company Cisco.

What are the spots offline?

A strong divide exists between the haves and the have-nots, and deprivation is an overwhelming factor. In some African nations' urban centres Internet connectivity is normal.

More than half of South Africans and Moroccans are online, and parts of other countries, such as Botswana, Cameroon, and Gabon, are easy to connect. Mobile phones are driving growth as mobile broadband prices over the past three years have fallen by 50 per cent.

But there are several places which don't keep pace. Around 30 to 40 per cent will get online in Tanzania, Uganda and Sudan. Just 7 to 11 per cent are online in Guinea, Liberia and Sierra Leone.

Less than 2 per cent have exposure in Eritrea and Somalia. Building a mobile hotspot in a small, off-grid village will cost three times the urban equivalent, reaching much more people and therefore offering a much higher investment return. There is still little desire for the internet in rural areas because people don't see the point: the web isn't serving their interests.

Is any of those parties offline?

There is a clear divide in age: the Internet uses far fewer older people than the younger ones. In Britain, where 99 per cent of 16- to 34-year-olds are online, according to the Office of National Statistics, the 75-and-overs make up more than half of the 4.5 million adults who have never used the internet.

There is still a significant gender divide. Men dominate internet usage in two-thirds of the world's nations. Globally, the number of women online is 12 per cent lower than men. Although in most regions since 2013, the digital gender gap has narrowed, it has expanded in Africa. There, the Internet uses 25 per cent less women than men, says the ITU.

In Pakistan, men outnumber women online by nearly two-to-one, while in India, 70 per cent are men. The divide represents predominantly patriarchal values, and the disparities they instil.

Some countries are bucking the trend, Jamaica in particular, where there are more women online than men. This may be because the West Indies University in Kingston enrols more women than men. The nation has the highest female executive ratio in the world.

Why is the entire planet going online?

A big challenge is having small, rural regions affordable internet. US tech firms are hoping to make inroads to expand markets. Google's parent company, Alphabet, has abandoned plans for solar-powered drones and is instead concentrating on high-altitude balloons to provide space-based internet access. SpaceX from Elon Musk and a company called OneWeb have their own plans to offer internet connectivity to everyone in the world through microsatellite constellations.

Facebook, which has seen its Free Basics service banned under India's net neutrality laws, has also abandoned plans for internet-beaming drones and is now working with local businesses to provide affordable mobile services.

For wireless broadband, Microsoft, meanwhile, uses TV white spaces – the unused broadcast frequencies. Another strategy is also gaining ground, Group networks. Usually, these mobile networks use solar-powered stations and are designed by and for local communities. Managed by cooperatives, they're cheaper than the alternatives, while retaining the area's expertise during income.

Windows Network?

Windows Networking is a mechanism whereby you set up a set up between various systems. It is important to agree on the type of network model that can be peer-to-peer or client-server before entering the process of setting up a Windows network.

All systems act like clients in a peer-to-peer network configuration since there is no process of centralization. Implementation is fine when there are no serious safety concerns. Other systems usually operate in case a system in the network is not working. If the network setup is that of a client/server, the central system will be a single computer, and it will be used as the server system. All other computers connected to that server are clients of the system. The client systems are able to access files, docs, spreadsheets, web pages and other resources on the server. The one downside in this type of network configuration is that if the central system fails, then all network systems can't function as well.

You need to pick a specific name for the client device as one of the steps involved in configuring framework within a network. Selecting a specific IP Address is also important, and assigning the same domain name to all network client device. To establish the communication network, such as hubs, switches, network adapters, routers, internal modems, cable testers and also a clipping tool. All necessary devices need to be put together. Among these is the hub which is the most important as it can be used as a central device and the hub must be linked to any system in the network.

When setting up and configuring each communication system to function as a part of the network, check how they operate. When the network is set up, install premium anti-spyware and antivirus software to keep network security intact.

Today Windows is one of the most commonly used operating systems. The more popular a given operating system or element is as with anything else, the more likely it is to be the target of people who will use it for their own ends. Like every other immensely popular operating system, Windows is no exception to the rule.

Windows operating systems and Windows networks are vulnerable to attempted attacks, so it is important to track them. While some Windows systems provide you with a basic method of monitoring your network, they don't help you see what kind of applications are running in the background or using the network.

If you need to discover and terminate some kind of programs that use your bandwidth or are using embedded malware, getting this knowledge handy is very useful.

Some monitoring of the Windows network can be accomplished using the built-in software and network monitoring tools that Windows 7 or

Windows 8 offers you. If you are just searching for simple network monitoring, you do not need to think about third-party network monitoring software, but you may need to use the Windows software to access the details you need.

In Windows 7, it is possible to take a look at processes running in the background and who is linked to your network. Making sure they're going to be there, what kind of load they're using and whether or not they're slowing down your service is another way the Windows network monitoring tools can support.

To track your windows network, all you need to do is go to the Task Manager for Windows. If you are interested in how active the network is, click on Performance and review the Ethernet or WiFi sections to review that detail. It is easy to see and easy to comprehend. You can also have your own IP address tested.

Your Task Manager will provide you with links to slightly more advanced network monitoring information that will give you all the information on each active part of your network. It will tell you how much data is sent and received, where it comes from and how much of an impact it has on the resources of the network. Note that these built-in tools have their limits. If you need more, you need to look deeper into the network and install some Windows monitoring tools from the outside. There is a large selection of free programs that allow you to take a closer look at all information on the Internet and that do not cost a dime. Much of it is even easy to install and easy to use. If you use Windows network monitoring tools, and they are not exactly what you are looking for, you should look for other tools that will help you take a closer look at your home or professional network.

Set up Windows for our network

Configure our computers for our home computer network

Now that all of the hardware has been configured for our home computer network, we now need to configure our computers to enable communication between us. Even though we installed our hardware, it is still useless unless the computer knows what to do with it and it is up to you to tell what to do with the hardware.

Routine technological activities such as driver installation (hardware controls program such as a network card) on your device are some of the things you have to do. In addition, you must configure each computer to be ready to share your files on your home network.

Note to wireless users: If you are using a wireless router on your network, you must first install the router. Although the installation procedures vary from manufacturer to manufacturer, most of them all have the same general configuration.

Hardware driver

Your network connections, regardless of whether they are ISA, PCI or USB connections, are hardware devices for which you have to install small software programs called drivers. Drivers help the operating system communicate with the hardware and indicate what and when to do it.

After physically installing the network adapter on your computer, Windows should automatically recognize it the next time you turn it on and request a driver installation. This cool feature in Windows is called plug-and-play and works while Windows starts. The plug-and-play function wants to install your hardware immediately and prompts you to provide the correct information for the correct installation.

The USB ports allow you to connect the device to the computer while it is on. Windows automatically detects it and displays the Add New Hardware wizard. This ability to install hardware while the computer is on is referred to by technicians as a hot install and is one of the coolest things about USB devices ... Got it? ... HOT installation ... The coolest via USB?

Come on, that's funny!

Oh, it doesn't matter!

There are times when the plug-and-play feature in Windows doesn't recognize your new hardware. In this case, you have to install the driver manually.

Protocols to initiate communication

Now that Windows has the appropriate drivers to communicate with our network adapters, it is time for our computers to start communicating. In order to communicate, our machine needs to use the same network protocol (the language in which computers interact is a technical conversation). Computer-to-computer communication protocols are of two types: TCP / IP or NetBEUI. Depending on your version of Windows, each will be installed automatically. Windows XP automatically installs TCP / IP. You must install NetBEUI in XP on Windows CD and vice versa if you use Windows 98 if you want NetBEUI in XP.

In order to communicate, every device must be equipped with the same protocols. The protocol and network adapter are combined in this installation. Services will begin online until every machine is able to speak the same beautiful language. Any job on a network you want to do, like B. Network access is referred to as file sharing, print sharing and network login.

Machines and Working Groups A new challenge is to connect and share information on our machines. In terms of Network Laws, the Microsoft network program is very systematic and needs to know who is who, what and when. For this reason, computers must have a name (each must be unique so that you cannot have two computers with the same name).

You must also assign a workgroup to each computer (the group your network is in so that each computer is in the same group). Windows Network Assistant If you are using Windows Me or XP, you do not have to go through In most cases, you can use the Windows Home Network Assistant to configure it.

The Windows Home Networking Assistant guides you through the process of setting up your network and also sets up the shared Internet connection for you. Many people don't like using this wizard because they say it complicates things (I can't say that I appreciate it too much). I'd advise you to do it all manually. It allows you to understand how much better Windows works.

Computer Virtualization

Today, more and more companies realize the benefits of cloud computing virtualization due to its flexibility, high performance, and cost-efficiency. Cloud computing significantly improves a company's bottom line. With cloud computing virtualization, shared servers provide computers, computers, and other devices with data, resources, and software so users can buy or provision a resource when they need it. The consumer charges only for the amount of services used and reduces costs considerably. The service costs rise as consumption increases. For times when unexpected traffic is normal, cloud storage is often very helpful. Since the cloud infrastructure is activated by virtualization, many platforms use technologies such as Citrix Systems and Microsoft. A company can run its cloud services without having to manually maintain and pay for storage partitions, bandwidth, networks, hardware, and data centres. The cloud server provider does all the work. All the tools you need to manage the server are available through a user-friendly control panel. The scalability of application and infrastructure management is quick and easy.

A virtual cloud computing platform provides the mechanism to manage all cloud resources. Migrating from the desktop to the internet clouds enables access from anywhere with an internet connection. In addition, cloud computing virtualization provides the infrastructure for a virtual development platform, applications, data storage and hosting applications. Advantageous Aspects of this technology include: flexibility, reliability, reduced IT costs, easy access via a web browser, high scalability, provision of resources when required, easy maintenance, improved implementation, measured resource consumption. Cloud hosting resources are very high and are shared by a large number of customers.

Open source web server technology with a service-oriented architecture is becoming the choice for companies that rely heavily on e-commerce. Cloud computing solutions offer companies a variety of advantages. More and more companies of all sizes are using the cloud to contain IT infrastructure costs. Cloud hosting can be used for a variety of projects, and users can use the service easily and efficiently at an affordable price. This innovative technology is expected to increase demand in the coming years due to its immense business value.

Virtualization against cloud computing

Among all the big debates, there is one more that can be added to the ranks: "Virtualization or Cloud Computing". Where are you in this ongoing debate?

Virtualization is a process that essentially enables businesses to do more with fewer devices by using certain software on their servers. If for any reason you've ever divided your hard drive into different partitions, This is a form of virtualization. By creating the different partitions, virtual versions were created, hence the virtualization of your hard drive. There are essentially three main versions of virtualization: server, storage, and network.

Cloud computing is a growing phenomenon of the Internet. If you do something on the Internet, you will likely do some math in the cloud whether you know it or not from editing documents with Google documents, cropping and sharing images in Flicker to filing taxes in TaxAct. Everything is cloud computing. If you store information in a web-based program for later retrieval, use cloud computing. Another example of cloud computing is the payment for external data storage.

Which is best for your personal or business needs? I will not take this responsibility for you. It depends on you. This article will help you understand the differences between the two and teach you better. Consider the following when considering the best data storage option:

Access: Have or want; that's the question. Although cloud computing has its obvious advantages, accessibility is not always part of it. Sure, it would be great if you could pick up and go out for a makeshift week, knowing that you can access all the information you need without dropping one of the constantly juggling balls. Unfortunately, access can be a problem from time to time, especially with busy servers and crazy internet traffic. On the other hand, the site's servers take care of it from time to time, right?

Security: Today, especially given the fear of September 11th, security is a big problem for most people. Your data, regardless of whether it's stored behind firewalls or off-site in paid data stores, is always vulnerable to attack by hackers who want what you have. The question is, what security do you trust the most?

Reliability: As every mechanic will tell you, your vehicle is just as reliable as its service and maintenance. The same applies to electronics. If you want to keep your IT department in the cloud rather than in the clouds, keep in mind that maintenance is a key factor. Maintenance costs go hand in hand with maintenance. With cloud computing, you don't have to worry about the cost of maintaining your hardware.

Costs: Pay for virtualization for IT servers, devices and personnel. You pay a monthly fee with the correct storage size for cloud computing. Of course, the more storage space needed, the higher the monthly fee, but you don't have to bear the high cost of buying the equipment yourself.

So what will it be for you? Is it virtualized or calculated in the cloud?

Cloud computing options for business growth

Cloud computing distributes computer capacity over several computers, which can be located in different locations. Cloud computing networks enable high computing power, and technology enables processes to run on multiple computers. When there is a sudden need for resources, the excessive workload is spread across other computers. The result is that the response time is not affected, which ensures that the webserver is functioning normally. Fundamentally, cloud computing is remote computing, in which shared servers provide software, resources and data at the request of computers.

The use of a cloud provides the infrastructure for developing a virtual platform, applications, data storage, hosting applications, virtual development platforms and applications that can be created either externally or on-site if required. This typically involves providing dynamically scalable, virtualized resources over the Internet. Resources and applications are managed via the cloud server network. In addition, this technology enables resources to be provisioned and configured when needed, and users only pay for the amount of resources they use. Users access the cloud through a web browser using web-based tools or applications, such as a program installed locally on their own computer.

This platform supports highly scalable, redundant, automatic recovery programming. Workloads are deployed and scaled by deploying machines or virtual machines. The cloud computing infrastructure is made possible by virtualization. Users have access to a computer and an Internet connection anywhere. It is a profitable technology because the cloud shares the cost and resources of a large group of users. Maintaining cloud computing applications is quick and easy, and the resources used are measured.

Cloud computing describes a new model for the improvement, use and provision of internet-based IT services. It is quickly becoming the most efficient way for businesses of all sizes to host their websites. Not only is it an efficient, reliable, and easy-to-use technology, it is also an affordable virtualization hosting solution. Cloud technology is expected to be the most widely used para-virtualization technology of any company that creates, maintains, and soon hosts on a flexible, high-quality server.

For those who have difficulty understanding business technology requirements, using the terms virtualization and cloud computing can be daunting. Fortunately, phrases are just a technological way to discuss shared resources. The ideas for these two concepts are limited to a few elements. To understand the two, you need to look at them individually and then compare them to see the benefits.

Because of these principles, the computer world has closed the circle. The start of the computers was forged using huge server rooms in which central computers were stored. Individual users have a terminal on their desktop that gives them the necessary access. The programs and systems they accessed were managed by the engineers who served the mainframes. In addition to advanced systems, this is almost exactly the same process as it is currently.

Virtualization and cloud computing work together and complement each other. The first is the idea of hosting software and disk resources so that individual users can get them over the network. For example, in a company with a thousand employees, it may take a third to use a word processor every day. Instead of finding out which individual computer a word processor needs, the software is deployed through virtualization in a controlled environment, and the network administrator provides the desired access.

The advantage of this process is the cost advantages due to licensing schemes and upgrades. The technician can use the virtual server to manage access and thus remove unused licenses. You can also update a single instance of the software if necessary. You save time on each computer to ensure that the update has been installed for each user.

Virtualization and cloud computing are often separated in discussions so as not to become too complicated. Think of the Internet as an example to fully understand cloud computing. By distributing this software to millions of computers and using it when the computer is idle, you can get the most out of the wasted computing power. The idea that is brought into a protected and managed environment is comparable because the cost will depend on the amount of data storage and processing memory that you need.

If you were to indicate how much computing power your company is consuming, you would be surprised that the answer is very small. With internal systems, you have to plan the maximum demand. In accounting processes, this often occurs at the end or beginning of the month. For the remainder of the period, a large number of computers are inactive for several hours at night, on weekends, and during the day. With cloud computing, you can eliminate the price of an internal system and reduce the cost of what you use instead of buying.

The simple truth is that virtualization and cloud computing eliminate the cost of staff, equipment, and computer software. By using programs that allow you to control license requirements easily, you no longer need to send technicians with your existing hard drive to install the latest update. Your IT costs can be controlled through these types of methods. With cloud computing, your data, along with daily backups, are stored externally in a safe place, which also overcomes the challenge of business continuity.

Solution To The Network Problem

Since the advent of the wireless network, people have switched from wired to wireless. To this end, consumers want to buy a laptop instead of a desktop computer so that they can easily use the Internet anywhere. Laptops, iPhones, and cell phones are now integrated into the WIFI network technology, which makes things much easier for you. There are no general network troubleshooting issues when using a wireless network connection. Here are some tips to assist you run with ease with a wireless network. First, check that all cables are connected to the router. You need to make sure that the power cord is connected or not. Also, make sure that all operational indicators on the router are lit. Sometimes network connection problems occur because the network cable does not lead to the router properly.

You also need to check that your WiFi adapter is turned on and that your laptop's indicator is lit and shows whether or not you are connected. Some laptops are available in red or blue, while others need to be activated from the computer. You can check whether your WLAN adapter is activated or not by opening Device Manager. If you are using a PCMCIA or USB adapter, you can also configure your network by removing and reinserting it.

Some cordless phones also disconnect wireless connections during use. Therefore, always use a phone that is compatible with your wireless network. Sometimes restarting your router and PC can fix this problem. A simple reset eliminates any anomalies between network connections and is effective instead of getting support from the ISP or router manufacturer.

Sometimes this type of problem occurs when you have the wrong device driver installed in your wireless network adapter. It can cause all kinds of problems, or your adapter will not work well.

Some factors can cause signal strength and affect the performance of your network. Typically, any device that operates at the same frequency level (2.4 GHz) as 802.11b or 802.11g can interfere with your wireless network.

Make sure that cordless phones, microwaves, and other electrical devices are at least 1 m from the access point. Monitoring signal output through a diagnostic tool is often a good idea. This way, you can determine how strong your signals are at different locations and whether other electrical devices are interfering. Run the utility when using the microwave or cordless phone and check if you notice a difference. Your access point is usually supplied with its own monitoring utility.

A problem-solving computer network is one of the top job descriptions for network administrators, system administrators, network technicians, and IT consultants. Various types of problems can arise in a computer network, e.g., For example, virus and spyware infection, hacker attack, unauthorized user access, and problems with connection errors due to faulty devices or network configurations. Below is a list of basic network troubleshooting commands built into Windows and UNIX-based operating systems, etc. Correct use of these troubleshooting commands can make a huge contribution to diagnosing and solving problems with your computer network.

PIPE

Ping is the main troubleshooting command and checks connectivity to other computers. For example, the IP address of your system is 10.10.10.10, and the IP address of your network server is 10.10.10.1. You can check connectivity to the server using the ping command in the following format.

At the DOS prompt, type ping 10.10.10.1 and press Enter

If you get the response from the server, the connectivity is OK. If you get a "Request

Timeout" error, access to the server will be problematic.

IPCONFIG IPconfig is just another important Windows order. This displays the computer's IP address, as well as the DNS, DHCP, network gateway, and subnet mask names.

Type ipconfig at the DOS prompt, and press Enter to show the IP address of your device.

At the DOS prompt, type inconfig / all and press Enter to display the detailed information.

NSLOOKUP

NSLOOKUP is a command based on TCP / IP that checks domain name aliases, DNS entries, and operating system information by sending a query to Internet domain name servers. You can troubleshoot the DNS of your network server

HOSTNAME

The hostname command shows you the name of the computer.

At the DOS prompt, type hostname and press Enter.

NETSTAT

The NETSTAT utility displays the statistics of the protocols and TCP / IP connections that are currently being established on the computer.

NBTSTAT

NBTSTAT helps fix NETBIOS name resolution problems.

ARP

ARP displays the IP address translation table and changes it to physical ones that use ARP protocols.

Finger

The Finger command retrieves information about a user on a network.

TRACERT

The tracert command is used to determine the path of the remote system. This tool also specifies the number of hops and the IP address of each hop. For example, if you want to see how many hops (routers) are involved in accessing a URL and what the IP address of each hop is, use the following command.

You can see a list of all hops and their IP addresses on the prompt, like tracert www.yahoo.com

TRACEROUTE Traceroute is a very useful network debugging command used to locate the server which slows down Internet traffic and shows the path between the two systems

ROUTE

Manual entries in the routing table can be made using the route order. Hopefully, the commands above will help you diagnose your computer's network troubleshooting.

Installation Of The Microsoft Windows Os

In this chapter we will learn how to set up a simple network with different versions of Windows. This tutorial uses Windows 7 Home Premium and Windows XP Home Edition but works just as well on Vista. We will share one folder from Windows XP to the Windows 7 computer, but the other one will work excessively.

On the XP computer

Click Start and look for My Workplace. Right-click on My Computer and go to Properties. Click the Computer Name tab and find the change button next to "To rename this computer or join a workgroup, click Change." Push the button. In Workgroup, choose a name for your new network and click OK.

Next we want to share some files. The proper way to go about this is to run the network wizard. Find the folder you want to share, e.g. B. My Documents and right click. Go to the Sharing tab and look for Shared Networking and Security. Under Network and Security you will see the new network wizard. Click on it and follow the instructions. When you are finished, restart the system.

After the restart, locate the folder you want to share and right click. Go to the "Sharing" tab and you will see a box titled "Share this folder on the network". Check the box and give it a common name. If you want other users to change files in your folder, select the "Allow network users to change my files" check box. That's it for XP now on Windows 7.

On Windows 7 computers

Go to Start and right click the Computer button. Click properties. When the "View basic information about your computer" screen appears, click Change Settings in the lower right corner. Look for "To rename this computer, click Change" and click Change. Paste the network name you selected for the Windows XP computer into the workgroup and click OK.

Windows 7 now tries to find the network and then asks if the network is public, at home, or at work. If this is the home network, click Start and so on.

Now you can access the shared files. Go to Start and right click on the Computer button. Click on a map network drive. Find the shared folder on your XP computer and click Finish when you find it. The shared folder is displayed as a network drive and can be accessed from the computer.

The word here about firewalls. If you use the built-in Windows firewalls, you shouldn't have any problems as they open the necessary ports for computers to communicate. If you use a different firewall, disable it (not recommended unless you have a different firewall between the computers and your router) or open the required ports manually. And that's it.

To share files backwards, name your Windows 7 workgroup as in XP, and then right-click the folder you want to share. Click Share with and then go to specific people. The process of mapping the drive is exactly the same in XP.

Every version of Microsoft Windows is installed through similar steps on a device.Although the installation process involves steps, it can vary between versions of Windows. The following steps and general guidelines will help you install Windows on your computer.

Note

If you are replacing your computer's hard drive, you will need to reinstall Windows.

If you are replacing the motherboard on your computer, you may need to purchase and install a new licensed copy of Windows. Microsoft has designed the current versions of Windows to be linked to the computer's motherboard when

Windows is installed. If you change the motherboard it may no longer be valid for the existing license or product key.

Tip If you want to upgrade your computer to a newer Windows version, the steps on this page will help you upgrade. The Windows installation process should recognize whether an older version of Windows is already installed on your computer and ask if you want to update or perform a new installation. When upgrading, the latest Windows operating system files are installed over the old ones and your files are preserved.

All newer versions of Windows, including Windows 98 , Windows ME, Windows 2000 , Windows XP, Windows Vista, Windows 7 , Windows 8, and Windows 10 are subject to the following steps. Except for earlier versions (e.g. Windows 95) these steps work as long as you are using the disk version. The diskette version is identical, but further steps are needed.

Test hardware compatibility Test the hardware on the computer to make sure it is compliant with this edition of Windows before installing or updating Windows on your computer. Microsoft offers a list of Windows-compatible products to check whether your computer hardware is compatible with the version of Windows that you selected.

If you find that one or more hardware components on your computer are not compatible with the selected version of Windows, we recommend replacing this hardware with compatible hardware. If you have compatible hardware on your computer, you can ensure that the Windows installation or upgrade process is successful.

Original Windows CD, DVD or USB drive

First you need an original copy of the installation CD, DVD or USB drive of the Microsoft Windows operating system. The installation CD contains an original product key for Windows which is required to activate Windows after install. If you have an OEM computer, the key to the Windows product is often at the computer's back or side.

If you have an OEM (e.g. Acer, Dell , HP, etc.) computer, there is no original Windows CD, DVD, or USB drive on the unit. Alternatively, it will reinstall Windows and all of the applications using a secret partition or a collection of recovery disks. This page's steps still work but you need a Windows copy. If your friend installs the same version of Windows that comes in with the system and is using a key to the app, you can borrow a Windows hard disk from your buddy. Notice With the first versions of Windows, a copy of Windows can not be downloaded to run on a device. You'll need to buy a physical Windows edition. You can download the Windows 10 authoring tool to build a bootable disk or USB memory stick, if you update Windows 10.

Note

Microsoft's website is available for access to Windows 10 only. Any other site reporting copies of other versions of Windows should not be treated confidently. These Windows copies are pirated and can include everything that, including spyware or malware.Install or update Windows

To start the Windows installation or update process, you must configure your computer to start from a CD or DVD before you boot from the hard drive. By changing the startup process, the computer must search for the Windows installation CD before attempting to boot from the hard drive.

Open the CMOS settings.

Change the computer startup order. Set the CD, DVD, or floppy disk drive as the first bootable medium when trying to boot from a floppy disk. Or configure the first boot device on your USB drive if you are trying to boot from a USB storage device. If the drive does not appear, leave the CD inserted and restart the computer. If the hard drive is in the drive, the BIOS should recognize and list it.

Save the configuration change and exit the BIOS.

After changing the boot order, the Windows installation process can be started. Insert the Windows disk in the CD / DVD or USD back drive.

Switch the machine on or reset. When the machine begins, the installation CD, drive and a message like press any boot key on the CD should be recognized. On your keyboard press any key to start the computer from your Windows hard drive or drive.

After the Windows installation begins, you should respond to several prompts. Select Yes or the appropriate option to install Windows.

Install note

Make sure you select the Full Installation option, not the Repair or Update option.

Update note

To run a Windows hard drive or drive, press any key on the keyboard.

After you start installing Windows, you should reply to a few prompts. Select Yes or the appropriate windows installation option.

Install Note Make sure you choose the Full Installation option, not the Repair or Update option.

Update Note If you upgrade to a newer version of Windows, select the Upgrade option instead of the Full Installation option.

When prompted for which partition to install Windows, select the primary partition that is usually the C: drive or one labeled "Unallocated partition." To upgrade Windows, select the existing Windows installation on your hard drive.

You may be asked if you decide to delete all content from your hard drive and then install Windows. We recommend choosing this option as it also formats the hard drive to allow the installation of the

Windows Operating System

The computer may need to be restarted several times during the Windows installation process. Restarts are normal. When prompted to restart, choose Yes.

When the installation process is almost complete, the Windows configuration options screens appear. You will ask on these screens to pick the time zone in which you live, your chosen language, and the account name you are using for accessing Windows. Choose the correct options and enter the necessary configuration screen information.

The Windows installation process will complete when the computer prompts you to log in with the account you created on the setup screens, or when it loads directly into Windows.

Final Windows and computer configuration

After installing Windows on the computer, you need to install the drivers and related software for the hardware on the computer.You can use the hardware-powered installation CD or download the drivers from the website of your hardware manufacturers.

Tip

You can download the drivers to another computer if you can't download drivers because your network card doesn't work after installing Windows. Then copy it and move it to your computer on a USB stick.

Computer Driver Installation And Upgrade

It is highly recommended to install the latest drivers for any hardware.

To determine which hardware drivers are required for installation, check the device manager and look for the exclamation mark "!" in addition to hardware devices. The exclamation mark means that drivers are required for this device.

After installing the required hardware device drivers, install any software program on the computer that you want to use.

Download and install available Windows updates. Upgrading Windows can improve the performance of the operating system, computer hardware, and software programs used. You can also improve security by fixing potential security vulnerabilities and deficiencies in Windows.

Windows home networks

You have set up a home network and all your computers use the same internet connection. It's great, but now we share everything else. Modern versions of Windows come with an easy-to-set-up and use method for sharing files and printers.

You may have experience with school or office networks. A network can make a big difference in the home and save money on peripherals. For example, you no longer have to buy a printer for every PC in the house. Everyone can point this out. You can also share files and documents between computers. You no longer have to burn a file to a CD if you want to move it to other computers.

Prepare the network

To prepare to set up the rest of the network, I recommend that you select unique and meaningful names for each computer on the network and put them all in the same workgroup. With these simple steps, you can identify and find any computer on your network. Open the system in Control Panel. Go to the Team Name tab. Your computer's name and workgroup are listed below. Click the Change ... button to give it a new name. Give each computer a unique short name such as "up" or "den" and assign it to the same work group. The default Windows workgroup is HOME, which is fine. Type START in the Workgroup field and click OK. Repeat this process for all computers on your network.

Share printer

In general, the most useful and time-saving feature of a home network is the ability to share printers. This is easy to set up, but unfortunately some printers on a network simply don't work. I've seen some Dell printers and some Hewlett Packard printers that couldn't be released for some reason. Most printers like to share on a network.

The first step is to correctly install the printer on the "server" PC. This computer must be turned on for instructions to print from other computers on the network. To make sure a successful implementation, open the printing and fax section of the control panel after printing a test page. Right-click your shared printer and pick Link ... Option. Option. Offered. Only click on the box next to this printer and type a name for the printer. Click the Attach drivers button if you have computers that run previous Windows versions on your home network. Place reviews next to the versions you want to activate. You may need to install additional drivers from the CD that came with your printer, or the drivers may not be available for these earlier versions to use this printer. Click OK and the printer can be shared.

Now we need the other computers to use the shared printer. Access the computer on which you want to use the shared printer. Now we have to connect to the other computer. There are several ways to do this. The easiest way is to enter the name of the shared computer in Internet

Explorer. Open IE, type the computer name with two backslashes in the address bar and press Enter. For example, enter "den" or "upstairs". You can also search My Network Locations to find them. Open My Network Locations, and then click Show Workgroup Computers.Open the printer's machine with a double-click. A firewall could block your attempts if you see a message that you can't attach. Please deactivate firewalls from third parties and retry.

Click on the printer, right now, and select Connect. A warning is displayed. Click yes. At this point the drivers will be downloaded and installed. The printer is now installed on this PC. Close these windows and open the Printers and Faxes icon in the Control Panel. The printer should appear there. You can make it your default printer by right-clicking and selecting Set as default printer. Print a test page. Repeat this process for all computers on your network.

Data exchange

Sharing files can also be very helpful. Sometimes we need to be able to access a document from anywhere in the house. Sharing a large file as video over the network can save a lot of time and effort when burning to CD. Some programs can even be run from another computer over the network.

Sharing a file is as easy as right-clicking the drive or folder on the workstation you want to share and choosing Sharing and Security. You can even share your entire hard drive by right-clicking on your C drive. If this is your first folder shared or if you share a sensitive area, a warning will be displayed. Click if you want to continue. Please check the box next to Network Share folder. Choose an appropriate name. The next checkbox decides whether users can change the files in their shared folder. This must be checked if users should be able to save files in this folder or edit files already listed. If this check box is selected, anyone can delete the files in this folder. If you have an unsecured wireless network, anyone on the street can read your files. If this second check box is selected, delete all files. When you are on a wireless network, make sure you have strict security settings and do not shareyour most confidential files.

In order for other users to access these files, they must connect to the shared PC in the same way as described in the Printer section. Enter the name preceded by two backslashes, or navigate to My Network Places on the computer. The shared folder should appear with the name that was selected during sharing setup. To make this shared folder more accessible, you can create a shortcut to the folder or create a network drive. A shortcut can be easily created by right-clicking on the shared folder and selecting Create Shortcut.

Network drives

A network drive makes the shared folder available as if a hard drive were installed on the local computer. Right click on the folder shared and choose Map Network Drive. Choose a drive letter. The checkbox Reconnect at login makes this device permanent. Otherwise, the drive will disappear when the computer is restarted. Click Finish to complete the setup. You should now have a drive that can be accessed like any other, but that displays files from another computer.

How To Update A Microsoft Windows Computer

Long-term maintenance of Windows Microsoft frequently releases new updates for Windows. We therefore recommend that you check and install the available updates. This way Windows can work better and protect your computer.

Also check the manufacturers' websites regularly for updated hardware device drivers. If you keep the hardware drivers up to date, hardware devices on your computer can operate at maximum performance and improve compatibility with other hardware and software on your computer.

How to make a copy of the Windows software

Nowadays CDs and DVDs are used much less than before because there are much faster and smaller storage media with higher capacities (e.g.

USB sticks). However, many users do not have (or had) a Windows installation CD. Here you can use an ISO image file. To create a USB flash drive (or DVD) with a copy of Windows, select your version of Windows below and follow the instructions.

Note

While each of these copies of the Windows software is free, you need a valid product key to activate and use it.

Windows 10

Windows 7 and 8.1

Windows 10

Open your browser and go to the Windows 10 installation media page.

In the Create Windows 10 installation media section, click the Download tool now button. Button.

Once the tool has completed the download, run and install it.

On the next screen, click the circle next to Create installation media for another PC, and then click the Next button in Windows.

Button.

Make sure the check box next to Use the recommended options for this PC is selected, and then click the Next button in Windows. Button.

On the next screen, select a USB flash drive (A) and an ISO file (B), then click Next (C).

The screen where you choose where to download an ISO.

Note

We recommend the USB stick option as this is a better and faster storage medium. In addition, many new computers do not have a DVD-ROM drive.

Find your USB stick in File Explorer or choose a different download location.

Once your download is complete, you can use it to install the Windows 10 operating system.

Installing the operating system of Microsoft Windows.

Note

If you want to download the ISO file, you must burn it to a DVD before you can install Windows.

Windows 7 and 8.1

The steps for Windows 7 and 8.1 are almost identical. The only difference is that you will be asked to enter your product key.

Open your browser and go to the Windows 7 disk image page or the Windows 8.1 disk image page.

Windows 7 users must enter their product key and then click the Verify button in Windows. Button.

Otherwise, select your edition (A) on the main page, click Confirm (B), select your language (C) and then click Confirm (D).

Options to create an ISO in Windows 8.1.

On the next page, choose a 64- or 32-bit download.

Choose 64- or 32-bit keys.

How to determine if you have a 32-bit or 64-bit CPU.

Once your download is complete, you can make a copy of the USB storage drive or burn a DVD:

Put the ISO on a USB stick

After opening the ISO in the file explorer you can drag and drop the file onto a USB stick.

The ISO file is copied to a USB storage device.

Burn a copy to DVD

In File Explorer, open the ISO script.

Right-click on the ISO file and from the drop-down menu select Burn Disk image. Option to burn a Windows image.

In the window that appears, select your DVD burner drive and click the Burn button in Windows 10.

So I delete my hard drive and start again

Most computers have a system recovery disk or a hard disk recovery process to restore the computer to its original settings and software. Resetting or restoring a computer can help resolve computer software problems, including corrupt program files and virus infections. Below are instructions on how to restore the original software to your computer.

WARNING

Restoring your computer will erase all information on the hard drive and make it new. Once the following steps are done, you cannot recover lost data. Make a backup copy of the files that you do not want to lose before proceeding with the recovery process.

Tip

For information about erasing a hard drive on your computer and not restoring the original software, see: Formatting a hard drive, SSD, or USB flash drive.

This is how you ensure that all data on a computer's hard drive is deleted.

Why can't I restore my computer using a recovery disk?

Erase the hard drive and reinstall Windows

For instructions on how to clear your hard drive and reinstall Windows, click the link below.

Tips

When you have an OEM computer (e.g. Acer, ASUS, Dell, or HP), perharps you have a hidden partition to recover the system and you don't need a hard drive to restore the computer.

Windows 10

Windows 8

Windows 7, and vista

Windows XP, and the year 2000

MS-DOS 5.0 +, Windows 3.x, NT 4.0 / 9x/ ME

Windows 10 Anyway

Open the menu on Start.

Choose the option Settings (seems like a gear).

Select Update and Protection in Settings pane.In the left navigation area, select the Restore option.

In the "Reset this PC" section, click the Start button.

Select the Keep my files or Delete all option, depending on whether you want to keep your files or delete all and start over.

Follow the instructions to start the recovery process.

Windows will reset, either keeping your files intact or deleting everything depending on which option you choose.

How to update Operating System for Microsoft Windows.

Windows 8 Read more

To open the Charms app, press the Windows key, and the "C" key.

Select Search option and type reinstall (do not press Enter) in the Search text box.

Choose the option Settings.

Select Erase All on the left side of the screen and reinstall Windows.

Click Next on Reset PC computer.

On the "Would you like to clean the drive completely?" Remove my files easily to perform a fast removal, or "Clean drive completely" to delete all files.

Click Reset on the screen on Ready to Reset Your PC.

Remove the hard drive, and reinstall Windows 8.

Windows 7, and vista

To recover a computer from Windows 7 or Vista, you need a set of computer recovery media, or an original Windows 7 or Vista install media. If you don't have a recuperation media package, please contact the device manufacturer to order a new collection or recovery media.

Notice

Make sure the computer is configured to start from the CD-ROM drive before you execute the following steps. See: Whether or not to boot a device from a CD or DVD.

Insert the installation CD of Windows 7/Vista into the CD-ROM drive, and restart the computer.

Tap a key on the keyboard when the message "Press any key to start from the CD" appears.

Press Enter on the welcome screen for Windows Installation.

Click any key on your keyboard, when prompted.

Choose your preferred language and other settings on the Windows Install page, then click Next.

Accept the terms and conditions on the License Agreement tab, and click Next.

Select Custom on Install Style computer.

Select the Advanced (Drive) option.

Delete all partitions for Disk 0. Upon deletion of all partitions, a single entry called "Unallocated space" will appear.

Click Disk 0 and then pick Next.

The installation process for Windows begins with the creation of a new partition, the partition formatting and the installation of Windows on hard drive. Before installing Windows the formatting process must delete the hard drive.

Windows XP, and 2000

You need a package of device recovery media, or an initial Windows XP or 2000 installation media to restore a Windows XP or 2000 device. If you don't have a recuperation media package, please contact the device manufacturer to order a new collection or recovery media.

Notice

Make sure the computer is configured to start from the CD-ROM drive before you execute the following steps. See: How to boot at a computer from a CD or DVD.

Plug the installation CD of Windows XP/2000 into the CD-ROM drive, and restart the machine.

Tap a key on the keyboard when the message "Press any key to start from the CD" appears.

To accept the terms and conditions, press Enter on the Windows XP Setup Welcome screen, and then press F8.

To format and install Windows XP, follow the on-screen instructions to pick a hard drive partition.

After configuration of the hard drive which wipes all records, click one of the links below to show the steps to Windows XP or Windows 2000.

When to upgrade Microsoft Windows Operating System.

MS-DOS 5.0 +, 3.x, 95, ME, NT, and 3.0 are available for download. Plug the disk or boot disk into the machine and restart the machine for the DOS prompt to be accessed. You can need to boot the machine with CD-ROM support in some situations, or press a key to boot from the hard disk.

Ms-Dos Prompt Format C:/S

Notice

If the command "format c:/s" isn't working, you may need to download the format.com file to your startup disk.

The machine asks: "Sure you want to delete everything on drive c:"If you agree, press "Y" for "Yes" and press Enter.

The computer then begins the formatting process. Make sure that no errors are found while formatting the computer.

I have bad sectors, groupings or missing tasks.

When the formatting is successful, type "fdisk / mbr" at the MS-DOS command prompt and press Enter. After typing this command, you should return it to the MS-DOS prompt without a message. This move is not mandatory but it is recommended.

Do you have any additional fdisk / mbr information?

Restart the device while the boot disk is still inserted at the MS-DOS command prompt, below are some steps to reinstall Windows on the hard disk.

Install older versions of Windows and DOS after formatting the drive

Windows NT 4.0

Windows 98

Windows 95 CD

Windows 95 disk

Windows 3.x

MS-DOS

Windows NT 4.0

Windows NT can be installed in various ways. We recommend installing Windows NT using the following steps, as we consider these steps to be by far the best way to install Windows NT 4.0.

First, we recommend that all users who want to install Windows NT use the / b switch, which allows users to avoid creating floppy disks. However, we recommend that the user create the disaster recovery disks if they have not been created after installing Windows NT.

Finally, before installing Windows NT, we recommend that you work smarter, which will make Windows NT installation much faster.

Attach the computer with the CD.

Form X: (which often has D: where x is the CD-ROM drive).

Type cd and click Enter to the Windows 95 directory on the correct drive.

Enter the Win / b once in X: \ WINNT >

To complete the installation, follow the on-screen instructions.

98 Windows

Installing the operating system of Microsoft Windows.

CD-based Windows 95

Place the machine with the Dvd.

Form X: (where x is the drive for a CD-ROM, sometimes it is D:).

In the appropriate drive, type cd win95 and press Enter to access the Windows 95 directory.

To start the installation, enter X:\WIN95 > setup.

To complete the installation, follow the on-screen instructions.

If you have issues during the configuration process, you can add additional switches to the configuration line. You will find these switches on our Settings Changes list for Windows 95.

Secure disk drive Windows 95

Connect the machine with the first Windows 95 floppy.

To start the installation, enter A:\ > and press Enter.

To complete the installation, follow the on-screen instructions.

Internet Windows 3.x.

Attach in the machine the first Windows 3.x floppy.

To start the installation, type A: \> setup and press Enter.

To complete the installation, follow the on-screen instructions.

Ms-Dos Ms-Dos

Attach the computer with the first MS-DOS drive.

To complete the installation, enter A: \> setup and press Enter.

To complete the installation, follow the on-screen instructions.

How to install Windows on a Mac

One of the advantages of using a Mac is that you can run MacOS yourself or install Windows if you only need to run applications and games for Windows.

Did you know that you don't need a copy of Windows on your Mac to run Windows applications? Learn how to run Windows apps on a Mac without Windows.

What Mac can Windows run on?

Depending on the Windows version you 'd like to run. Windows 10 will still be able to operate on every new Mac. Yes, since late 2012, most Macs have supported this. The list of compatible devices on the Apple website is given below.MacBook was introduced in 2015 or later

MacBook Air was introduced in 2012 or later

MacBook Pro was introduced in 2012 or later

Mac mini was introduced in 2012 or later

iMac was introduced in 2012 or later

iMac Pro (all models)

Mac Pro was introduced in 2013 or later

Your Mac must also have at least 64 GB of free space when installing Windows on a Boot Camp partition. However, since Windows needs 128 GB, Apple suggests creating a 128 GB partition.

Boot Camp Against Virtualization

There are two main methods when you need to install Windows on your Mac. The option you choose generally depends on the type of software you need to run.

The first one provided by Apple with the Boot Camp Assistant installed on each Mac is called "Dual Boot" because you can start (or "boot") your Mac on Windows or MacOS.

Boot Camp Assistant can divide your Mac hard drive (or solid state hard drive) into two sections called "partitions". Leave macOS on one partition and install Windows on the second partition. Only click on the Alt key on your keyboard to select the operating system you want to run when starting your Mac.

If this method is used to install Windows on a Boot Camp partition, the Mac is successful as a basic Windows PC, with all Mac processor and graphics card capacity and memory (if any) being used only to run Windows.

This is the perfect way to play Windows games or to run high-end design tools and graphics with all the resources you have.

The only downside to Boot Camp is that all standard Windows Mac apps are no longer available. This means you have to shut down Windows and restart macOS if you want to use Mac applications such as Apple Mail and Photos.

Like the other "virtualization" method this can be useful. Instead of separating the hard drives for macOS and Windows, including ParalleLs Desktop or VMware Fusion, using a virtualization program to create a "virtual machine," Read the best VMS app for Mac for more options. It's running itself on macOS.

The virtual machine (VM) is basically like every other Desktop program that runs on the Desktop. The virtual interface therefore imitates the function of a PC so that Windows can be installed on a virtural computer and then Windows is installed.

You can use this option as well as any of your ordinary Mac apps on a Mac, so you don't have to double boot MacOS-Windows as you did again. This is definitely the most convenient option. But virtualization also has disadvantages. Running Windows in a virtual machine means that you are effectively running two operating systems at the same time. Therefore, you need a lot of processor power and memory to get adequate performance when running your Windows applications.

However, newer Macs still perform well when Windows is running in a virtual machine, and only 3D games and high-end graphics applications need the extra performance you can get through Dual Boot with Boot Camp.

How do I get Mac Windows?

You can download it from the Microsoft website, as "Pic Disk" and often as a "ISO File" file, if you are going to run Windows 10 on your Mac

ISO files for Windows 7 and 8.1 can also be downloaded. However, these Windows versions were sold on the hard disk originally. Unless you've still got the original hard drive, the ISO file on the hard drive with the installer would probably be quicker to build. It's pretty easy, and Apple treats this choice on its website as well.

You need to run Boot Camp or your virtualization program before you can install it after getting Windows installation files.

What to do with the boot camp?

The Boot Camp Assistant is an Apple program for installing Windows on your Mac. You can find the wizard in the Utility folder in the Applications main folder on your Mac. Before you run the wizard, however, there are a few things you need to do in Windows at Boot Camp.

Apple recommends that your Mac's internal hard drive (or solid-state drive) has at least 64 GB of free space to install Windows. 128 GB is actually recommended!

You may also need a memory card with at least 16 GB of storage space for the additional driver software that Windows needs to control components such as the monitor and camera on your Mac, as well as your Mac keyboard and mouse (which of course is the case) are different from conventional ones Windows mice and keyboards). However, some Macs can download these required drivers.

A paid copy of Windows and the license number are expected to be issued. New Mac models and Catalina Macs are only running on Windows 10, but older versions can be used on Windows 7 or Windows 8.1 as well. The website of Apple helps you to verify which versions of the Windows Mac will run.

The method is based on the Windows version used.

How To Run Windows On Mac From Boot Camp

Once you've completed these preparations, you can run the Boot Camp Assistant and install Windows on your Mac. You should do this.

Step 1: Open the Boot Camp Assistant.

If you run Boot Camp Assistant for the first time, you are prompted with a number of options. The first option is to choose the ISO image you want to use. Click the Select button and navigate to the button that you created or downloaded. This will copy your Windows ISO file to the USB storage so you can install Windows.

Step 2: Download the driver software

The next Boot Camp assistant may tell you that the driver software for Windows will also be downloaded to the USB storage device. However, only drivers for Windows 8.1 and Windows 10 are downloaded. If you want to install Windows 7, which is still used by millions of people around the world, you'll need to go back to the Apple Compatibility Chart website to find drivers, follow the instructions you need for your Mac, and follow the instructions to copy the drivers to your USB memory stick.

Step 3: partition your hard drive

To allocate space for Windows, Boot Camp needs to split your Mac's hard drive into two separate sections called "partitions". This is can be seen below the panel with the normal MacOS on the left and the suggested Windows on the right.

By default, the Boot Camp Assistant offers to create a small Windows partition with a size of only 40 GB. However, you can use the slider (the point between the partitions) to adjust the size of the two partitions as needed.

When your Mac has more than one internal hard drive or SSD, one of these hard drives can only be assigned to Windows.

However, Boot Camp does not work well with external drives that are connected via USB or Thunderbolt. It is therefore best to use your normal internal drive if possible. When you are connecting the external drive to a Mac to back up Time Machine, delete it, because it may be somewhat confusing to Boot Camp when an external drive is detected while installing.

When you are finished, you can start the process by clicking the Install button at the bottom.

Phase 5: Windows update

If your Mac drive is partitioned, Boot Camp shuts your Mac down and starts a Windows USB Storage installer. The directions to install Windows can be followed simply. When Windows starts, additional Boot Camp drivers from the memory card are also needed to be enabled.

Step 6: run Windows

Once that's done, you can simply "dual boot" between MacOS and Windows by pressing Alt (also known as an option) on your keyboard when you turn on Mac. When the Mac starts up, both partitions with MacOS and Windows are displayed on the screen. You can select the desired operating system.

How To Run A Virtual Machine Windows

Virtualization systems such as Parallels Desktop and VMware Fusion provide a good and scalable alternative to the dual-boot solution of the Boot Camp.Instead of dividing your Mac's hard drive into separate partitions and then installing Windows on the Boot Camp partition, these programs create a "virtual machine" or VM, which is just an application that runs on the Mac and as a PC.

You can then install Windows along with all of the Windows applications and software that you need to run on the VM. The VM can run with other Mac applications such as Safari or Apple Mail, so you don't have to switch between the two operating systems because Boot Camp requires it.

These programs are not free, so you'll need to purchase a copy of your preferred program and provide your own copy of Windows (although both Parallels and VMware offer trial versions that you can refer to to determine which ones are concerned) . They prefer).

There is also a free virtualization program called VirtualBox, but it is quite complex and difficult to use. Therefore, we first focus on using Parallels and VMware to install Windows. Proceed to the VirtualBox section when you feel ready for the challenge.

For more information on the best virtual machine software for Mac, click here.

Run Windows on a Mac with Parallels

Parallels Software (version 15) costs £69.99 /$79.99 and is more vibrant than VMware Fusion graphical design but the two programs are of the same basic method. You may use a disk installation or an ISO file to build a new VM on your Mac.

The current Windows PC can also be linked to your Mac, and a Mac VM that is a precise copy of your PC including Windows and any Windows applications needed can also be developed. You can build a virtual machine to double your Boot Camp partition if you are already using Boot Camp. This is a convenient choice for quickly reviewing some files and/or running programs without having to shut down both Mac and Server. Launching Windows.

You may use both programs to change a variety of essential settings after you have determined how to mount Windows.

Use VMware Fusion to run Windows on Mac

VMware is a little bit more complicated because a window with many settings appears to new users a little bit daunting. Parallels makes it simple for beginners to provide many predetermined choices, such as Microsoft Office or high performance 3D games or design tools.

VMware costs £70.96 / $79.99 but if you upgrade from previous launches, there are discounts.

Execute Windows to VM: Hardware

You can change the hardware settings of your virtual machines as required with both VMware Fusion and Parallels, as if you were choosing a real Mac or PC for your actual hardware.

You may also install more core devices on your VM to optimize performance in your Mac with a multi-core processor (for example iMac Pro with up to 18 processor cores). Additional memory and space may also be allocated, and the VM video memory used on games and other graphical applications may also be extended.

Parallels and VMware have certain options, for example, for connecting external devices like a hard disk or bluetooth speakers to your Windows VM. You can also find out how your VM communicates with macOS on your Mac, by sharing certain directories and files that you need for work or sharing music or images libraries.Run

Windows On Vm: Software

An important aspect when running your VM on your Mac is the way it runs on the Mac desktop.

By default, both Parallels and VMware operate their virtual machines in one window, giving you a kind of "Windows window" in which the Windows desktop is displayed in a seaparate window above the Mac desktop. It is also possible to extend the Windows desktop to fill the entire screen, making your Mac look like a normal PC (while you can use Command key to switch to Mac applications).

However, a better option for many people is the ability to hide the Windows desktop completely, so that individual Windows applications, like normal Mac applications, appear on the Mac desktop alone.

The number of options available here can be a bit daunting, but the best thing about virtualization technology is that you can't really damage a VM. You can save various versions of your VM just as you can save different versions of a document in Microsoft Word. This way, you can experiment with different settings to determine which options are best for you, and then revert to an earlier version of the VM at any time.

How To Run Windows On Mac For Free

Here is an alternative way to run Windows on your Mac: Use Oracle VirtualBox to run Windows as a virtual machine. This section is from Nik Rawlinson.

Download the latest issue.

Find the downloaded image on your Mac, mount it, and double-click the VirtualBox.pkg file to install the application.

After the installation is complete, start VirtualBox in your application folder.

Download your Windows 10 Copy as described above so that you can reach it via the VirtualBox installer in a convenient location.

You can pick the operating system to update from the upgrade version menu by clicking on the New button in the VirtualBox toolbar. Give the name of your new virtual machine, in this case Windows 10.

Select Continue. Click on start.

Set up enough resources: when Windows runs, it is like a machine that is running macOS and is isolated from the rest of your Mac. To do this, you must 'move' resources from your Mac that your Mac cannot access during service of the virtual machine. Memory is the most significant. The more memory you add to the Disk, the faster it is running.

Creating a virtual hard drive: when you install a virtual machine, you save it in a box that you use on your Mac as a virtual hard drive not just the operating structure but also its programs and files.This is handy because it means that your Windows and MacOS assets won't get confused, but it also means that much of your hard drive is out of MacOS range.

If you click Next, you will be asked what type of unit you want to create. Stay with VDI (VirtualBox Disk Image) unless you use this Windows installation with another virtualization application like Parallels Desktop.

The VirtualBox can delete or use the memory immediately if needed, by increasing the Windows drive's size over time when your files are growing and the area of installed applications are expanding.

Choosing the latter is a good idea. So, if you don't have a particular reason to instantly waive the entire number, leave Dynamic's save option and click Next.

Windows Install: Your new virtual machine has now been created. You only need to install Windows on it now. VirtualBox new gives you an overview of the structure of your virtual machine and allows you to move from one tab to another if you configure multiple virtual environments.

To start the installation process on Windows, click Start.

Finally, your installation file has to be found. On the slot on the back of our Mac Mini we saved our download installer on the SD card. You need VirtualBox to tell the location where it is and then, when you click Start, you click on the folder icon of the map and choose an ISO file. By clicking on Open, you will go back to the setup screen by clicking Start to open the image of your disc and use it as the setup media.

If the language is selected, the installer will know whether you update or select a custom installation from an older version. Select Custom while configuring a completely new virtual machine, and then on the next screen make sure that drive 0 is selected as the installation drive (this should be the only option).

The virtual machine restarts a few times during installation before you are prompted to configure your settings. You can choose Quick Setup that accepts all of Microsoft's default settings, including using Bing as a search engine, automatically installing updates if available, and sending your browsing history to Microsoft.

If you do not want this, click the Customize button and change the settings manually. Next, you need to tell Windows if the computer is yours or your company's. You know the right answer here, but the second choice is probably the most appropriate if you're a private or small business owner.

Click Next and enter the details to sign in to your Microsoft account. If you do not already have an account with Microsoft, click Create One.

You will be asked in the last two steps whether you want a PIN to replace a password, and whether you want to save your files on OneDrive or the local virtual machine. When you have decided what to do, Windows will restart the desktop one last time before it appears.

May I have macOS running on a Windows PC?

What about the opposite scenario? Is macOS capable of running on a PC?

To put it another way: no. One such irony is that while Microsoft is known for its violent business practices, Apple is responsible for that particular dead end. Though you can run Windows on any X86 device, Apple only provides Mac devices with its own macOS program.

The logic is clearly commendable: macOS is designed to run on Apple's own hardware, and performance on any old machine will not be as good as that. This is one of the reasons you'll never run a Mac with low performance.

But you can also say that Apple is building hardware software to sell. MacOS Excellence is a perfect feature when it comes to Mac sales and you don't want to share it. So, you need to run

Windows on your Mac if you want to experience the best of both worlds.

How to configure and install a Desktop printerA computer printer will only work if you have installed the supplied drivers and software. If you have lost your printer's CD, you can download the drivers for your printer and install them using the drivers. On our printer driver page you will find a list of printer manufacturers and links to the associated driver pages.

Connect the printer to the computer

Usb

Attach the printer with a USB cable, a parallel cable or SCSI cable to the device, and then plug in an electric outlet. The USB cable close to the example picture is used by most home computer printers today.tip

If it is a network printer, connect it to a wireless network or to the RJ-45 connection.

Note

A laptop works just like a desktop computer and, if available, can use one of the connections mentioned above.

Note

Smartphone and tablet users have a printer that can wirelessly or via the Internet connect to devices for printing.

Install and configure the printer

The program that the Windows or the operating system instals a printer must be used with any printer.

Once everything is linked, switch on your computer.

Insert the printer CD. Insert the CD. Open My Machine, double-click on a CD drive, and then press the update or setup file when the CD is not running automatically. Run the downloaded installation file once you have downloaded the drivers. Follow the installation wizard and your software will be installed when finished.

Test the printer to make sure it works.

Computer without a CD drive

You can download the program for your printer from the printer driver page of your computer if your drive is missing or the CD is lost. You can run the driver installation file once you download the drivers

My operating system has no drivers available

No older printers can be compatible with newer operating systems. For starters, a printer made years before Windows 10 is published can not support it. If the drivers are not specified on a printer's driver tab, this printer is not compatible with your operating system or Windows version. Install an older version of the drivers for the operating system and it might work. However, you should purchase a new printer for full support.

Install a printer with drivers only

You can install the printer driver by following the steps below if you want to install only the printer and no other software software programs.

Tip

A list of printer drivers and software can be found on our printer driver page.

Note

If you installed the printer according to the steps above, these steps should only be necessary if errors occur.

Open the Control Panel while the printer is connected and turned on.

In Control Panel, double-click the Printer or Printer and Fax icon.

In the Printers window, click the Add Printer icon.

After completing the above steps, read the Windows Printer Assistant. Click Next to start the wizard.

The next choice is to mount a local printer or network printer. If the printer connects to your computer directly, pick the Local Printer connected to the computer and click Next.When asked for the location of the printer driver, find the directory for your drivers or point to the printer CD.

Test the printer

You can print a self-test page in Windows after installing the printer to verify the printer is working.

Benutzers of Microsoft Windows

The control panel is opened.

Double-click the symbol Apps and Printers, or Printers and Faxes.

Right-click the printer to check and then press Properties. If you don't see your printer you won't get your printer installed.

Click the Print Test Page button inside the Printer Properties window.

When the printer is able to print a test file, it must mount and configure the printer correctly. If you can't print in other applications, however, there may be issues with the software you are trying to print from.Understanding Network Cabling Basics

If you are in a room with tech-savvy people, it is normal for the few of us around the world to remain illiterate. Computer illiterates nod wisely and follow the statements. "Oh, your connection cable is not working properly? I hate it when mine do it, especially the purple one. Thankfully, the following articles give you an summary of network cabling and standardized cable networks. It still may sound a bit like a nerdy party fool, but at least you can get the basics of the chat.What exactly is network cabling? Basically, your computers can communicate with each other, with the Internet, the printer and other devices. Cables are one way to send information. And a network generally includes everything that wants to be connected and exchange information. There are different types of network cables, and most systems offer a variety to meet all of your needs. Each structured cabling system has its own design due to the architecture it has to work with, the products used, the support of the products, the precise provision of the system and the manufacturer's guarantees.

A structured cabling system consists of many different smaller systems that work together for one main purpose. Most data devices are stored in a telecommunications room. The point at which the building is connected to the outside world is classified as an entrance area. At this point, the cabling must be changed frequently from inside to outside, whereby fire-resistant cables must be considered depending on the building regulations. The equipment rooms house the rest of the necessary equipment and serve the users in the office or building. There will be backbone cabling that will connect signals to other areas of a building. Master cables handle all main traffic and can also be laid between buildings. In the telecommunications room, horizontal wiring is connected to every socket on the floor. The last subsystem is the work area components, which allow people to connect their machines and devices to the sockets of the horizontal cabling system.

Many different types of cables are used within these subsystems. The most common is a combination of twisted pair cables, coaxial cables, fiber optic cables and Ethernet crossover cables. These few hardly scratch the surface of everything there is to choose from. However, the systems use a combination of these. Ethernet crossover cables may sound more familiar, since Ethernet was the only way to connect a computer to a network before the wireless connection spread. Crossover cables allow computers to connect using their network adapters, eliminating the need for network routers and switches.

The American National Standards Institute provides standards for US cabling companies. USA Follow and maintain. They define what the cable layer should look like, where it should be connected, where the layer should be located, etc. These standards help to ensure consistency between so many different network cabling providers and to maintain user-friendly, industry-wide documentation. Understand.

Networking in the sense of Dictionary.com is an association of people who have a common interest and were founded to provide mutual support, useful information or the like. Networking can be an important social and life skill that catapults you to success in any traditional or private business.

If this is the case and we continue to see Top Earner after Top Earner has used this technique, why are so many others neglecting this powerful tool? I think part of it is due to the fact that most people don't feel like they have what it takes to network like big dogs.

Before I continue, I want to make something clear to everyone. YOU already know how to connect and have done it all your life. You just never figured out how to refine the process.

Still, I'm not going to point out a few simple steps, the simple steps most big winners don't tell about networking.

These steps are simple and duplicable.

Step 1 - get out of there

Make yourself accessible to others. I know that we all work on our website and we want our social media websites to look perfect. But remember that those who know you personally are the most beneficial for you. This is because those you know know you personally and can name a face.

It's easy to get out of there. Attend a party, attend a business event or training seminar, and join an organization.

It is no longer enough to meet new people and take part in social events.

Step 2: get ready

This means that you should investigate which events are beneficial to you. Research the organizations or people who will be there. When you know what to expect and are informed about potential contacts, stand out from the others. When you're prepared, you can focus more on people. This is the key to a powerful network!

STEP 3 - Be Confident

When you network, you have to be confident. Get close to people and introduce yourself. Don't wait until they get close to you. Don't spend too much time with people you already know and leave your comfort zone. If you push your limits, make sure you keep meeting new people and adding them to your network.

STEP 4 - Don't sell, connect!

Please don't make the mistake of selling people when you first meet them! This makes you appear opportunistic at best, or aggressive and interested at worst. In both cases the wrong signals are sent.

Trying to close the deal also gives you more time to focus on your new connection. Now I'm saying this because you're considered the best person to talk to and people remember you more when you ask them questions and let them talk about themselves. People are selfish by nature and will take every opportunity to let people know what they are about and what they like to do. Use this to your advantage and collect as much information as it is willing to give you. Then you can solve their problems and support their passions. You will be your new best friend and you will sing your praises.

STEP 5 - Specify value

Always be ready to give 10-20 times more than you get. If you let them know that you are the reference boy / girl and have skills and knowledge that others can benefit from, they are more willing to come to you for advice and suggestions and to tell your friends about you .

Check these 5 simple steps frequently to create a powerful network that adds value not only to your life but also to your business.

Remember that the network aspect of the network is a long-term obligation to know more about yourself and others and what you can do together, what you can't (or can't) do on your own. A healthy and active network is a great resource that is available at a low personal cost. It can help you achieve a number of goals that would otherwise be too difficult or unreachable. Networks can play a key role in connecting you with a wider range of people who can help you achieve more, whatever "more" is for you.

Networking is an essential skill for many people today. And in American companies, you can make or break your career. Developing good skills with people is not always easy. In some cases, it may be necessary to adapt your behavior to the circumstances. Most importantly, if you neglect this ability, it's like operating a machine without proper maintenance; finally breaks.

Studies show that many people use informal networks to make progress. Others say that networks are just another word for "how to play the game". In my opinion, networking dominates the art of people's good skills. It is a clear illustration of his personal character. Many executives say they prefer to speak to employees in a less formal social environment. Because it allows them to see the real person.

Successful professionals have good networking skills. Part of networking is knowing what's important. To be more precise, it is to know who the important people are. These skills are relevant in marriage, in social groups, at work or just in everyday everyday situations.

A leader's interpersonal skills can determine whether people are willing to follow him or her. Communication style can make a difference in the world. What you say or don't say can affect employee morale. In today's workplace, non-verbal messages can also affect the bottom line.

Speaking of impact: Networking has always been a source of wealth and power. Joseph of Egypt (Old Testament) used his networking skills to explain Pharaoh's vision. As a result, the wealth of ancient Egypt increased. Machiavelli used networking to master the art of mixing war and management. This way he could stay in power for many years. Networking has become an everyday part of today's business environment.

In terms of networking and personal character, I want to leave you an important metaphor. It is the illustration of "Foxes and Lions". In the natural sense, lions are considered strong and powerful. You are bravely moving through the jungle. Lions often remind me of autocratic leaders who use their power to get what they want. They only act sensibly when they are in the midst of a very powerful leader (who beats them).

On the other hand, foxes trust their "wisdom". They survive because they are aware of the danger. They are small, but otherwise prevail. Foxes move carefully through the forest. They remind me of smart leaders who coexist among people (regardless of rank). These leaders have respect for powerful leaders. At the same time, they show respect for caretakers and cleaning staff.

To build an effective network, you have to "see" the big picture. Networking begins inside: that's how a person thinks. A positive self-image begins with you. This affects how you interact with others. Respect everyone regardless of status. Help others when you can. Be resourceful, share your knowledge. This will make it a win for many people.

Your generosity is worth its weight in gold. You also never know how help can help you. As my grandfather used to say, "What comes is turning."

It is important that managers understand the benefit of a strong network and good skills with people. However, it is so important that they do not abuse their power. The best leaders always try to create a positive culture. In addition, they maintain the respect and self-esteem of others.

The secret of networks is to help other people. Think of the metaphor of power against wisdom: it is better to be a fox than a lion.

Network basics

1. The Internet Protocol (IP) is the main communication protocol in the set of Internet protocols for transmitting datagrams across network boundaries. Its routing function enables network connection and essentially establishes the Internet.
2. TCP is one of the primary TCP / IP network protocols. Whereas the IP protocol handles only packets, TCP allows two hosts to communicate and to share data streams. TCP guarantees data transmission and also ensures packets are delivered in the same order they were sent in.

3. UDP (User Datagram Protocol) is a communication protocol that provides a limited amount of service when messages are exchanged between computers on a network that uses the Internet Protocol (IP). UDP is an alternative to the Transmission Control Protocol (TCP) and is sometimes referred to as UDP / IP together with IP.
4. OSI (Open Systems Interconnection) is a reference model for the communication of applications over a network.The OSI reference model assists providers and developers in the development of the software programs produced and digital communication products and allows direct comparisons of communications resources possible.

The main concept of OSI is that the communication process between two endpoints in a telecommunications network can be divided into seven different groups of related functions or layers.

Every user or program that communicates is on a computer that can provide these seven levels of functionality. In a particular message between users, a flow of data flows through the layers on the source computer (according to OSI), through the network, and then through the layers on the receiving computer (layers will soon be shared).

Please note: This model is used by all providers to manufacture network devices that must meet the same standard. This is important because the devices should work together. If someone (provider) uses its own standard, there is a possibility that the device is not compatible/interoperable with other devices in the network. The user/client will not prefer the device because he does not want to be dependent on a product. Nobody likes monopoly. The current device that works together and is compatible with other products is considered the BEST.

Network Basics: Stateless Firewall

These firewalls use stateless packet filtering techniques. They do not maintain a status for the packets, as is the case in the stateful firewall. They have a set of rules and compare packets against these rule sets to filter packets.

The match rule decides whether a package is allowed or not.

Stateless firewall advantage: it uses less memory since the status of the packets does not have to be maintained.

Disadvantages of the stateless firewall:

1. The CPU utilization is high because you have to search the entire rule set for each package.

2. The control parameters are corrected after input into the device, which is ineffective in some cases.

Example: For clients behind a firewall to be able to receive responses from DNS servers on the Internet, for example, the firewall must accept incoming UDP packets. However, the port number on the clients can be dynamically assigned from 1024 to 64 KB. The stateless firewall cannot accept this dynamic information. To activate an important UDP-based service, a stateless firewall enables UDP packets for all ports between 1024 and 64 KB.

This opens security gaps. For example, an attacker could configure a UDP daemon on a compromised host with a port between 1024 and 64 KB, e.g. B. 5000. The attacker can connect to this host via port 5000 to control it remotely, even if a stateless firewall protects this host.

The basic guideline for designing firewall rules is to reject everything except explicitly allow what we need. However, the stateless firewall has to open its door further because it cannot process dynamic ports. This error significantly reduces the security protection of the firewall.

I have heard before that the difference between "successful" and unsuccessful people is that the "unsuccessful" person does not do what the successful person did or will do. How can we turn it into basic network concepts? Why do I apply and what is the purpose of the networks?

In today's economy, we are all looking for unique ways to reach and touch new people. I like to call it effective networks. With networking, the time it takes to build relationships affects your future. What is the alternative? Advertising!

Unfortunately, advertising costs have skyrocketed and I can understand why. Many advertising media such as newspapers, postcards, Value-Pak e-mails, etc. have problems between the economy and the Internet because people who would normally advertise have cut their budgets. The advertising dollar is usually the first place to cut back in tough times, and I actually think advertisers have raised prices for those who continue to advertise to stay the same because less and less money is spent. However, I consider advertising to be very passive, hoping against hope that someone can see your ad and need what it has to offer.

I know the advertisers looking for advertisers who call me seem desperate. They tell you that there is an audience of "x number of thousands". Sounds great

Now be honest, when did you last pour over a newspaper or postcoupons and then act? You should cut out the coupon and never call or avoid using it. EX: of 150,000 mailed, how many have children? (Certainly there are some industries that do not have much with advertising but not many). And how many of these families will have a child involved in Marshall Arts? How many people are involved in a plan already? And how long will ONE child be interested in the recoupment of the money spent on the single ad if you enrolled your mailing? Eighteen months?

We all know that the best thing we have to sell is the slice of bread! So who wouldn't save money, earn a free donation, or come to the event you are promoting? The frustrating reality is, because it is YOUR universe, not theirs, that you think this. In fact, I think that it is a very small number that even looks at the offers, typically less than 1%. It is also important to make a commitment of at least seven times, before you can get a return of 1 percent, to complicate it even more. Please pay the promotional costs 7 times. This is a huge money to get 2 or even 3 clients, and most people spend the dollars once, twice and again and have no answer and they just quit. They don't get a response. A publicity agency is the only winner. Statistics tell us that if you stayed on, somebody would jump on board at the end, but you would end up with the cost.

MPLS and VPLS Networks Basics You would probably have used the words MPLS and VPLS networks if you've searched out Internet service providers. MPLS stands for the swapping of multiprotocol labels while the VPLS stands for the network access of the virtual private local area. In short, it is your preference to turn multi-protocol label if you want anything to boost your business data transfer. You may choose to have a virtual private, local network area service if you just want to boost connectivity and speed for data transmission in your home.

One of the characteristics of MPLS is that it uses a much shorter pathway marker for transferring data and communication. Long addresses for networks are rarely available. In fact, this system is the framework on which different access technologies are based. Some of the technologies you are familiar with, including DSL, might also be access technologies.

The advantages of MPLS are many, but most of them will optimize the benefits that corporations are able to achieve. Every second counts for many companies and every second they can save helps to boost their profit margin. The swapping of multi-protocol labels is at least time-saving. It enables the owners to circumvent routing tables and scale their own networks effectively.

Also, the switching of multiprotocol labels is flexible. Business owners can allocate their customers different levels of traffic. More importantly, it is also highly secure and can work at various layers.

Basically , there are three methods for swapping multi-protocol names. The first is a point-to - point device Layer 2. Secondly, an Internet Protocol (IP) VPN will be used for Layer 3. The last option to discuss here, however, is virtual private local local network service. This is also the second option.

Lastly, Layer 2 functions. The Ethernet is also used as a network. You are crucially aware that VPLS is just one part or service provided by the interruption of multiprotocol labeling.

If multi-label switching has an IP backbone, VPLS is using the backbone multi-protocol name. If you only have less than 100 websites to operate, your needs can be served more than by virtual private local area network service. Of course, management would also be simpler. At the other hand, flipping multi-protocol labels will prove to be the right option for you to handle over one hundred or even more than a thousand sites.

Multi-protocol label swapping is therefore the best choice in terms of width and length all alone. But if you need to weigh your budget and just want a safer way to access data in your house, the more realistic alternative is the virtual private local network service. The MPLS and VPLS networks have certain parallels, but they have a major impact on pricing due to the few variations.

When you want to start a career in networking data, most people need some basic training to understand the basics. If you do not take this course as part or equivalent of a university degree course, you will need to find the means to lay the foundation. Most IT consulting technology companies will provide training courses for beginners for networking.

It is important to address the reason of registering or embarking on an online training course or instructor-led training course. Many people can easily pursue online education and find a training system that suits their educational style online. Others prefer listening to an teacher and answering questions on their own. Naturally, online or classroom theory lessons are never enough if you want to learn the data networking skills needed. There must be a practical aspect to the class and I think this is better served by an instructor-led, high-quality course with real-world classroom equipment. Some training companies compromise that equipment is available in central locations via a terminal server and that students just need to log in and can configure remote networking equipment. This works well, particularly for those students who have worked before or at least saw the equipment with the equipment. Unfortunately the networking of data does not just involve the configuration of networking equipment such as the router, the switches and the server. A high quality teacher with practical expertise in network equipment and cables is the remedy for the purpose of access to a network of warts and all. I always considered and still think of Cisco CCNA courses as an excellent basis, but some people do not always want a particular course for the seller with the choice at its end to be certified, subject of course to adequate examinations.

How about content, what about content? Okay, any beginner introduction to network training should give the student a strong foundation in core TCP / IP protocols with realistic presentations that should require the use of some kind of network analyzer. Theoretical explanations will help the students. To grasp the idea of layered networking, the TCP/IP and OSI networking models should be clarified. Popular protocols, interfaces and standard media of the LAN (Local Area Network) and WAN (Wide Area Network) should be covered and used in practical classroom exercises.

In order to enable the studants to understand the building blocks of the networks, the start of a networking training course will encourage them to grow gradually a classroom network and attach physical devices and connections as the courses progress. The classroom will use routers, Ethernet switches, hubs and servers, to make students feel fully networked.

The routers, layer 2 switches and layer 3 switches are still present on all modern networks as the core building blocks of a network with various peripherals, such as working stations, servers and firewalls. More specialized training will be offered on other network peripherals, such as VoIP telephones, IP PBXs and wireless connections.

A strong 50% of any basic information networking course is reserved for practical activities aimed at improving knowledge acquired from theoretical lectures. The course length will depend on the level of knowledge and experience you want to learn from this initial exposure to data networking. In the UK most courses offered by popular trainers are usually 2-5 days long and I would probably recommend 4-5 days because the lesson might not be enough time for the good. I personally will also be looking for a training course in which the provider provides appropriate help either via e-mail or telephone.

How can I set up a working group or small home network?

One of the benefits of your home or small business networking computers is that multiple computers can all access similar files , directories and printers. The owner of a computer create files in two step, directories or a linked printer accessible for those on the network (a mechanism called "sharing"). This multiuser capability has been introduced.

Others access files, folders, or disks on the network.

To facilitate this multi-user access, we recommend that you first set up a workgroup and make all computers that share or access shared resources a member of the workgroup.

What is a working group?

A workgroup can be described as a group of computers that are connected to each other via a network. This grouping is done within the Microsoft® Windows® operating system, where the members of the workgroup assume the same workgroup name (although each computer in a workgroup must have a unique computer name). Computers in a work group communicate directly with each other and not

Requires a server to manage network resources.

A workgroup can be created for use in a small office or home network, making it easier for different computers to share files, printers, and other network resources.

Once a workgroup has been created, it will appear under My Network Locations (available on the desktop in Windows). The ability to view an entire workgroup simplifies viewing and access to shared resources.

Note that while a workgroup is a group of computers that are connected to a network, they are not the same as a network. You could connect a computer to your network without being a member of a specific work group. The same computer can also share its resources and access the shared resources of the computers in the other workgroup. However, the computer is in a separate work group (see "My network locations"). To make it easier to see computers on the network, it's easier to assign them to a single workgroup.

Set up a work group

It's easier to set up a workgroup while you're setting up your network. When you set up a network with Microsoft Broadband Networking products, the process is particularly easy. The Microsoft Broadband Networking Configuration Wizard has screens that guide you through the process of setting up and joining a workgroup.

Tips for deployment

Here are several other issues to be taken into consideration when setting up the working group:

If you are running the Windows XP or Windows 2000 operating system, you must have administrator rights on your computer before you can set up or join a workgroup. For more information, see Windows Help.

If you previously set up a workgroup when installing a computer on your network, you can now set up new network devices from that computer with a network setup diskette. In this case the workgroup name will appear in any new network configuration on the Workgroup Names tab. If not, then write down. If you are configuring a wireless network with Microsoft broadband network products and there is no workgroup name, the configuration wizard displays the name of your wireless network as the name of your workgroup (the set ID) of services or SSID). Although the workgroup and the network are not the same, they can use the same name for simplicity. You can also write another name. When adding other computers to the workgroup, make sure that everyone uses the same workgroup name.

If you previously named your computer and workgroup in a previous file and printer sharing setup in Windows, these computer and workgroup names should appear on the appropriate pages of the configuration wizard. You can keep these names or enter new ones. Make sure that all other computers in your workgroup have unique computer names and use the same workgroup name.

If you have not previously configured a workgroup name or wireless network name, the default workgroup name MSHOME appears on the Workgroup Names page. You can use this name for your work group or enter a new name.

Adding A Computer To Your Workgroup

You can connect computers to the working group after setting up your network and working group. For different Microsoft Windows operating systems the process varies slightly. Enter the same working group name on all machines you add to the working group to be seen in my network locations together.

Note: Do not appoint your workgroup for the machine without consulting the system administrator who manages your area if a computer that is a domain member already exists.

For example, if you have a portal that is a domain member at work, do not delegate it to a working party without obtaining advice. When you are trying to reconnect to your domain at work, you can remove your domain membership from your computer.

Those are the protocols to create a computer working group.

To designate a working group of a device on Windows XP OS click Start, click on the Control Panel, and then double-click Framework. If the system icon does not appear, click Performance and Maintenance, and then click System.

Click the Computer Name tab.

Click Change, and in the Workgroup field, type the name of the workgroup that you want to join.

In the field "Computer Description" enter a new name, if you wish to modify the name of your computer to easily recognize it under the other computer names at "My network locations." However, note that a certain device name is needed for certain internet connections. If you have been given a device name by your Internet Service Provider (ISP), do not change it.

Click Start, click Control Panel, then double-click System to designate a workgroup on a device inside the Windows 2000 operating system.

Click the ID tab for the Network.

Click Properties and type in the Workgroup field the workgroup name you want to join.

In the field "Computer name," if you want to rename your computer to allow other computer names to readily recognize it in "My Network Locations," enter a new name. However, note that a certain device name is needed for certain internet connections. If you have been given a device name by your Internet Service Provider (ISP), do not change it. How to specify the workgroup of a computer in the Windows Me or Windows 98 operating system

Click Start, choose Settings, and then Control Panel.

Double-click Network and then the Identification tab.

In the Workgroup field, enter the name of the workgroup you want to join.

To modify your device names so that they can easily be found in "My network locations" under other device names, enter a new name. However, note that a certain device name is needed for certain internet connections. If you have been given a device name by your Internet Service Provider (ISP), do not change it.

Working group names and computer conventions When developing names for your working group or machine, you can use these naming conventions.

Names for the working group A working group must consist of fewer than 16 characters for each computer working group Unlike the name of the computer in each workgroup.In general it has no one:; "< > * + = \/?, Computer name Computer name must: In general there are no characters:;Be unique in the workgroup (no other computer in the workgroup can have the same name)

Be different from the name of the work group.

Usually it must be less than 16 characters.

Usually it doesn't contain any of these characters:; : "<> * + = \ |?,

In certain circumstances, everything is activated

Are you in need of a logo design for your company? Why not try a logo maker? Paste your website into this great online marketing directory

Use a work group

After you set the names of your workgroup and your computer, you can configure file sharing between files, folders, and printers in your workgroup. For more information and instructions on sharing files and printers, see File sharing settings and Print sharing settings.

You must be signed in to the network to access your workgroup and shared resources. This is automatically achieved by logging on to your computer in Windows XP and 2000. You will sign into the network separately when starting your machine in Windows Me and Windows 98. An alternative network access password can be set.

Use of work groups in computer networks

In computer networks, a workgroup is a collection of computers on a local area network (LAN) that share resources and responsibilities. The term is most commonly used with Microsoft Windows workgroups, but it also applies to other environments. Windows workgroups can be found in private households, schools and small businesses. Although all three are similar, they don't work exactly like domains and homegroups.

Workgroups in Microsoft Windows

Microsoft Windows workgroups organize PCs as local peer-to-peer networks, making file sharing, Internet access, printers, and other local network resources easier.

Each computer that is a member of the group can access the same resources that others share and, in turn, can share their own resources if configured to do so.

Both members will use a appropriate name to join a working party. A common category called WORKGROUP (or MSHOME in Windows XP) is automatically allocated for all Windows 10 computers.

Users may change the name in the Control Panel for the workgroup administrator. To find the Change button on the Computer Name page, use the System applet. Workgroup names are handled separately from machine names.

To access shares on the other PCs in your community, you can use the name of your workgroup to which the machine belongs, and the account username and password.

Working groups on Windows are able to accommodate many machines but operate better with 15 or less. As the number of computers increases, a workgroup's LAN becomes difficult to manage and must be reorganized into multiple networks or configured as a client-server network.

Windows workgroups versus home groups and domains

Windows domains support local client-server networks. A specially configured computer called a domain controller that runs a Windows Server operating system serves as the central server for all clients.

Window Domains

More computers can be handled by Windows domains as workgroups as central shares and access control can be monitored. A client PC may be a Windows domain or a workgroup, but they are not both. Assigning a machine to the area excludes it from the working group automatically.

Corporate domains may include network interface transfers to the broader corporate domain.

The business groups and home network groups are different methods of grouping machine in a network. THE Distinction BETWEEN A Community and A WORKING GROUP.

Domestic network groups, working groups and regions are different strategies for network management of computers.

The domain or working group must be included in all Windows PCs including Windows 7. Such machines may be used in a home network. in a home network.

You don't have to engage in a homegroup, but in Windows 7 this eliminates network conflicts. At home, your computer can be part of a home network group and a work group at the same time. At work, your computer is generally part of a domain.

Your computer cannot be in workgroups and domains at the same time.

Working group

Below are 5 typical characteristics of the different working groups from the domains and the home network group.

In a work group, all computers are pairs. No computer is in control of another.

Each computer has a number of user accounts. To log on to a workgroup computer, you must have an account on that computer.

There are usually about 20 computers in a workgroup.

A work group is not password protected.

It is important to have all computers in the same local network.Home group

Below are two typical characteristics of different home groups from domains and work groups.

Computers in a home network must belong to a work group, but can also belong to a group at home.

A homegroup is password-protected, but you only need to enter the password once by adding your computer to the homegroup.

Domain

Below are 6 typical characteristics of different areas of the home network group and the work group.

Computers are arranged in a domain in such a way that one or more computers are servers.

Network administrators use servers to control other computers.

You can log on to any computer in a domain if you only have one user account in the domain.

It is not necessary to have a user account on every computer to log in.

You can probably make only limited changes to the configuration of a computer because network administrators often want to ensure consistency between computers.

There may be thousands of computers in a domain.

Computers can be on different local networks.

The association between a domain, a work group and a home network group

Computers on home networks are generally part of a workgroup and possibly a home network group, and computers on workstation networks are generally part of a domain.

The work group or domain must be included in computers running the windows network. Computers with Windows can also be included in a home network category in a home network, but are not needed. This is the difference between a domain, a work group and a home network group. If you have any further questions, please feel free to leave a message in the comments section.

How do I know if the workgroup or domain is part of my computer?

If you have entered a working group or domain your machine can be checked: Home> Right-click Computer> Properties

- In the configuration of computer name, domain and work group, the work group or work domain is displayed followed by the name (see figure below).

Windows 7 workgroup name

If you see the word Unified next to homegroup, your machine must belong to a homegroup, go to Start > Control Panel > Show the status of the network and tasks.

Windows 7 Home Group Features of the peer network working group: There is no other computer access.

A number of user accounts are available on each device. You need to have a network account to sign in to a workgroup network.

In the working community normally just around 20 machines.

Password is not covered in a working party.

The local network or subnet must be the same for all computers.

Characteristics Of A Domain

Protection managed centrally by the servers and policies for all computers in the domain.

Any time the domain is accessed, domain users need to have a password or other credentials.

Users can sign in to any system on the domain without setting up a local account on this machine.

Computers in a domain are more restricted and cannot install programs without permission from the network administrator.

There may be thousands of computers in a domain.

Computers can be on different local networks.

Characteristics Of A Home Group

A computer in a home network can belong to both a home network group and a work group at the same time.

A home network group makes it easy to share photos, music, videos, documents, and printers with others on a home network.

A homegroup is password-protected, but you only need to enter the password once by adding your computer to the homegroup.

A home network group will help you set up your home network for easy sharing.

Now you understand the differences between home groups, work groups and domains. Continue with the previous tutorial on easy file sharing in Windows 7.

Microsoft Homegroup

Microsoft introduced the homegroup concept in Windows 7. Homegroups are designed to simplify workgroup management for administrators, especially homeowners. Instead of an administrator having to manually configure the released user accounts on each PC, the HomeGroup security settings can be managed via shared login.

In addition, HomeGroup communication is encrypted and makes it easier to share individual files with other HomeGroup users.

By joining a home network group, no PC is removed from your Windows workgroup. The two methods of sharing exist side by side. Computers running versions of Windows earlier than Windows 7 cannot be members of HomeGroups.

To find the HomeGroup settings, go to Control Panel> Network and Internet> HomeGroup. Connect Windows to a domain using the same process that you use to join a workgroup. Instead, choose the Domain option.

Other computer workgroup technologies

With the open source software package Samba (which uses SMB technologies), Apple MacOS,

Linux and other Unix-based systems can join existing Windows workgroups.

Apple originally developed AppleTalk to support workgroups on Macintosh computers. However, this technology was removed in the late 2000s in favor of newer standards such as SMB.

Windows 10

Note

The home network group has been removed from Windows 10 (version 1803). For more information, see Windows 10 Deleted Homegroup (Version 1803).

After installing the update, you cannot share files and printers with HomeGroup. However, you can still perform these tasks using the features built into Windows 10.

Share your network printer to learn how to share printers in Windows 10.

For information about sharing files, see Sharing files in File Explorer.

What Is A Homegroup?

A home network group is a group of PCs in a home network that can share files and printers. Using a group at home makes sharing easy. You can share your home network community with others, including images, music, videos, documents and printers.

You can protect your home network group with a password that can be changed at any time. Other people can only change the files you share if you give them permission to do so.

Select libraries (e.g. my photos or my files) you wish to share after you have built and entered a home network community. You may stop sharing those files or directories and then share more libraries.

The following windows are available for the homegroup network Windows 7, Windows 8.1, Windows RT 8.1 and Windows 7. You can join a homegroup on a Windows RT 8.1 PC, but you cannot create a homegroup or share content with the group on the home. You might be able to enter a home network community under Windows 7 Starter and Windows 7 Home Basic, but you can not create one.

Build a home community

Open HomeGroup in a search box at the taskbar by typing homegroup to then pick HomeGroup.

Choose Homegroup Creatment > Next.

Choose the libraries and devices that you want to share and choose Next.

A password is displayed: Print or write it down. You need this password to add more PCs to your home network group.

Choose Finish.

Remarks

When there is already a home network party in your network, it will be asked to join it rather than build a new one.

You can enter a homegroup if your Computer belongs to a domain, but you can't build it. The libraries or devices of other homegroup computers can be accessed, but the homegroup can not share libraries or devices yourself.

You may join a Windows RT 8.1 homegroup, yet you can not create or share your homegroup content. After creating a homegroup, other Windows 7, Windows 8.1, Windows RT 8.1 or Windows 7 PCs can join your network.

Add your other PCs to the home network group

After someone in your network creates a homegroup, the next step is to join it. You need the password for the home network group, which you can get from any member of the home network group. All user accounts except the guest account belong to the home network group. Each person controls access to their own libraries.

You can enter a homegroup on the Desktop, which you want to connect to your homegroup:

Remark:

A homegroup can not be available if you don't see a room for entering a password. Make certain that someone built a homegroup, or that you can make your own homegroup.

Open HomeGroup in a search box at the taskbar by typing homegroup to then pick HomeGroup.

Choose Enter Now > Next. Now.

Choose the libraries and devices that you want to share and choose Next.

Enter the Homegroup password in the field and pick Subsequently.

Select Terminal.

Search for home group files

Your home network party computers are displayed in the explorer tab.

Sharing libraries links to other PCs for homegroups

On the searchbox on the taskbar, open File Explorer and then pick File Explorer.

Pick a person whose libraries you want to access from the user account name of HomeGroup.

Click the file list to navigate with a double or double click on the folder, and then double or double click on the file or file you want to use.

In the file list, tap or double-click your desired library and then tap or double-click your preferred file or folder.

Notes

PCs that are turned off, hibernate, or asleep are not available as part of the home network group.

If you have made the homegroup files or folders available offline and you are not connected to the network, the files or folders will no longer appear in the Libraries window. Open the network folder to find it.

Share libraries and devices or stop sharing

You choose libraries and computers that you want to share with other members of the homegroup if you build or enter a homegruppe. Libraries for reading access are initially written.This means that other people can see or hear what is in the library, but cannot change the files in it. You can adjust the access level at any time and exclude the sharing of certain files and folders.

Only people belonging to the home network group can see shared libraries and devices. You can share individual libraries, devices, or files and folders with specific people in your home group or with everyone.

Note

Please note that children using group computers at home have access to all shared libraries and devices.

Share devices and entire libraries

Open HomeGroup in a search box at the taskbar by typing homegroup to then pick HomeGroup.

Change what you say with your homegroup.

Select the collections, applications and Next > Finish with the homegroup.

File or Folder Sharing How

When entering File Explorer in a search window on the taskbar, then choose File Explorer and open the File Explorer.

Pick the element and pick the Sharing List.

Select an option under Community Share. Depending on the Computer connected to the network and what sort of network it is there are different networking options.

Choose the person's account to share stuff with somebody.

Choose one of the homegroup sharing options for every homegroup. (Select libraries to share with all members of your homegroup)

To prevent files or folders sharing with others, pick the Sharing tab, and then stop sharing it.

To change the access level for a file or folder, click on the Sharing tab, and choose the Homegroup (View), or Homegroup (View and Edit).

When you have to share a spot, such as drive or directory folder, use Advanced Sharing option.

The USB cable can be connected with a home community of printers. Printers You can use the Print dialog box from any other program when you share the printer, just as with a printer that is connected directly to your PC.

Share or stop sharing with the homegroup your printer

Open HomeGroup in a search box at the taskbar by typing homegroup to then pick HomeGroup. Select Change what you share with the homegroup.

Next to Printers and Devices, select the Shared or Unapproved option (the Shared option is used by default).

Choose Next> Finish.

How to print on a home group printer

Open the Print menu of the application you want to print from (e.g. Microsoft Word), select the home group printer, and then select Print.

Note

To use it, the PC connected to the printer must be powered. Adjust the homegroup configuration if necessary

After your homegroup is built, you can change the settings at any time:

Open HomeGroup in a search box at the taskbar by typing homegroup to then pick HomeGroup.

Choose the system you would like.

These are the parameters you can modify:

Definition of Settings

Choose libraries, printers and computers you want to share with your homegroup. Switch what you share with your homegrowing group.

Enable all network devices including B. TVs and consoles to enjoy my rising material

Use this setting for content sharing for all network users. For instance, a digital frame or a network media player will share images with you.

Remark:

Content exchanged is not secure. Anyone with your network linked

Shared content is not secure. Shared content is not free. You can receive your share content from everyone linked to your network.

Please show or print your password for Homegroup. Display your password for Homegroup. Send them this password if anyone else wants to enter the homegroup.

Change Password

Change your password for the homegroup. All other PCs in your home group must enter the new password they generate.

Leave the group at home

Leave your group at home. You cannot delete a group in the apartment, but if everyone leaves the group in the apartment, it disappears. Then you can set up a new homegroup if you want.

Change the advanced sharing settings

Change network discovery, printer and file sharing, HomeGroup connection, and advanced security options.

Start troubleshooting the homegroup. Solve homegroup problems.

What Is A User Account?

An ID for an person in a computer or computer system is a user account. For computer entities , for example, user accounts can also be generated. B. Running application service accounts, system accounts for system files and process storage, and system management root and admin accounts.

A user account with more permissions is a privileged account than a regular user account. E.g. network accounts, operation reports, master accounts, manager accounts and system accounts.

Interactive account: A user interface standard

An interactive account or standard user account is also the standard account for a individual. Users like these will normally log into a machine with a password and use it for running programs.

Non-user account

The term non-user account is sometimes used to refer to all user accounts that are not standard user accounts.

Privileged account management

Privileged accounts, especially root and administrator accounts, grant general privileges on computers. They can be used to steal information, change important data, change system settings and hide their own actions. They can also be used to install and remove software and to update the operating system. Monitoring privileged accounts is therefore very important to prevent employee cybercrime and detect malware.

Privileged access management is a technology for controlling and monitoring access to privileged accounts.

Types of user accounts explained on the computer network

This guide describes the forms of computer network user accounts. Study in detail all user accounts forms such as your device account, your user account, your guest account, your super user account, community account, your local user account, and your remote user account, and your network user account. Every user who uses the system must have an individual user account. With a separate user account, the user can save their files securely and customize their user interface.

Types Of User Accounts

Regardless of the operating system used, user accounts are used to authenticate, track, register and monitor the services. When we install an operating system, some important user accounts are created automatically, which we can use to access it immediately after installation. You generally create four types of user accounts during installation. System account, super user account, normal user account and guest user account.

System accounts

These accounts are used by various services that run on an operating system to access system resources. The operating system uses these accounts to verify that a particular service that requests system resources can access those resources. Typically, the services create the required accounts themselves when they are installed. The services use these accounts after deployment, to access the required resources. You never need to know these accounts unless you are a machine or network administrator.

Account for Superuser

This user account is the operating system with the highest permissions. This user account is referred to as the admin account in Windows. This is known as the root account on Linux. This user account will do all the privileged activities with the operating system , for instance. For example, system files should be updated, new software installed, existing software removed, services started, services stopped, new user accounts created and current user accounts removed.

Normal user account

This user account has moderate permissions. This user account must not make any changes to the system files and properties. The operating system enables this user account to only perform the tasks for which it is authorized, e.g. For example, creating files and folders, running applications, adjusting environment variables, etc.

Guest user account

This user account has the lowest privileges. You cannot make changes to system files or properties. This account is generally used to access the system for temporary tasks, e.g. For example, suffering from the Internet, watching movies, playing games, etc. In Windows, this account is created automatically during installation. On Linux we need to create this account manually after installation if necessary.

User account against group account

A user account is an individual identity of a user, while the group account is the collective identity of all users belonging to a certain group. Grouping enables system administrators to effectively manage systems. In a company, for example, all users in the development department can belong to a group called developers. Once the group is created, the administrator can create and configure various security rules and applications to ensure that only users in the developer group access the resources of the development department, such as: B. SQL Server, language API, source code compiler, etc.

Group accounts are only used to manage user accounts that are similar or require access to a specific resource. In contrast to the user account, the group account does not have login functions. A user can belong to a single group or multiple groups.

Local User Account Vs. Network User Account

The user name and password of the local user accounts are stored on the local computer. Local user accounts are linked to physical computers. As explained above, each operating system creates some user accounts during installation. By default, all of these accounts are considered local user accounts.

The user name and password of the network user accounts are stored on a central computer, commonly referred to as a server. In contrast to local user accounts, network user accounts are not linked to a specific system. Depending on the configuration, a user can log on to a specific computer in the network or to any computer in the network.`

The local user account and the network user account are used to access a fully functional operating system.

Remote service account

The user name and password for these accounts are stored on a remote computer. These accounts are used to access a certain service or application on a remote system remotely. Examples of remote service accounts include FTP accounts, email accounts, and website accounts.

App profiles anonymous

For this account to log in, no password is needed. This account has all available accounts the lowest privilege. This type of account is usually used for the public sharing of data via a service that usually requires login access.

An instance is that the FTP server requires a user account to access something. If an administrator wants to allow someone to download the data stored in a specific folder on the FTP server, they can set up an anonymous account and set their default location in that folder. Once the anonymous account is activated, users can download all files and folders stored in this folder.

That's it for this tutorial. If you have ideas and/or comments on this tutorial, please let me know. If you like it, don't forget to share this tutorial.

Administrator and different user account types:

BTA London IT Consultancy System Administrator Fotor Most of us know the administrator profile and the general user profile of our Computer. Administrators equate themselves with God and consumers equate themselves with the general population.

What about domain manager accounts, domain user accounts, or local groups, however? Many other profiles provide various levels of access to machines, servers and network configurations. To maintain network security and ensure that everyone accesses the areas they need to do their jobs, knowing one another's accurate skills is essential.

Here are some of the user profile settings that are most common and often misunderstood.

Who's going to be a network administrator?

There should be no regular user account with administrator network access. Users who have administrator access as part of their normal user account can inadvertently do harm if, for example, they are infected with a virus that deletes data.

A Windows network typically has a "Windows Active Directory domain" that contains user accounts and manages the permissions for each user when they log on to the network.

If a user needs special permissions, they should be given details about an administrator account that has the required level of access.

Domain Administrator Accounts

For users to carry out administrative tasks, users who occasionally need admin access should create special administrator accounts with sufficient network access and have credentials assigned to users. A common username for an account administrator is ... Manager! Manager! Only imagine. Imagine

Note it's a good idea to deactivate the built-in default admin account and create a different name for an admin account.For example the network administrator.

Administrator accounts are used by users to perform tasks that require special permissions, such as: B. installing software or renaming a computer.

These administrator accounts must be checked regularly. This must include a password change and confirmation of who has access to these accounts.

Windows domain administrator groups

In a Windows network there are several security groups that have high access to different parts of the network. These groups should be checked regularly to ensure that there are no normal users as members, only administrators. The standard groups are:

Administrators

Domain administrators

Schema manager

Business administrators

Manually may have been produced other groups with high access level. Those should be reported and included in the review process.

Accounts For Domain Service

There is a separate type of user account, the service account, with restricted access to the components of your network. Service accounts are user accounts which are used for administrative work on a server such as a backup or managing the anti-virus software. Services such as an Administrator's account credentials can never be enabled. Your network must have at least one dedicated service account.

Accounts Domain Guest

Windows has Guest's Regular Account. These guest accounts are for criminals the first point cf contact and must be immediately and permanently deactivated. It shouldn't have a simple guest name if a guest account is needed.

Domain User Accounts

These are the normal user accounts that employees use in their day-to-day work to log on to a computer and do their normal work. You must not have any special permission that could lead to damage or loss of data. These user accounts are typically members of a security group called a domain user.

In some cases, users have to be granted special or administrative permissions. This should be limited to local administrator access (they are administrators only on their own computers and not in the domain).

Local accounts

They are domain accounts-like, but just local access. A computer or a server may be accessed locally. Local accounts may be admin, user accounts, and guest accounts. Integrated administrator and guest user accounts should always be disabled on workstations, and integrated guest user accounts should always be disabled on servers.

Local Groups

On computers and servers there is a default safety category known as administrators. Membership should be confined to the Domain

Administrators group.Importance of user accounts

Our data-driven economy is developing rapidly at a pace that is difficult for data security. The industries balance the customer's access to the desired information and the protection of the data from violations. User accounts can be compromised and allow access to large amounts of confidential data. Data security tactics must have masking capabilities. An intelligent system for analyzing threat risks and effective security measures throughout the company are an important source of comfort. The TrustMAPP Security Dashboard is designed to easily visualize and act on complex security challenges regardless of who you are in the company.

Cyber Security Keeps Executives Awake

Industry leaders in the US admit that cyber security keeps them awake at night. Businesses as well as national security can be endangered by persons from a foreign or national state or a terrorist organization. A breach of security can affect areas including financial institutions, power grids, technology and medical confidentiality. Cyber security issues related to national and economic security are discussed by senate committees.

Access Control On User Accounts

Each organization must do its part to keep pace with the evolution of the institution's technological fabric. Controlling access to user accounts is an important step in the right direction. Think about the impact of a user account violation on a person who has access to multiple areas within the company. A compromised user account can collect data from a variety of confidential information.

Questions about access to information policy

Does your policy protect data in different sources and languages?

Can you customize access to data based on user role?

Does your security platform work company-wide and analyze it in any application?

Can your data policy ensure that sensitive data is respected or masked in real time?

Can you visually assess attempts to access data to identify a suspicious pattern of activity?

Data security tactics

By using an information security platform like TrustMAPP, companies can visualize data security tactics on a practical security panel. You can monitor access to user accounts and protect yourself against user account violations that can result in loss of income, loss of trust, loss of business, and loss of sleep.

How do I change my password or username?

Below are the steps for changing your username or password in major operating systems, online services, and other locations.

Note

Unless you are the administrator or root, you must know the password for the account before it can be changed.

Change username and password in Windows 10

Change the password

Press the Windows key, enter login options, and press Enter.

In the Password section, click the Change button.

Check your account by entering your Microsoft PIN.

Enter your current password (A), choose a new password (B), confirm your new password (C) and click the Next button (D).

Change the username

Note

You can only change the names of local accounts, not the names of Microsoft or administrator accounts.

Click Windows key, form panel control and enter button.

Select profiles for consumers.

Once again, click User Accounts.

Select Access Another Account in the center of the browser.

Pick the account you want to update its name.

Choose the Account Rename.

Select a new name for a new account (A) and then click Rename (B).

Edit your Windows 8 username and password

Charm menu of Windows 8

Password modification

Click the windows and "c" key to open the Charms menu and choose Settings.Under Settings, select Change PC settings.

Select Users in the PC configuration.

Select the Change Password option to change the password for your local Windows account.

Change the username

Open the Charms menu on the Windows desktop by pressing the Windows key plus the C key and selecting Settings.

Under Settings, select Control Panel.

Select user accounts.

In the User Accounts window, select Rename Account to change the user name of your local Windows account.

Change the username and password in Windows Vista and 7

Change the password

Open the control panel.

Click Add or Remove User Accounts.

Click the account you want to change.

Click Change Password.

Change the username

Open the control panel.

Click Add or Remove User Accounts.

Click the account you want to change.

Click Change the account name.

Change the user name and password in Windows XP

Change the password

Open the control panel.

Double-click the User Accounts icon.

Select the account you want to change.

To change your username, select the Change my name option or create a password, or Change my password.

Remark:

Only the administrator password in Safe Mode can be changed for Windows XP Home users.

Change the username

Open the control panel.

Double-click the User Accounts icon.

User Accounts button double-click.

Select the account you would prefer to change.

Edit my name by tapping.

Enter your new name and press the Rename button.

Edit the Windows 2000 user name and password

Password modification

By pressing the Ctrl+Alt+Del + Windows option, Microsoft Windows 2000 users can change their username. Click the "Password Update" button in this browser.

Please enter your old and new password.

User change

You must have an account with administrator rights in order to change the name of a Windows XP user. If you sign in as an administrator or have an administrator rights account, follow the following steps.

Open the panel power.

User and password icon by double-clicking.

Check for "Users must enter the name and password of the user in order to use this device."

Choose the account for which the user name will be changed and click Properties.

The user name of the properties can be changed.

Modify the Windows 95, 98 and ME username and password

Password modification

Follow the following steps to update your Windows 95, 98 or ME login or user setup.

Open the panel power.

Passwords icon double-click.

Click the Modify Windows Password button in the User Properties tab.

Remark:

You can change the Windows password using the Control Panel User icon.

User change

Using the User icon in Control Panel to adjust the device settings in Windows 95/98. But the real username can not be modified this way. We advise you to copy your current user name and use the new user name if you need to change the username. The following steps are given.

Open the panel power.

User's icon with a double-click.

Tap on a Copy button and pick the user you would like to copy.

To create a new user account, follow the wizard.Change the username and password on Apple macOS X.

Change the password on macOS X 10.6 or higher

Log in with an administrator account.

From the Apple menu, choose System Preferences.

Select Users and Classes from the Display menu.

If it seems to be closed, you might need to press the lock button. Enter the password for the administrator.

Select the Account you would prefer to change.

Click Password Reset or Password Update.

Enter the new password and Verify the new password in the fields.

Click on the Reset Password or Change Password button again after entering the new password.

Modify the macOS X 10.3 password to 10.5.8

Link to an account administrator.

Pick Machine Preferences from the Apple menu.

Pick Accounts from the View tab.

If it seems to be closed, you might need to press the lock button. Enter the password for the administrator.

Select the Account you would prefer to change.

Click Password Reset or Password Update.

Enter the new password and test the current field password.

Press the Reset Password button again after entering the new password.

Select OK if there is a dialog box.

Modify the macOS X 10.2 to 10.2.8 password

Login to an account administrator.

Pick System Preferences from the Apple menu.

Pick Accounts from the View tab.

If it seems to be closed, you might need to press the lock button.

Select the Account you would prefer to change.

Choose the User Edit option.

Enter the new password in the New password and Verify fields and click OK.

If a dialog box appears, click OK.

Change the password on macOS X 10.1.5 or earlier

Log in with an administrator account.

From the Apple menu, choose System Preferences.

Select Users from the View menu.

If it seems to be closed, you might need to press the lock button.

Select the Account you would prefer to change.

Choose the User Edit option.Enter the new password in the New password and Verify fields and click Save.

Change the Apple iPad password

Change Password

Go to Settings on iPad.

Choose General

Choose Password Lock.

Choose Change Password.

Change username and password on Linux and Unix and most variants

Change the password

Almost all versions of Linux and Unix and their variants have access to the password command. Enter this command in the request to change your password. You must know the current password before you can change the password to a new password.

Change the username

To change the user name, you must have root or superuser access.

Use the vipw command to change the user name of an account.

Use the chfn command to change user settings. BIOS password change

Change the password

The system password that appears immediately after you turn on the computer and the CMOS or BIOS password are changed in the CMOS settings.

Change the username

The computer BIOS has no username, just a password.

Change of Internet user name and passwords

Changing your Internet user name or password is based on your Internet Service Provider (ISP) and your guidelines for changing your user name and password. With most ISPs, you can change your password frequently as needed. Often, however, you cannot change the account username.

As each web service provider is different, we suggest contacting the company to change the username or password for additional support.

Change forums and online accounts

As in the Computer Hope forums, in most forums, users can only change their password through account or profile settings. However, in most companies you cannot change your username. Generally, you need to create a new account. If you need additional help changing your username or password on another website, we recommend that you contact the company or webmaster who controls this website.

If you can't access an account online because you don't know the username or password, look for a link on the account sign-in page to retrieve a forgotten username or password. This option allows you to find your username or password or reset your account password.

In Windows, how do I create a new user?

Tip: tip

For build new accounts, you must have an administrator password.

In Windows 8 and 10, build a user

Click Windows key, form panel control and enter button.

Select profiles for consumers.

Once again, click User Accounts.

Select Access Another Account in the center of the browser.Click Link at the bottom left of the Current User Accounts field to add a new user in Windows 10.

Click Add New User in the PC Settings at the bottom of the window.

In Windows 10, next to Add a family member or add another person to this PC, click the Add icon.

Follow the instructions for a new user account development.

Tip

You can choose what type of account to create during creation of the account: the standard user or the manager.

In Windows Vista and 7, create a user

Open the panel power.

To delete user accounts, click add or delete.Click Create New Account.

Enter the name of the account you want to use and the type of account. For most accounts, we recommend using "standard user".

Finally, click the Create Account button.

Tip

During account creation, you can choose the type of account to create, either a standard user or an administrator.

After creating the account, name, password, picture, parental controls and other settings can be changed by clicking the account in the list of accounts.

Create a user in Windows XP

Open the control panel.

Open user accounts.

In the User Accounts window, click the Create New Account link.

Enter the account name and click Next.

Select the account type. We recommend using a "restricted account" for most accounts.

Finally, click the Create Account button.

Tip

During account creation, you can choose the type of account to create, either a standard user or an administrator.

After creating the account, name, password, picture, parental controls and other settings can be changed by clicking the account in the list of accounts.

How do I change the user in Windows?

In Microsoft Windows, multiple user accounts can exist on a single computer. Alternate accounts let you separate your settings and preferences from other family members who log on to the same computer.

Windows 10

Press Ctrl + Alt + Del and click Change User.

- OR -

Click on Start

Click your username or icon at the top or center left of the Start menu and select the user you want to use. Also, you can log out and then log in to the user account you want to use.

Windows 8

Press Ctrl + Alt + Del and click Change User.

Windows Vista and Windows 7

Press Ctrl + Alt + Del and click Change User.

Change users in Windows

- OR -

Click on Start

In the Start menu, next to the Shutdown button, click the right arrow and choose Change User.

Share resources

There are a lot of cases whereby you need to print a job from different computers, use data that may be on another computer, or communicate with someone who uses a different computer. One way to do this is to save the data you need to print, use, or send to a floppy disk, switch to another computer, log on, and load the data from your floppy disk.

On the other hand, if the computer and printer are connected by a cable and can communicate with each other, you have a network. You can do all of this without having to go anywhere.

One of the advantages of a network is that groups of computer users can share data, software, and even hardware (e.g., a printer or a modem). Most organizations that use many computers have connected them together as a network. In fact, networks have become commonplace since people can provide hardware and software to build simple, low-cost networks within their own four walls.

Microsoft XP Home Network configuration wizard

What you need a network card

In order to create a network, you need at least two computers (if you don't share your resources it is unwise to have a network). Each computer must have a network card (like the one shown here). The interface card is installed in the computer in one of the special expansion slots.

In a simple network, simply use a special cable to connect computers via their interface cards. However, the cables must have the correct connector type in order to be connected to the interface card.

Special software is required for computers to communicate with each other. You can share a printer or modem, play games, or send messages over the network.

LAN and WAN

If the network computers are in a small area, for example. B. This is referred to as a LAN or local network in a single building (for example, a school network). Network computers can share data and send messages, as well as terminals. One of the network computers can have a modem that can use the Internet on all computers on the network.On the other hand, a wide area network (WAN) covers a large area. For example, computers in a large supermarket chain may be in stores across the country, but all are connected to a central computer via telephone lines (or more specialized cables). With WANs, people can communicate in different places and exchange data and information.

Advantages And Disadvantages

Advantages

Messages can be sent to other people on the network very quickly. These messages can contain images, sounds or data (so-called attachments).

All computers on the network can share expensive things (such as printers or telephone lines to the Internet) without having to buy a different peripheral for each computer.

The same data can be used by everyone on the network. This prevents issues in which some users may be older than others.

Network maintenance, once established, is a complete work which requires network technicians and monitors to monitor.

Disadvantages

- Networking can be a costly and complicated task. The larger the network, the higher the cost.

- Security is a real problem when many different people can use information from other computers. Protection against hackers and viruses increases complexity and costs.
- Once configured, network maintenance is a full-time job that requires monitoring by network technicians and monitors.

The main goal of computer network maintenance services is to ensure that the networks are up and running at all times. Various methods must also be followed to protect the network from unauthorized access. Network security has become a problem for companies, as hackers lurk in the network and try to steal important information. Some of them might even try to make money selling their business information to their competitors.

Network administrators are always looking for threats and compromises to security. The main task is to prevent any type of unauthorized access and network downtime. However, users can do a few preliminary troubleshooting steps before addressing issues with their network administrators.

Here are some tips for maintaining your computer network:

Network problems: Network problems are some of the most common problems that users face. System failures can lead to loss of productivity, and companies cannot afford to experience such cases frequently.

Some of the reasons for network problems are:

Some problems on the end server

Problem with switch, router, hub etc.

Wiring error

Problem with your workstation

In addition to these common problems, there may be other complex reasons that are preventing you from accessing your network. Some of them are:

Rights access permissions

Discrepancy with login and authentication

Conflict with an application or software

Firewall problems

When we encounter network problems, it's always good to be able to perform basic troubleshooting. Sometimes we find it difficult to find network administrators for immediate help. It can be very helpful to learn some basic steps to maintain your computer network.

It is often sufficient to restart the system. However, it is good to clear the cache and cookies before restarting the system. Basically, these are temporary internet files and other files that accumulate on your system over a certain period of time. You get information about the files and websites that are accessed in different sessions. It is always recommended to keep the system clean by deleting it periodically, preferably before logging off.

You can also check whether the physical connections are properly connected or not. You can remove the connection cables and plug them in again. If you don't have administrator privileges, you cannot diagnose the problem beyond these few troubleshooting steps.

You can then request a problem ticket from your computer's network maintenance team for further assistance. Depending on how much downtime in your system can affect the overall productivity of your company or organization, you may need to mark the priority status for troubleshooting.

There are many companies that offer maintenance services for computer networks. As a rule, companies conclude contractual contracts. Your main task is to ensure that the network is always active so that your company's productivity is never compromised.

Troubleshooting

Patience is crucial when solving computer problems. Being frustrated or not making notes will prolong the problem-solving process significantly. Take note of things that can alter. Have you developed a new hardware or software piece? Has there been a terrible ordeal? All of these problems may be part of the root problem and so take careful notes. Make sure you put into writing any error messages before you click on "Okay" or restart your computer. Note the programs you were conducting at the time carefully. If the message appears in a windows box, more information can also be given by clicking Details.

A colder restart of the machine is one of the most common methods of solving troubles. Shut down whole windows until the computer is absolutely turned off. Wait for 10 seconds and turn the computer on again. It is recommended that you control certain devices concurrently when your computer is shutdown if your computer has a printer, external hard drive, or other devices attached. In most cases, you would like to control these devices again before turning your computer on.

Do you take a specific action, such as starting a program, accessing a particular function, or using a computer to make the problem repeat?? In problem solving, taking this carefully into account can be invaluable. In order to track the problem, verify that every stage of the way still exists when you use the elimination process. It would be easier to resolve if the problem is straightforward and repeatable. It can be very difficult to overcome random problems. Be vigilant of user behavior and usage habits when troubleshooting problems. What changed most importantly, before the problem itself became apparent.

You will probably have an issue with your power supply if your machine isn't activated. Test the outlet at which your machine is connected by connecting a different unit to the same outlet. Make sure any faults are corrected if this is on a power strip. Typically, there is a switch or button to reset a power strip from a drive. You probably have a bad power supply if the outlet tests OK, and you hear nothing moving inside your Laptop when you turn it on. This part will be substituted by a professional technician.

When you start your computer, you can conduct a self-test power (POST). If hardware is apparently in trouble, an error code is displayed and the machine speaker can deliver a beeping sound. The error codes and number / length of the bips may vary depending on the particular problem. For instance, sometimes, a memory-related problem would show a 201: memory error. Any issues associated with the memory will start with a 2 in the error code. If you start up, your machine issues a series of beeps that show a hardware problem. The BIOS program can detect hardware problems and transmit error sound.

The size and length of the beeps can differ according to BIOS manufacturer and hardware. For example, an Award BIOS code will be a long beep and will be followed by two short beeps at once for a video card problem.

Also be sure that your important documents and files are protected by a backup solution. The safest choice is to provide a completely automatic backup and a backup that protects the data in a separate safe place if a fire or a natural disaster happens.

Make sure to write the particular error code message like prog.exe triggered an invalid page failure at module xw32.dll at 0.147: ffccddee, when your computer is entered in a "Blue Screen" (often referred to as BSOD or Blue death screen). Your technician would be helpful in getting that info. If your computer restarts or shows a blue screen during the playback, the video processing or other CPU-intended tasks you may have a heat problem. Ensure that the system is placed in a cool position, that the heat sink does not contain any staub and that all supply units operate correctly. Using compressed air to eliminate waste from fans and heat sinks to mitigate heat problems. Ensure that the dust is removed, not just carried into a bath deeper. Modern device cooling systems may be influenced by a layer of dust.

One piece of hardware has to be turned off every time the hardware is resolved. For example, exchange one memory module. Verify that the reason is still there for the mistake. If it does, reset the original component and add another one. The defective part will probably have been detected if the problem is resolved. Troubleshooting is a responsive removal process. Swap hardware components, leaving an infrastructure part or software part one by one. Make sure that you update your hardware or software just one update every time. If the issue is not fixed, the shift will still be reversed.

When solving a network connection problem, attempting to connect to various types of resources is critical when defining the problem. Seek to pin a nearby machine or a printer if you can't connect to the Internet, for example. Ensure that the firewall of a device does not block pings. You know that when you can access local resources the network interface, cable and switch is fine. The problem is the router, the modem or the web.

Problem solving is the process of solving a problem or identifying a problem from a problem. Troubleshooting often involves the process of remediation, which involves a technician following a series of steps to identify or correct the problem.

Overview of computer troubleshooting

Below is a short rundown on your computer's basics for troubleshooting. Anybody should follow these measures in order to recognise or fix most computer issues. Does the computer turn on?

If the computer or display doesn't turn on, you can quickly determine that the computer is connected or has some other hardware problem. Follow one of the links below for steps to resolve these issues.

Any error message?

If you receive any error messages, make a note of the error and look for this error message. Computer Hope and millions of other websites have error message documents that explain how to fix them.

Restart the computer

If the computer is acting strange, is frozen, or is experiencing errors and can boot, restart the computer. Restarting the computer can often solve many computer problems. We recommend that you do not do any of the following until your computer restarts.

Has new hardware or software been added?

If new hardware devices have been connected to the computer or if new software has been installed, this might be the cause of your problem. Remove the hardware or uninstall the program and restart the computer. If the problem is resolved, this is a good sign that the new hardware / software has caused the problem.

Did the computer move?

If your desktop computer was recently moved, something in the computer may have come loose. A cable may be loose, or modular hardware such as RAM or GPU may need to be reconnected.

You can open your computer case to check your hardware for loose connections. Before you touch the hardware in your computer, always make sure that the computer is properly turned off and physically grounded. Grounding ensures that the electrostatic discharge does not get from your fingers to the hardware and damages the circuits.

How do I open my computer case?

Have there been power cuts or thunderstorms?

Power overload

A computer that is not powered by an uninterruptible power supply (UPS) cannot shut down properly during a power outage or failure. Failure to shutdown a computer properly can result in data corruption and, in some cases, hardware failure.

When the computer is not connected to a surge protector, an electrical surge may damage the computer hardware. This type of damage is particularly likely if there have been recent thunderstorms or blackouts in your area.

Reconnect and check the power cables

Power cord connections

Problems may arise if the computer does not receive enough power or if the power supply is interrupted. Unplug the power cord from a power strip or UPS and plug the computer directly into a good electrical outlet.

Is it a hardware or software problem?

When troubleshooting, it is important to determine whether the problem you are experiencing is caused by hardware or software. When you determine the cause of the problem, you can better understand the direction of the steps to be taken.

Update the drivers or install the latest patches

Hardware manufacturers often release updated device drivers and firmware to keep their hardware compatible with technological changes. If you have a hardware problem, make sure that the latest drivers for this device are installed.

Likewise, your machine might also have a patch for your operating system and software to help you fix any problems. Make sure the applications and operating system are up to date.

How Microsoft Windows upgrades a device.

Malware and viruses are checked

Computer viruses and malware can lead to a number of problems from slowing down to not running the OS.

Note

It is very common for people to quickly assume that a computer problem is a virus. However, it is much more common to have a different software problem and not a virus or other malware.

When was the last time the computer ran without problems?

If the computer was previously running and Microsoft Windows is running, you should run Windows System Restore to revert the computer to an earlier date. Restoring the system does not delete any data and restores the configuration as before

What does hardware troubleshooting mean?

Hardware troubleshooting verifies, diagnoses, and identifies operational or technical problems within a hardware device or device. Your goal is to solve physical and / or logical problems and problems within the computer hardware. Hardware troubleshooting is done by a hardware or technical support technician.

Hardware troubleshooting processes primarily aim to solve computer hardware problems using a systematic approach.

The process begins by first identifying the problem and finding various problems that can cause the problem, and ultimately leading to the implementation of a solution or alternative.

Hardware troubleshooting is typically done on hardware devices installed on a computer, server, laptop, or related device.

Some hardware troubleshooting processes include:

Remove, repair and replace defective RAM, hard disk or graphics / graphics card.

Clean the RAM / Video Cart slot / connectors and fan from dust.

Tighten cables and jumpers on the motherboard and / or components.

Software related hardware problems, e.g. B. Update or install the device driver.

How to fix hardware errors on your own desktop computer

Often a device that cannot be switched on was unintentionally disconnected or, theoretically, a cable has come loose. The following checklist is intended to remove a power connector or a disconnected cable as the source of a system that cannot be turned on.

* Check that all switches are turned on. Check the back of the microcomputer case. There is often a power switch on the back of the PC next to where the power cord is connected to the laptop. Make sure it's in the correct position.

* Check that the voltage switch is set correctly. In the United States USA Must be set to 110V / 115V. You will also find the voltage switch on the power

supply, which is usually located on the back of the computer, close to the power cord.

* Make sure the PC power cord is securely connected to the back of the desktop computer.

* For laptops, make sure that the transformer is firmly connected to the laptop.

* Run the power cord from the back of the desktop computer to the outlet on the power strip or on the wall and make sure the outlet is absolutely hot. You can test this by taking an approved work tool such as a lamp and testing the actual outlet that the laptop is plugged into to make sure it really works.

* If you have an operational indicator or another L.E.D. If the monitor in the PC case does not display a screen, the monitor may not be powered or the video cable may have been disconnected. Make sure the monitor power cord is securely connected to the back of the monitor. Track the power cord from the back of the monitor to the

electrical outlet and be sure it's plugged into an electrical outlet.

* Check that the video cable from the monitor is attached to the back of the monitor and that the other end is connected to the video connector on the desktop computer.

* Still out of luck? Try to disconnect and reconnect all cables. Remove all cables from the laptop, including power, monitor, mouse, keyboard, printer, network, and other connected devices. Make sure you know where the cables go again! If not, label them.

* Now plug in all cables again and try to switch it on again.

Troubleshoot PLC hardware

The programmable logic controller, better known as PLC, plays a role in almost all automated manufacturing processes. The PLC is an electronically programmable device that enables almost unlimited combinations of relays, contacts and time circuits to control industrial machines of all types and sizes. It is essentially a computer that can withstand a hostile manufacturing environment. It was developed to replace the complex system of relays, cam switches and other electromechanical circuits. In late 1970s, the first PLCs were introduced and became more and more popular after their publication.

PLCs are now manufactured by numerous large manufacturers, including Siemens, Allen Bradley, Koyo, Fuji, Telemecanique and Mitsubishi and many others. PLC programming is carried out using proprietary software from the respective manufacturer. There are several slight variations between the labels, and software between the PLcs is not compatible and logical programming is very similar. The ladder system is the script that is saved in the PLC. The ladder program problems can be very complicated, and it's a very different matter. However, the hardware problems are very similar and can be easily diagnosed if you know a little about each model and its input and output settings.

Hardware failures of the brain or the main processor are rare. With an illuminated error display on the front of the PLC, the visual diagnosis can be carried out more frequently. A failure of the internal power supply would be possible if the PLC display or the power display does not light up and the technician would check whether the correct voltage is applied to the current terminals. Some PLCs are equipped with an internal fuse that can also fail. These problems are not as common as an input or output port failure.

The inputs and outputs in various configurations and voltages are available. Both AC and DC are available in the same unit individually and at times. The digital and analog inputs and outputs can be configured as transists or as dry relay contacts. It is necessary to define the PLC specifications on both the input and the output side. At the time of troubleshooting, too, the correct PLC software should be available.

Firstly, the light inputs and outputs should be correlated with the software in real time. A failed or disabled input is indicated by a light input that can not be displayed correctly as the power supply input in the program. An illuminated connection on the output side which doesn't drive the correct output voltage may mean one of two things: the output failed openly, or the typical output connection is fed with incorrect voltage. The only way to check this is to use a multimeter that is set to the correct voltage scale.

In general, troubleshooting PLC hardware problems is not complex, but must be properly addressed because both hardware and software must work together harmoniously so that a PLC can perform the intended tasks.

Network performance problems due to incorrect cabling

If the network efficiency of your organization is not where it should be, many factors need to be considered: so many users are trying to access resources simultaneously, more and more devices are being linked wirelessly, and some part failure. Waypoint and so forth. It can be hard to determine the problem sometimes.Be sure to consider your cabling when troubleshooting the cause of network performance problems. This can be the culprit, causing bottlenecks, sluggishness, stains, or even complete downtime.

Below are some of the most common cabling issues that cause network outages and what you can do about them.

Where potential problems can lurk

Outdated backbone / incoming wiring

The cable that enters the building from your Internet service provider (ISP) connects your network to the Internet. If this masterpiece does not meet the current bandwidth standards, major bottlenecks can occur.

If you try to work at too high a speed or bring too much bandwidth over a cable that is not properly designed for this capacity, users will notice and business will be affected.

Wrong type of structured wiring

Manufacturers must evaluate cabling based on performance and capabilities (e.g. Category 6 or 6A cables). Manufacturers must at least also meet suitable performance standards, such as those set by TIA. There are manufacturers that go beyond specifications, meet industry expectations and provide more coverage for that bandwidth specifications. It is important to remember that

If the cabling exceeds the minimum standards, you can achieve higher network speeds without having to fully update the cabling. If the cabling simply meets the minimum standards, network speeds cannot go much beyond what the cable rating indicates.

It is important to be vigilant and do reasonable research when it comes to cable ratings and standards. For example, simply because a cable is called "Class 6A" does not mean that it meets expectations of efficiency. The level of compliance may be insufficient, or the cable may be poorly made and can not achieve the resulting efficiency.

In other cases, the age of the cabling system can be to blame. The installed cabling may have been the right solution to meet the requirements and expectations of 15 years ago, but can no longer cope with the increase in network traffic.

Provider compatibility issues

Problems can arise when connecting cabling and connectivity from different manufacturers. Using connectors from one manufacturer, cabling from a second manufacturer and patch panels from a third manufacturer can lead to compatibility problems, for example. If the components are not designed and manufactured to work consistently, there may be performance issues.

If you invest in high quality, high-performance cables, but use connectivity solutions with lower performance levels, you have a weak link. The cable, no matter how well designed and manufactured, cannot develop its full potential with plugs, plugs, patch panels, etc. They are not designed to endure it.

Poor quality connecting cables

Based on what we've seen, patch cords can be the most common cause of network performance issues.

Similar to mix & match providers, investing in a high quality, high performance cabling infrastructure, choosing lower quality patch cords to save a few dollars can impact network speed and performance. They may not meet standards and cause signal degradation.

Improper installation

Another aspect in avoiding network performance issues is to ensure that your installer is qualified and certified properly to operate with your chosen cable system.

If the installers are not properly trained, it is very likely that your cabling system is not properly installed. This can result in excessive bending, improper air resistance, a cable that is installed too close to sources of noise (heavy machinery, motors, etc.) or a cable that is not properly finished or polished. The lack of details about front-end installation will lead to costly and time-consuming network performance problems in the future.

Lack of education

People are sometimes asked to take on tasks with which they are unfamiliar or familiar. This can also cause network performance issues. Depending on how an undertaking is planned, the IT team, which already has a lot to handle, is responsible for the formal cabling system:

cybersecurity; Hardware, software and applications for all employees; Device problems; etc.

The team may be familiar with hardware (switches, routers, servers, etc.), but may not know how the individual components of the structured cabling system affect the corporate network. (Of course, this depends on the background and the training.)

How to fix network performance issues

If you notice network problems and believe that your cabling is to blame, you must first determine the bandwidth that you want to control. What network speeds do you want to achieve?

For example, once you know the answer – 10 G or 100 G – the next question is: The form of standardized cable system(s) are in place? The response on the question will help you narrow in. Starting with backbone cabling, and working your way down to your IT rooms from the MDF and IDF, check the type of cabling system in place.

For example, if you encounter Category 5e cabling somewhere along the way and attempt to move 10 G speeds across your network, you have just found the problem: your built cabling was not designed to accommodate this speed.

If everything looks good after analyzing the cabling of the backbone, MDF, IDF and IT room, it is time to check the patch cords. If they are obsolete or are made cheaply or poorly, try to replace them with a good quality patch cord and see if that improves performance.

Belden's Reliable Cabling Solutions ensures that every cable and connectivity solution it manufactures is designed not only to meet industry standards but to be above those standards. You can rest easy knowing the network can meet future needs in terms of speed and bandwidth.

If the symptoms we mentioned above are encountered by your network – sluggishness, bottlenecks, unexplained downtime – and you're not sure why, we can help you diagnose the issue. Or, if your on-site team simply wants some assistance in evaluating the current cabling network (or what may be expected in the future), we can also assistance with that.

Then when you're ready to update your cabling system Belden will help you make a good, cost-effective, efficient, safe then future proof cabling decision. Learn more here.

How to troubleshoot rising wireless issues

In the past, we had a look at how to mount and configure wireless networks. We are mindful of the fact that managing and operating a wireless network is so difficult. Wireless networks' growth has led to the development of more complex and robust networks. Many of the men, worldwide, use wireless networks for different purposes. However, as the success of these networks has increased, a number of issues have also arisen associated with them. Such problems that arise when the network is running or when the devices are in use. All of these issues require an efficient method of troubleshooting and resolving certain problems.

To ensure their smooth running, it is absolutely important that you know numerous ways in which you can troubleshoot the wireless systems. You may experience a variety of wireless network issues related to interference, signal power, incompatibilities, configurations, latency, form of encryption, bounce, SSID mismatch, Incorrect location of switches and incorrect channel. It is really important that you consider these problems and figure out successful ways to ensure they are removed. Below is the process to get rid of each of these problems and troubleshoot the network in detail.

Interference

One of the most influential issues wireless networks have to face is interference. We are aware that wireless devices operate through the transmission of signals in the form of radio waves. That is why any system near a WAP that generates radio, or even microwaves, appears to cause interference. The interference contributes to signal disturbance. It can also allow the signal to stray from its original path and cause weak signals to be received by the client. That is why it is important to position the WAP and the client in a location where radio waves are not transmitted by electrical devices. Besides this, you should also make sure there are no metal objects near where you set up your wireless network, because metal objects do appear to interrupt signals. Making sure there is no interference is really important so that the client can get the full amount of signals and get the best output.

Signal Quality

The consistency of the signal that consumers receive is one of the most important aspects to consider when building up a wireless network. This implies that you must ensure that the signals are extremely effective to the customer. The location of the WAP is absolutely essential in this respect. You will keep the WAP in a central position to ensure the signals are received by all the clients. You will also suggest using the most suitable type of antenna. If the signal is to be received in all directions, for example, you will consider using an Omnidirectional antenna. Additionally, your wireless network should also be configured in such a way that unauthorized clients can not connect to it. Also, you should also be mindful of the fact that, if you are close to the WAP, you continue to get high signal power. Also, the signal strength could be reduced if there are lots of walls between the WAP and the client.

Configurations

The protection factor impacts the way wireless networks are designed. Many of the people always hide their SSIDs in order to add an extra security layer to their network. They do not, however, think this may make things very complicated for the company. If the SSIDs are concealed, then there is a lengthy process to locate it on the computer of the client and then make other settings to connect to it. It is one thing that people try to avoid because in this situation any client will have to have a set of instructions that they will have to follow in order to connect to the network. It would be much safer to publicly broadcast the SSIDs but the password is strong enough to increase the protection. This password would still need to be transmitted to the clients, but it will be much less of a concern than full instruction communication.

Incompatibilities

A crucial topic to focus on is also the topic of compatibility between various wireless standards. We are aware that 4 different types of wireless standards exist; 802.11a, 802.11b, 802.11 g, 802.11n. The devices configure these wireless standards according to the frequency at which the device transmits the signals. The key challenge, however, is that any two devices that want to connect over a wireless network need to have the same wireless standards. This is a very significant criterion. However, the best solution to tackle this problem is to use backward compatible devices. Such systems are capable of communicating with all other wireless protocols. This will ensure that performance problems aren't present. If the devices are not backward compatible, you should wisely select the type of wireless standard to be configured to ensure compatibility on each device.

Incorrect channel

Frequency selection is normally achieved using channels. It's important to remember that you have a frequency band available from which to pick the best frequency for your network. A channel consists basically of a variety of frequencies that are mixed together. Such channels are created to increase the bandwidth that is supplied to the customer. However, all of these should be placed on the same channel to allow the WAP and the client to communicate. This will ensure the client chooses the signals emitted by the WAP. You should take other precautions, too, though. When setting up channels, you should make sure that you pick the chancel that does not contain a frequency spectrum that is being used by any other system in the region around. This is done to prevent duplication and to stop some kind of intervention. Besides this, you should also ensure that the wireless network and the client operate on the same channel, otherwise no link can be created. For wireless networks the most appropriate channels are 1, 6 and 11.

Latency

The time it takes for latency to relay wireless signals to the customer from the WAP. The lower the latency, the greater the network effectiveness is. There are a variety of factors that influence a network's latency and allow the signal reach its destination in more time. Most of the factors that we mentioned above can lead to problems with latency. Interferences can cause disruption to the signals and reach their destination late. Additionally, WAP positioning and antenna type selection can also lead to variability in latency. Therefore all these considerations must be taken into account when dealing with problems of latency.

Encryption style

Nowadays it is very important to move the data in an encrypted form over a network. This will improve data protection and anyone intercepting the data would not be able to decode it in any way. There are a range of protocols that provide the wireless networks with protection in this regard. However, the main issue that needs to be considered is that both the WAP and the client should be set to the same type of encryption. This means the protocol that provides encryption at the WAP should be the same that provides encryption to the client. Unless the form of encryption is not the same then the WAP and the computer will not be able to communicate. Besides this, you should always make sure that the type of encryption used is the most suitable for the necessary circumstance, as different encryption protocols have different security styles.

Bounce

We know of the fact that wireless signals are transmitted in the form of radio waves. This indicates that such waves have the ability to bounce off reflective surfaces, such as metal surfaces. This allows the radio waves to bounce off the surface if there is some point between the WAP and the client. This will result in a poor signal being received at the device. It is important to carry out a check to make sure that there is no bounce in the signals, therefore, the client receives the highest strength of signals. However, the first step should be to make sure that there is not object, particularly a metal object, between the client and the WAP. If there is any, you should consider adjusting the location of your WAP to ensure maximum signal power.

SSID Mismatch

SSIDs are referred to as Service Collection Identifiers. Whenever a wireless network is deployed, its SSID is broadcasted in the surrounding areas which lie under the range of the network. Any computer in this field can search for this SSID in the list of available networks in that area. In reality, this SSID is the name the network gives. Through choosing SSID from your network and entering the necessary details to get to the network, customers will connect to the network. Nevertheless, the problem of SSID mismatch occurs in the crowded field, where a range of WAPs supply wireless signals. It that be difficult for the customer to decide which network is yours. For example, if your customers have problems connecting to your network, they probably try to connect to another network in the area. In this respect, the client 's computer should be tested for network information in order to let the client know the network to which they are to connect. So, to avoid any such issues, you can make sure that your SSID is distinct from the other networks in the network.

Incorrect switch location Also known as a Wireless switch is a WAP. There are a number of issues that occur because the WAP and its antenna are incorrectly positioned. Which can cause the client to receive weak signals and experience poor functionality of the network. It is important that you place your wireless switch and its antenna in the right position to prevent this. You should ensure that the wireless switch is positioned in a central position from which it is possible to transmit the signals in all directions. You may also attach the antenna to a wire and position it in a location where the WAP can not be positioned to ensure the maximum signals are received. If it is not possible to find the best location to set up the switch, however, you can also contact other organizations offering special services to ensure that all switches and customers are positioned so that the received signals are optimum. This is essential in situations where the network contains a lot of WAPs.

Wireless network troubleshooting process is of high importance. Before you start the troubleshooting process, you should be able to identify the actual reason the problem occurs. You will have in-depth information about the operation of wireless networks and their components in that regard. To allow it to function perfectly, you should make sure that all of the issues discussed above do not occur within the network. In the event that any related issue arises, you can use the knowledge provided in this chapter to eliminate these problems. You should know that more than one issue can contribute to a question, too. Therefore, you can thoroughly test the program after you have completed the troubleshooting process. Bear in mind that if you don't conduct this delicate process with precision, this may result in generating new problems while removing a previous problem. When you keep all of these factors in mind and follow the suggested steps, you'll definitely be able to master the wireless network troubleshooting process.

Conclusion

Network Security Problems

Your non-profit or library depends on security to complete its work, and unexplained software crashes and error messages can put a stop to your work. When this happens, it is tempting to automatically contact tech support. However, there are easy steps you can follow to solve machine problems on your own, or at least narrow down their triggers before you make the call.

Try those troubleshooting tips the next time you have a software problem in the order they are listed below. Chart the actions carefully. That way, if a call to tech support is necessary, you'll at least have a clear idea of what doesn't cause the problem.

1. Give up RAM by leaving other programs up.

Uses Random Access Memory (RAM) for each piece of software. The more apps you run on your computer, the more RAM you 're using. This can be especially troublesome if you use older machines which don't have much RAM. The first thing you should do is close all other programs, if a software program refused to load or run slowly.

To find out which open applications can hog your RAM, you have tools for viewing this information on both Windows and Macintosh operating systems (OS). hit Ctrl+Alt+Delete in Windows, then select the option Start Task Manager. Click the Processes tab from the window that appears then press the Memory menu object. This sort out all processes that are open based on the amount of RAM they use. Clicking the End Process button can shut down a runaway process. You may want to do some work on the process before you do that, to make sure you don't unintentionally interrupt a vital process or system.

In Mac OS X, using the Task Monitor (in older versions of OS X, called the Operation Viewer). Go to Applications > Utilities and access the Activity Control. If the Activity Monitor is called up, sort programs based on RAM usage by clicking on the column "True Memory." 2. Computer restart.

Problems with software may arise from a dispute with other programs or simply from difficulties that the software experienced when starting up. Often shutting down the software and restarting it will fix those problems.

2. Switch off your machine and restart.

If restarting the troubled program does not solve the problem, try rebooting your computer. If the machine has rebooted completely, restart the program in question to see if the problem has been fixed.

3. Using the Web to find help.

Whatever software problems you encounter, chances are someone else's happened. It is possible you will be able to find help on the Internet. Check for answers: In your search engine question, provide the name and version of the software system, the problem you have encountered and the circumstances in which the problem occurred. If you have received a particular error message, enter the exact text of the error message along with the code name.

Check the vendor's website: most software vendours, including frequently asked questions, product documentation or user discussion boards, offer some sort of product assistance.

Check out more websites: TechSoup's article "Learning about technology online" lists a number of websites offering technology tutorials, articles and forums for discussion.

4. Delete any improvements recently made to the hardware or software.

Changes in software and hardware can sometimes cause problems with software, such as: conflicts with other software: newly installed software can conflict with other software. Symantec Norton Antivirus for example may conflict with competing antivirus products. So uninstalling the other antivirus product could solve your problem if you have recently installed another antivirus program and Norton Antivirus does not work correctly.

Computer configuration updates: Undo any recent changes to the configuration and try to restart the program on your computer.

The Windows Control Panel, for example , includes a "Set Program Access and Defaults" option, which allows you to disable access to certain applications. Here the program may not run if you accidentally disable access to a program.

Conflicts with new or unsuitable hardware, such as scanners and printers. If you have attached new hardware to one of your computers recently, consider disconnecting the hardware to see if this will fix the software issue.

5. Uninstall, then reinstall the app.

Software issues often occur due to the insertion, modification, or deletion of essential program files. A lot of Windows applications, for example, use Dynamic Link Library (DLL) files to perform basic tasks. Many programs may often use the same DLL script. If you recently removed one program from your computer, you might have removed DLL files you were dependent on from another program. Similarly, it might add or upgrade DLL files to a program. Applications that depended on those DLL files can become unstable or fully cease working.

To make sure all the correct files are intact, you can uninstall the problem program fully and then reinstall it again. Even if you disable a program using its built-in uninstall wizard (if one is included), Searching the System Files folder for some sign of the program on your hard drive — usually on the C drive — and removing some files or directories you find is always a safe idea.

Test to see if a new version of the software is available until you reinstall. The vendor or developer may have bug fixes published that correct the issue you're experiencing.

6. Scan for Program fixes.

Software vendors can also repair bugs by releasing patches — small software changes that address known problems. Even if you are using the current version of the app, there might be a more recent patch available for that version.

7. Scanning the virus, and malware.

Viruses, spyware, and other kinds of malware (or "malware") can cause software to freeze, crash, or stop working altogether.

If tips 1 through 8 have not helped solve your software issue, you might also want to find and uninstall viruses and malware using both antivirus and malware tools to search the system. Use the most robust scan mode available, and remember to restart your computer if the antivirus or anti-malware programs have detected any risks.

8. Checked on firewall for a fight.

Instead of a centralized hardware or software-based firewall, some organizations may install individual firewall software on each computer. Personal firewalls can be a big protection against hackers and other security threats but can cause software disputes as well. Firewalls also show messages asking whether a program can run or block it. Therefore the personal firewall may be unintentionally told to block the running of a program. Check the firewall setup to see if the troublesome software has been added to the firewall blocker list of programs. If so, change the firewall settings to make the system run, then check to see if there are still issues with your software.

9. Boot up in Safe Mode.

Some program malfunctions can be due to OS settings or other problems with the computer. Windows and Mac operating systems both provide a troubleshooting feature known as Safe Mode. Safe Mode deactivates non-critical programs and devices, which in turn simplifies problem solving.

Most Windows computers require that you enter Safe Mode when booting your device by pressing the F8 key. Enter Safe Mode on a Mac when your computer boots up (or starts immediately) by pressing the Shift key.

Start the troublesome program once your computer is in safe mode and try to replicate the problem you had in normal mode when your machine was in. If you do not have the same problem in safe mode, there is a good probability that the problem has been triggered by your OS or other program, not the device from which you're troubleshooting.

10. Hard-drive defragment.

A final move in troubleshooting may be to defrag the hard drive of your computer. Defragmenting rearranges the hard drive's file structure so the machine works more effectively. Defragmenting is likely to be most effective if you encounter sluggishness on your computer overall, as defragmenting is intended to make the whole system run faster. Know defragmenting a hard drive only applies to computers running Windows.

Most recent Windows versions — including XP, Vista and Windows 7—include an advanced method for defragmenting the disk. Go to Start > All programs to boot from > Accessories > Machine Tools > Disk Defragmenter: Defragmenter. Be aware of the time-consuming defragmentation of a hard drive, so be sure to perform this task when you'll be away from your computer for a few hours. You know what to do when your screen goes blank? What if your speakers do not seem to be able to close an application, or do they not hear any sound? Don't panic any time you run into a computer problem! There are a variety of basic methods of troubleshooting which can be used to fix these problems. In this lesson, we'll teach you some simple things to try while troubleshooting, as well as how to fix unique problems you can encounter.

General tips to bear in mind

A lot of different problems with your machine will cause a problem. No matter what causes the problem, troubleshooting will always be a process of trial and error — in certain cases, you may need to use several different approaches before finding a solution; other problems may be easy to fix. To get started we recommend using the following tips.

Write down your steps: until you start troubleshooting, you will need to write down every move you take. But stop making the same mistakes. You know exactly what you were doing this way. It would be much better if you ended up asking other people for advice if they knew just what you already did.

Take notes on error messages: if your machine receives an error message, be sure to write down as much information as possible. You can use the experience later to find out whether other people have the same error.

Check the cables at all times: If you have issues with a specific piece of computer equipment, such as your monitor or keyboard, checking all associated cables is a easy first step to ensure they are properly connected.

Restart the machine: If anything else fails, rebooting the system is a wise thing to do. This will fix many basic issues you might find with your computer.

Using the elimination process If you have a problem with your computer, the elimination process can allow you to find out what's wrong. That means you're going to make a list of items that could cause the problem, and then try them out to remove them one by one. If you found the root of the problem with your computer it will be easier to find a solution.

Scenario: Let 's say you 're trying to print out invites to the birthday party, but the printer won't work. You have some ideas about what you can do and you work through it one by one to see if any potential triggers can be excluded.

Second, you check that the printer is powered on and connected to the surge protector. It is, so that's not the issue. You then check that the printer's ink cartridge still contains ink and that paper is loaded into the paper tray. Things look perfect in both cases and you know the problem has nothing to do with the ink or paper.

Now, you want to make sure printer and computer work properly. If you have recently downloaded an update to your operating system, that can interfere with the printer. But you know there have been no recent changes and the printer was working yesterday so you'll have to look elsewhere.

You search the printer for the USB cord and you will find that it is not plugged in. You must have unplugged this unintentionally when you had something else plugged into the unit earlier. If you plug in the usb cable the printer will start working again. It looks like the printer issue is solved!

This is just one example of an problem you might experience while you are using a computer.

Simple solutions to common problems Use basic methods of troubleshooting such as closing and reopening the machine, problems can be overcome several times over. It is best to seek such simple solutions before resorting to more drastic measures. If the problem isn't solved yet, then you can use other troubleshooting methods.

Problem: Power button won't start computer Solution 1: If your machine doesn't start, check the power cord to make sure it's securely plugged into the computer case and power outlet backwards.

Solution 2: Insure it is a working outlet when plugged into an socket. You can also plug your outlet into another electrical unit, such as a lamp, for checking.

Solution 3: When plugged into a surge protector, verify that the system is turned on. The surge protector can need to be reset by turning it off and then turning it on again. The surge protector may also be plugged into a lamp or other device to check that it is working properly.

Solution 4: Unable to charge the battery while using a laptop. Move the AC adapter into the wall then attempt to turn the laptop on. If it doesn't get going yet, you may have to wait a couple of minutes and try again.

Problem: Solution 1 runs slowly on an application: Close the software and reopen it.

Solution 2: Update to framework. To do this, click the Help button, and find an alternative to the

Updates list. If this alternative is not found, then another suggestion will be to run an online search for application changes.

Problem: An application is frozen Sometimes it may get frozen or stuck. When that occurs, you will not be able to close the window, or click any buttons within the software.

Solution 1: Compel stoppage of demand. On a Desktop, to open the Task Manager, you can press (and hold) Ctrl+Alt+Delete (the Control, Alt and Delete key). On a Mac, press Command+Option+Esc, and hold. You can then pick the non-responsive task, and press End Task (or Quit Force on a Mac) to close it.

Solution 2: Reboot your PC. If you can not force an application to stop, then all open applications will be closed by restarting your computer.

Problem: All computer programs run slowly

Solution 1: Execute a virus scanner. In the meantime you can have malware running which is slowing things down.

Solution 2: You can run out of hard drive space at your computer. Attempt to remove any unneeded files or programs.

Solution 3: You should run Disk Defragmenter while you are using a Mac. Check out our lesson on Securing your Machine to learn more about Disk Defragmenter.

Problem: The machine is frozen.

The computer also becomes totally unresponsive or frozen. When this occurs you won't be able to click on the machine anywhere, open or close programs, or access shutdown options.

Solution 1 (Windows only): Windows Explorer reset. To do so, click and hold down Ctrl+Alt+Delete to open the Task Manager on your keyboard. Next, from the Processes tab find and pick Windows Explorer, and press Restart. To show the Processes tab, you may need to select More Info at the bottom of the page.

Solution 2 (only on Mac): Restore Finder. To that end, press the Force Quit Applications dialog box on your keyboard and hold command+Option+Esc. Next, pick Finder and search, then press Relaunch.

Option 3: Push the Power button and hold. The Power button is normally positioned at the computer's front or side, traditionally indicated by the power symbol. To force the machine to shut down press and hold the Power button for 5 to 10 seconds.

Solution 4: You should unplug the power cord from the electrical socket if the device still won't turn off. The battery can be replaced by using the laptop so that the computer is turned off.

Note: After testing out the other ideas above, this approach should be your last resort.

Problem: While using a wired mouse or keyboard, the mouse or keyboard has stopped working Solution 1: ensure that the mouse or keyboard is properly plugged in.

Solution 2: When using a wireless mouse or keyboard, make sure that the mouse is turned on and its batteries are charged.

Problem: The sound does not work Solution 1: test the level of volume. Click the Audio button in the screen's top-right or bottom-right corner to make sure the sound is turned on and the volume up.

Solution 2: Test the controls on the audio player. A lot of audio and video players should have different audio controls of their own. Make sure the sound is switched on, and the volume in the player is turned up. iTunes Solution 3 screenshot: Check out the cables. Make sure the external speakers are connected to the right audio port or USB port and are plugged in, turned on. If you have color-coded ports on your computer, the audio output port is normally green.

Solution 4: Attach headphones to the machine to find out whether the headphones allow you to hear sound.

Problem: Blank Solution 1 is the screen: the machine can be in sleep mode. Press any of the keys or Click the mouse to wake it on the keyboard.

Solution 2: Ensure that the display is attached and turned on.

Solution 3: Ensure that your computer is plugged in and switched on.

Solution 4: Make sure that the display cable is correctly connected to the computer tower and display while you are using a laptop.

Solving more complicated problems You might need to ask someone else for advice if you have not yet found a solution to your problem. We'd suggest searching the Internet as an simple starting point. Many users may have had similar problems, and solutions to these problems are also shared online. If you have a anyone who knows a lot about computers they can support you.

Understand that most computer problems have easy solutions though it can take some time to find them. A more drastic approach may be required for difficult issues, such as reformatting your hard drive or reinstalling your operating system. If you think you may need a solution like this, first we suggest that you consult a specialist. If you're not an expert in programming, it's likely that trying such ideas will make things worse.

How to use the built-in assistance of your machine Often someone needs to seek support. Luckily it's usually easy to find when you want help with a computer program. Somewhere, most programs have a support feature, and learning how to use them will make a major difference. You might not discover everything you need but the built-in support of your machine is a great starting point.

Different applications incorporate support functionality in various ways. Others are like digital guides that are included with the software that you can access with a menu while others are links to the website of the developer help. Yet they're still built with the same thing in mind: helping you understand the program's functionality and solving problems on your own.

How to access coordinated aid Most services have one of two ways to receive built-in assistance. Adobe Photoshop Elements for example has a Help menu with a variety of options. Many of these choices will open the support page for Adobe in your web browser while others will access functionality inside the software itself.

Many programs have a support icon, usually near the window's top-right corner. Microsoft Office 2013 for example has a small question mark icon which opens the help file.

Help file features Support files can be arranged in a variety of ways, such as a contents table, FAQ, or searchable database.

In Office 2013, a search box is what you can see when you open the support page. You type keywords in the search bar, just like a search engine, and it shows topics related to the keywords you entered.

Although built-in support can be helpful, it may not always provide the details that you want. If you cannot find what you're looking for or do not understand what you've found, usually you can ask someone you know, do a search on Google, or contact support staff. It may take a little extra time and effort, but learning how to find solutions on your own is a valuable skill — and with practice you'll be getting better at it.

Do Not Go Yet; One Last Thing To Do

I would be very happy if you would write a short review on Amazon if you liked or considered it useful. Your encouragement makes a difference, and I personally read all comments to get your input and make this book even better.

Thanks for your help and support!

www.ingramcontent.com/pod-product-compliance
Lightning Source LLC
LaVergne TN
LVHW051346050326
832903LV00030B/2882
9798653453373